VOX·ROX

Written by Shaun McClure and Lauriat Lane III

Book Layout Designer – Jason Redway

Editing - Niall Chynoweth

Proof reading – Hilary Wells, Mike Mee, and Lee Fogarty.

All interviews by Shaun McClure, Hilary Wells and Lauriat Lane III

Erasure, Yazoo and Madness images/Album covers (where not licensed from Alamy) are licensed courtesy of BMG Rights Management (UK) Ltd

The Lurker's images used courtesy of Peter Haynes – Peter Haynes photo by Nick Atkins

Woody and Madness images used with permission of Grace Fairchild with our thanks.

Special thanks to Bekah Zietz Flynn at Sub Pop Records, Dan Earl at BMG, Derek Birkett, Joshua Cooper and Paul Johannes at One Little Indian, Kris Maher at Universal Music, Howard Wuelfing at Howli' Wolf Media, Caroline Borolla at Clarion Call Media, Monica Seide-Evenson at Speakeasy PR, Christian Fighera at Two Gentlement PR, And Lucy Boughton at PR Police. We also want to thank the staff at Wax Trax! Mute Records and Stiff Records, without whose help we couldn't have written this book.

CONTENTS

WESTERN MUSIC POST-WAR TO LATE 1970s:
CHANGES AND TRENDS

Are there such things as musical genres? Perhaps a better way to express these new types of music would be as trends, and certain trends clearly emerge at certain times in history. But why did these trends come into being? Several seemingly unconnected things coming into play at once is the usual answer.

Social change is key. During the period with which this book is concerned this change involved new waves of immigration, the availability of leisure drugs, and shifts in financial climate, good or bad (bringing either optimism or despair). Also seminal were changes in technology that allowed easier access to music and new methods of making it. And of course, a good dollop of influence from established musical styles and other elements of popular culture also moved things along. The seeds are many, the fertilisers complex, and the flowering still incomplete.

It is important to look at the momentous effect World War II had on many aspects of culture in the in the first half of the twentieth century. The war itself was a tragedy, but out of the suffering came several technological breakthroughs brought about by the race to superior armament. One such revolution was the development of smaller, lighter electronics and communication devices

that were made cheaper than ever before and produced in higher numbers. This was to have a knock-on effect in domestic entertainment.

People also changed after the war. In the late 1940s and early 1950s they began to demand a better standard of living than what had previously served. They wanted more leisure time and consumer items that were affordable. This demand coincided with a manufacturing base much expanded by the war that could mass-produce items, therefore making them cheaper. Many factories were repurposed post-war to fit these needs. General Motors, as one significant example, turned their manufacturing away from aeroplane and tank production to refrigerators and cars. Gramophones and radios were already relatively common though too expensive for most families. The post-war years brought these into the price range of more and more people. A battle between two vinyl record competitors to find a standardised format ended with CBS's 33.3 rpm albums and 45 rpm singles replacing the previous 78s.

As the 1940s ended and the 1950s began, live music was still dominated by big bands such as The Glenn Miller Orchestra (although Glenn Miller himself didn't survive the war) and this

was largely due to the volume needed to entertain large numbers of people in dance halls. This was before the availability of electronic amplifiers.

In regard of radio and vinyl sales, crooners such as Bing Crosby and Perry Como were still as sought after post-war as pre-war. Swing music, popularised by the members of the Rat Pack—Frank Sinatra, Sammy Davis Jr, Dean Martin & co.—was also very popular. Jazz musicians such as Louis Armstrong, Nat King Cole, and Duke Ellington amongst others were selling lots of records and a more dance friendly version of jazz called bebop, led by Charlie Parker and Dizzy Gillespie, was starting to gain traction in places like New Orleans.

Country and western music, itself a form of Cajun and folk music, began to gain popularity around this time. Though it had its fans from its origins in the early 1920s, it was only when the livelier honky-tonk sound developed that artists such as Hank Williams, Patsy Cline, Johnny Horton and a young Johnny Cash come to prominence. This arguably influenced a nascent rock and roll sound just beginning to surface.

In 1954 Wynonie Harris released the song 'Good Rockin' Tonight.' Originally written and released by Roy Brown in

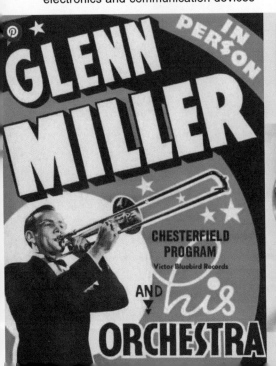

1947, the record is considered one of the many contenders for the first rock and roll song. Another close contender is Goree Carter with his song 'Rock Awhile,' released on Houston's record label Freedom Recordings. Then, in 1951, the song 'Rocket 88' (recorded by Ike Turner's band at Memphis Recording Service) was released as a single credited to Jackie Brenston and His Delta Cats by Chicago's Chess Records. In the same year, Billy Ward and the Dominoes used the slang term 'rocking and rolling' as a euphemism for sex in the song 'Sixty Minute Man'.

Around this time radio disc jockey Alan Freed launched his *Moondog Show* on Cleveland radio station WJW, featuring a mix of jump blues, up-tempo jazz, R&B, and western swing. Freed would frequently use the term 'rock and roll' to describe the type of music played on his show, which gained the term traction in the music press. It was Freed who organized and promoted the Moondog Coronation Ball, arguably the first true rock concert.

Bill Haley and his Comets began to create the rock and roll sound as we would know it today. Their single 'Rock Around the Clock' from 1952 is widely held to be the song that brought rock and roll to mainstream audiences. Others such as Buddy Holly and Gene Vincent would follow and performers such as Fats Domino would show that this music was not the sole domain of white performers (as would Little Richard). It was becoming big business. This shift to the mainstream, along with the success of Marlon Brando's movie *The Wild One* in 1953, set the stage for several decades of rock and roll music and brought with it the look of leather jackets, jeans, and quaffed hairstyles. In 1954 the Top 40 format emerged on radio entertainment (*American Bandstand*) as a standard of achievement for musical performers and helped promote rock music and pop music worldwide.

Elvis Presley began his music career in 1954 at Sun Records. This company was at the time attempting to merge rock and roll and country and western music with blues (popular in the southern states of America) and bring it to a much larger audience. The mixture of his music and his provocative stage style made Elvis one of the biggest stars of all time. 'Heart Break Hotel' alone sold over ten million singles. Sun Records would later release music by Johnny Cash and Roy Orbison.

1958 saw the breakthrough of funk and soul music. Funk emerged from earlier blues music, with a slightly slower downbeat and highly danceable sound. Motown Records, originally created to market and sell jazz records, found a flourishing nightclub scene in its home city of Detroit and soon recruited a seventeen-year-old Smokey Robinson to join a growing roster of song writers. The success of Jackie Wilson's hit 'Reet Petite' gave Berry Gordy the capital to launch the label, but it was not until 1961 that Motown Records gained its first number one with The Marvelettes' single 'Please Mr Postman' (later covered by The Beatles and The Carpenters). Rock and roll received a blues and gospel influence too; Sister Rosetta Tharpe's records had a huge effect on the development of this style of music.

Rock and roll became a youth movement and this coincided with teens having for the first time a reasonable disposable income, and these youths were directly marketed to and recognised as having their own culture. 1955 saw the first fully-transistorised radios and record players becoming available and with the further price drop this brought they were suddenly coming to be owned by teenagers.

The UK were a little behind the USA in their development of popular music in the 1950s and it was only towards the end of this decade that American rock and roll rose in popularity. Teddy boys (so called because they dressed in Edwardian clothing) signalled one of the first appearances of youth culture in Britain. They gravitated towards the music of Gene Vincent and early UK rockers like Billy Fury. By now the 1960s were in motion; Lonnie Donegan was a big hit with his skiffle music, especially the single 'My Old Man's a Dustman,' though there was seemingly not much happening locally to inspire what was emerging as a teen movement.

But new bands with new ideas began to form in Britain, often with a cockiness that wasn't seen before: groups such as The Beatles, The Who, The Kinks, The

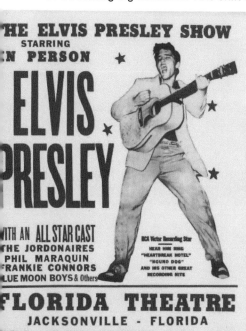

Faces, Cream, and The Rolling Stones. It is noteworthy that many of these influential rock and roll bands came from port cities such as Liverpool and London, whose residents would regularly meet American sailors and so listen to records with a black influence—music that simply wasn't available elsewhere in England at the time. Radio stations like the government-owned BBC Radio 1 were very conservative and didn't respond to the needs of teens. This gap in the market was soon filled to some extent by Radio Luxemburg (although it would transpire that they were sponsored to play music by only a small number of record companies, such as PYE). Radio Caroline, using converted fishing boats to broadcast from international waters, was soon on air and playing music more suited to younger listeners—often difficult-to-purchase American singles. Many of the DJs that broadcast on Radio Caroline would later move to Radio 1.

Synthesised music was being made many years before even the most basic of electronic keyboards, and from what seems an unlikely source: the BBC Radiophonic Workshop. Delia Derbyshire, an electronic music pioneer, created what is considered the first purely electronic tune, the *Doctor Who* theme.

In the mid-sixties Britain began to create its first teen music shows, such *as Ready, Steady, Go!* and of course *Top of the Pops,* which helped generate interest in rock and roll and other emerging musical trends. In fact, it was

Britain that now led the world in music as well as fashion, and a new trendiness and optimism followed the post-war gloom. This led to the so-called British invasion of America, when English bands toured there and became internationally famous.

New teen movements—the Mods and Rockers—established a longstanding rivalry. Rockers were basically teddy boys on motorbikes and would set the stage for later bike gangs. Mods (short for 'modernists') had their own roots in London jazz—particularly around Carnaby Street—and American beatnik culture. Crucially, they were focused on certain clothing styles, donning smart suits and nice shoes, though they soon began to identify with bands such as The Who and The Small Faces. Much was later made of the Mods–Rockers rivalry, which seemed to be exemplified in massed fistfights and was popularised and then mythologised in cult movies like 1979's *Quadrophenia*, though in reality these mass brawls were few and far between.

The mid-1960s saw dissatisfaction with governance on both sides of the Atlantic. Gone were the heroic struggles of Western nations to overthrow fascism as the governments of these countries were now perceived as being led by corporations (particularly arms manufacturers) into unjust wars in Korea and Vietnam. This warmongering spawned a peace movement fronted by younger rebellious citizens, often tied up with the easily identifiable

hippies and their embrace of alternative religious traditions and social drug use. The mores of hippy culture would inspire psychedelic rock bands such as The Grateful Dead, early Pink Floyd, Jefferson Airplane, and, of course, The Beatles, who were at the time evolving into a new beast. An offshoot of the hippy movement was a folk music revival where performers such as Simon and Garfunkel, Donovan, Patty Smith, The Seekers, and Bob Dylan rose to prominence.

In the mid-to-late sixties we see the full flowering of rock and roll in a wide range of styles across the world. This included hard rock and the genesis of what would become heavy metal music as exemplified by major bands like Led Zeppelin, Jimi Hendrix, Iron Butterfly, Deep Purple and The Doors. We also see bands like The Rolling Stones, The Who and The Kinks trying out a range of styles, from the older and more jubilant party songs to grittier teen rebellion anthems like The Who's 'My Generation', The Rolling Stones' 'Paint It Black' and The Kinks' 'You Really Got me'.

During this period the confluence of art and technology would engender experimental rock (later 'art rock'). Probably the best-known examples of this are found in The Beatles' later work, influenced by Paul McCartney's growing interest in the use of tape loops and altering sounds electronically. Post-production manipulation would make possible their concept albums *Rubber Soul* and *Sgt. Pepper's Lonely Hearts*

Club Band. In America, Frank Zappa's Mothers of Invention were mixing styles and using instruments in interesting ways while The Velvet Underground were charming Warhol's Factory-goers with avante garde performances in New York's underground. And alongside all this existed scores of lesser-known artists who began in the sixties to stretch the boundaries of music and create new modes of performance art. The Residents among these were quietly adapting from making films to making electronic-led guitar music.

Blues now had a new face in reggae, which stemmed from the early ska music of Prince Buster, Desmond Dekker, and Millie Small. Originally successful in the West Indies with Bob Marley, Peter Tosh, and Bunny Wailer leading the line, it soon grew in popularity and hit the mainstream charts. Motown was going from strength to strength, with top acts The Supremes (featuring Diana Ross), The Jackson 5 (with a young Michael Jackson), Stevie Wonder, and Marvin Gaye.

The sixties ended on a high note with the legendary Woodstock Rock Festival in 1969. This saw performers such as Jimi Hendrix, Joe Cocker, The Who, Janis Joplin, The Grateful Dead, Santana, Crosby, Stills, Nash & Young, and other legendary bands play to a massive outdoor audience in upstate New York. But at the start of the 1970s we see a sinister downturn. Following on the inevitable breakup of The Beatles were the sudden deaths of Janis Joplin, Jimi

Hendrix and Jim Morrison, seeming to signify an end to the maverick rock and pop of the decade. Then came a few years of pop- and folk-oriented melodic bands with the likes of The Carpenters, Bread, Elton John, and John Denver all dominating the charts. Several singer-songwriters previously based in the Brill Building in New York (a famous creative hub of singers, songwriters and record companies harking back to the 1940s) went solo; names like Carole King, Neil Diamond, Phil Spector, Sonny Bono, and Burt Bacherach.

Pop later crystallised in the form of Michael Jackson, who left the Jackson 5 and became one of the world's most successful performers. Electronics evolved further: the Moog, though invented and used by several bands from the mid-60s, became smaller and less expensive, notably attracting the attention of Brian Eno (then of Roxy Music) and Pink Floyd and other bands later associated with progressive or prog rock. The first music featuring overtly electronic sounds would begin to appear in mainstream charts. 'Popcorn' by Hot Butter would sell highly in several countries, reaching number 7 in the UK. Hip-hop emerged in inner-city America, taking inspiration from West Indian 'toasting' or 'chatting' over recorded music and forming the basis of modern rap. Mid-70s hard rock had evolved into glam rock with artists such as David Bowie, Marc Bolan and T-Rex, as well as Mud, Wizzard, Mott the Hoople and Sweet, experimenting with new guitar sounds and outrageous costumes and

make-up—it was camp and fun.

Towards the end of the 1970s disco music became briefly popular, spawning the flared white spandex suits of The Bee Gees and Earth Wind and Fire. This coincided with the first uses of the sequencer, a piece of digital equipment that could accurately control several electronic devices at once to form complex electronic music. Making deft use of these, Giorgio Moroder would produce several hit records for such artists as Donna Summer. Proto-electronic bands like Cabaret Voltaire and Kraftwerk would conduct their own experiments with the technology, and there began the development of industrial and electronica (more about these later).

Arguably, some of the bigger bands (with wealth) became self-indulgent. Prog rock, with its tendency to produce longer and longer singles and often bewildering concept albums, had lost its excitement and vigour and the music scene was starting to be seen as cosy, musically elitist and out of touch with the mainstream. Bands such as King Crimson, Yes, Yello, and others, set the tone.

But there was one more genre to emerge before punk came in to smash all established norms, and one that was itself born from prog rock: art rock. It is with this that we begin.

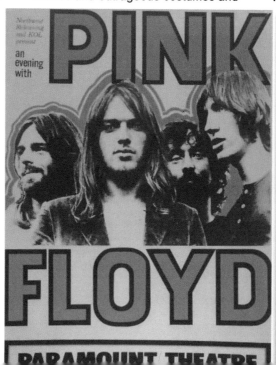

ART ROCK

Art rock is a kind of experimental music where the performance and the presentation are as important as the music itself. Clever songwriting is prioritised over catchiness, and the result is a sound that is more 'thinkable' than danceable. Sharing some of the seriousness and the classical and jazz influences of avant garde music, art rock is perhaps more accessible than purely experimental styles.

A greater accessibility can be attested by the massive popularity of what could be called early art rock: albums like *Rubber Soul, Sgt. Pepper's Lonely Hearts Club Band, The Velvet Underground and Nico,*. These forerunners would be followed by such notable bands as King Crimson, The Moody Blues, and Pink Floyd.

10cc and Godley and Creme, with their sophisticated pop sounds and later video work, are probably among the better-known bands that can be placed under the aegis of art rock. The Residents, who cut their teeth in primitive video in the 1960s and pioneered aspects of electronic music and bizarre stage performances long before such ideas would occur to other artists, have remained in willed obscurity. We speak to both bands next.

10cc/Godley and Creme

Interview with Kevin Godley

Kevin Godley is a songwriter, percussionist, and singer known for his work in art rock band 10cc and subsequently Godley and Crème. After meeting Lol Crème at art college and working with him in several Manchester groups, Kevin and Lol joined forces with Graham Gouldman and Eric Stewart (also active in local bands) to form 10cc in 1972.

As a band 10cc had an almost unique arrangement, being formed of two partnerships who each wrote music all four would then play together. Also uncommon was the incredible versatility of these four artists, with every member being a multi-instrumentalist, writer, and producer.

In the early 1970s 10cc were one of the UK's most successful bands with five consecutive Top Ten albums from 1972 to 1978. They also had twelve Top Forty singles during this time with standouts 'Rubber Bullets' (1973) and the classic 'I'm Not in Love' (1975). 'I'm Not in Love' broke the band internationally whilst also being technically superb, creating an atmospheric, moody, and ethereal sound that had rarely been heard before.

Just as they were hitting the big time internationally with hits like 'Life is a Minestrone' and 'I'm Mandy Fly Me' Kevin and Lol made the difficult decision to part ways with 10cc to form Godley and Crème and to expand into other areas, including music video direction after making their own ground breaking videos for their own records timed nicely as MTV emerged as a music video channel. The first outside production was for Sting's single 'An Englishman in New York,' and this was followed by videos for Ultravox, Duran Duran, and many others. They also made the video for their own hit single 'Cry' which used innovatory fading techniques to switch between a series of singing faces. Music was still a huge focus for them, however, and in addition to 'Cry' (number 19 in the UK charts) they had hits with 'Under Your Thumb' (number 3) and 'Wedding Bells' (number 7).

Godley and Crème officially ceased working together as a band after their *Goodbye Blue Sky* album of 1988. The original members of 10cc occasionally collaborate on albums and live shows, and Kevin recently released *Muscle Memory* (2019), an album which was the result of remote collaboration with artists from across the globe, some of whom he has never met. He has also developed apps to facilitate remote collaborations and user-generated music videos.

Alamy Photo Library

I have always thought that 10cc didn't cultivate an image as such?

We never even thought about it. I think it was probably because we weren't in the thick of it. We were working outside of London, which was, is, and probably always will be, the centre of the music business in the UK. We were stuck out in the outskirts of Manchester and there wasn't much of a scene going on there particularly.

We were four guys who were interested in making interesting music. The thought of constructing an image for us never really entered the picture. We were obviously aware of what was going on elsewhere, with people like Gary Glitter, Sweet, and all the other maniacs that were out there, but it never really appealed to us because we were too focused on audio.

You all played instruments and you were all proficient song writers. Did that cause any conflict because all of you could do everything?

Strangely enough it didn't because, I suppose, we all had our basic roles, which were the instruments that we played. But I could only ever play drums and sing. The others could maybe play bass, keyboards and guitar, so that was never anything

that impacted on me, so I never had that problem. What we did was always decided by who could do it the best and it was a very democratic way of working.

So, for instance, if there was a song that was written on piano then the person that played it on piano in the first place got to play it to begin with, because he was more familiar with it. However, if one of the members of the band that could play the piano could contribute a better version of it, then he would be the one that would play the piano. The trickiest bits were the vocals because all four of us were singers. What tended to happen was each of us would audition for the role of lead singer for the song. One of us would go into the studio and attempt to sing it, and if it wasn't so good the rest would hold up a sign saying 'Next'. So that was kind of how we approached everything we did.

What was your favourite 10cc song?

Gosh! Well, it's a very difficult question to answer because there are lots of favourites for different reasons. I suppose the obvious answer would be 'I'm Not in Love' because it turned out so much better than we expected it to. The original version, the first recorded version, was pretty crappy. We all agreed it was

pretty crappy, so it was shelved. It was only when we came back to it when I suggested doing it with all voices that it took on a life of its own. The production produced itself after a while and that was our most successful song.

There are other songs such as 'Somewhere in Hollywood'. Those are also favourites for different reasons because as songwriters they challenge the songwriting process, and I felt that we pushed ourselves to the limit on those tracks.

So how did you get that ethereal sound on 'I'm Not in Love'?

Once we'd agreed that we were going to go for an all-encompassing vocal sound, we then had to figure out how to do it. There were only four of us, so rather than hire a choir, which was the obvious option, we decided we'd do it ourselves.

Myself, Lol and Graham went into the studio, stood around a mic and sung a note that was needed for the song, just one note for as long as we could sing it. We did that note sixteen times on the sixteen-track tape recorder, mixed it down to two tracks on the quarter inch tape recorder, and created a tape loop out of it. We did that for every note that we'd need for the song. It took about three weeks to do. We recorded each of the loops back onto the sixteen track so effectively that the sixteen-track machine became a voice sample instrument. We used the faders on the control board to create chords on the notes that we'd sung. We'd fade them in and out through the backing tracks, which we'd done with an electric piano, electric guitar, and a Moog synthesizer bass drum. We just faded them in and out to that rough backing track and that's what created the sound.

We were one of the first bands to get hold of a Moog synthesiser when they came into the UK, but we didn't use it that much and we didn't use its full capabilities. We used it, like a lot of people did, to create odd effects here and there. I think the reason we used it on 'I'm Not in Love' was because it meant I could play a bass drum in the control room. That's where the electric piano and the guitar were being played so we could all be together in the one space, rather than be out in the live area and on full kit. We probably mostly used it to add effects or to simulate sounds that we couldn't get using ordinary instruments. We had lots of other hits too of course, and I'm proud of them all.

To fast forward quite a bit, why did yourself and Lol leave such a successful band?

We were almost unique as a band in that we had somehow gravitated towards two songwriting partnerships. You had myself and Lol doing what people have described as 'clever art rock,' and then Eric and Graham had their own style that was a bit closer to mainstream pop. Both were liked and both were good in my opinion, but I think myself and Lol just got a bit frustrated with the touring, and we always had big ideas.

Godley and Creme were an instant hit – did this surprise you at all? And do you think that your video for 'Cry' helped this?

I think a lot of the music that we wrote when we were with 10cc was very cinematic, very filmic, and it was our way of making films with sound. We didn't have access to the equipment to make films with back then, so we did sound things instead. But once we were on our own—as Godley and Creme—we started recording our own music. We weren't a touring band, we were just two guys recording, so we couldn't go out and promote them as a band. We figured it might be interesting to make little films to promote them, although there weren't that many places where they could be seen – this was before MTV and other such channels.

We had an idea for a film for one of our early singles, called 'An Englishman in New York', and we went to the record company with the idea, fully expecting them to say 'Piss off.' But they said 'Yes, why not? But you can't direct it on your own as you've never done it before, so you have to get a proper director in.' They got one in for us and we made the film and we learnt a lot about cameras, editing, lighting, everything really, during the process. At the end of that whole thing, we looked at each other and thought 'Hang on a minute; whatever this is, we can do some interesting things with this stuff called video.'

Not many people were doing it and record labels didn't know if there was any value in them. Before then they had only been used because a band wasn't available to appear live on some show or other, so various people made interesting little films instead as a substitute. That's how it all started for us. It was the first time we'd been in at the beginning of a movement, because when we got into music it was already well in its stride. Here was something interesting and new happening. I think we helped to form it in some way.

Our hit Godley and Creme single 'Cry' did take us by surprise to be honest, but it came at a time when music videos had started to be… not commonplace as such,

but something that people began to take seriously. They used to only use them on places like *Top of the Pops* when a band wasn't available, and usually on shows such as *Top of the Pops* they'd get a dance troupe to do a performance with the music in the background, but this had become a bit dated. The 'Cry' video allowed me and Lol to experiment with film as well, and since we were from an art school background, it was a new thing to try, and suited our experimentality. We used fades to different faces singing the song, from us to much older people and people from different cultural backgrounds and even children and then back again, and it was quite striking, and I think that set the tone for us really. That video not only set us on the road for a separate musical path but also the video side of our work too.

Do you think your lack of any formal training in filmmaking helped?

We shared that approach with Orson Welles, strangely enough. What he did was quite revolutionary at the time, but he did it because he didn't know he couldn't! No one told him he couldn't and, because he didn't know the rules, he just made it up as he went along. He made things that he thought would look good, and that's pretty much what we did. We bent the technology to our needs.

You've made videos with many diverse people, from Marti Pellow and Wet Wet Wet through to Snow Patrol and some reality show winners like Will Young, and the Frankie Goes to Hollywood 'Two Tribes' video. How was it and what was the creative process? Did you have the majority of the say or did the artists have input as well?

It's a selfish process. Obviously, it involves listening to the music a lot and just kind of freewheeling with it. I wanted to see if I could come up with something that was what I would like to see and felt that it would be appropropiate for the music and also would be something that the artist could carry off. Then, I would assume that it's worth pitching that idea. Often, I didn't but sometimes I did. It had to fulfill those criteria, the first being 'Is it something that I would like to see?' Because if it doesn't exist yet, is this idea fermenting something that would be interesting? That's pretty much the process once you've actually thought of the idea.

There's then a number of things that you have to do, and it's the same now as it was then, even though there is so much more noise now. You think of the idea, and you talk to your producer, who has to go and tell you whether the budget is sufficient to

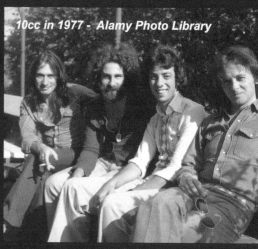

10cc in 1977 - Alamy Photo Library

make your idea work. Then, chat with the video commissioner—who is the person from either the label or the managment company who had commissioned us to come up with the idea—to see if they felt that this might be something that the band might like. You pitch it, and then you wait and wait and wait. Then, nine times out of ten they come back and say 'We've actually changed the track, we're gonna release this one instead' or they say 'Let's do it!' There are so many moving parts to the process.

To go back to your initial question, it's just a matter of sitting there and thinking or allowing the music to touch you in some way, and I suppose if you've been doing what I've been doing for a while it's kind of an automatic process. If you have a feel for it, you know something will come eventually, and that's how it works.

Video editing software is amazing, but do you think having that level of power to manipulate film now (often quite easily) can make the process worse?

I wouldn't say it's worse. What I would say is that I would prefer to live in what I would call a 'digi-logue' world, where there could be a combination of the best of digital and the best of analogue. Editing video, to me, is very much like playing an instrument, and it always has been. It's a very musical experience, and initially editing suites were very analogue places; if you wanted to cut between two shots you pressed a button, and if you wanted to mix between two shots you operated this little paddle. You could modulate how you actually did that by hand, and that's all disappeared. It's now been taken away and replaced with a guy sat next to you punching in numbers, which isn't quite as satisifying and takes longer.

Everything takes longer now because you can defer making a decision. You have a good shot, and you think 'Well, let's shave a bit off both ends of the shot and maybe

Left to right - Eric Stewart, Kevin Godley, Lol Creme, and Graham Gouldman - Alamy Photo Library

let's try the shot here instead of there, let's flip it left to right, turn it upside down'. In other words, your choices are infinite so you're using the ability to try it in lots of different ways. So inevitably, something that used to take us 24 hours to edit now takes three days. The job expands to fill the time allotted to it. You've got three days to edit, so it will take three days.

I think the other major difference between now and the earlier days is that there never used to be a critique process from the client. A director was hired because they'd made some good films and whoever was hiring you recognised that you had a particular way of looking at the world that may be appropriate for the song. So, you were given the song and you went away and did it and handed it in and that was it. There was no 'Well, we need a little bit more of the singer and you know the drummer looks a bit pale so can you maybe give him a bit more colour'. There was none of that kind of involvment from the commercial powers that be. That is so much more dominant today than it was with the marketing departments. Everybody thinks they know what works.

They are trying to make an artistic decision by committee, basically?

Yeah, in a word. That happens across the board. It happens at the beginning,

the middle, and the end. Which is why I don't do many of them anymore because it's harder to be as creative as one used to be as everyone's so cautious. It's crazy. It doesn't make any sense to me why everyone's cautious. 'We want to be really edgy and do something really dark,' but what they really mean is they want something that's as close to the last thing that their artist did that was a success. We've reached saturation point.

Are a lot of the artists very protective of their image?

I think it depends on who the artist is, and I think a lot of artists are totally in control of what they do and they are the people that you deal with. Some other artists are controlled by management and record labels, and they've become 'hit machines.' You know you have to do something cool but not that cool; it has to be within the scope of what people anticipate from you.

Whole World Band – can you tell us more about that please?

That came from a music special for the BBC back in 1989. They were running a two or three week special about environmental concerns, and they were looking for an idea to show communities and countries working together but at a musical level. The series was called *One*

World Fortnight, and they wanted to do a kind of Live Aid concert thing with people from all over the world appearing. But that had kind of been done, so my idea was to film what I called a 'chain tape'. The idea was to begin a piece of music in one location and film it taking place, then take that footage and the sound around the world, adding artists as we travelled. I never for one second remotely expected them to green light it, but they did. So, there was a programme that went out called One World, One Voice in 1989 on BBC2.

Around 2008, I'm thinking about the potential of the internet and what it could and couldn't do, and I figured 'What if one could actually do that without travelling? What if you could put a piece of music up, a little filmed clip of somebody playing the guitar and singing, and then what if someone in Guatemala could add an overdub to it in sound and picture, and then someone in Scotland could add drums to it in sound and picture?' That's the genesis of the idea and that's how it works, and so Whole World Band came from *One World, One Voice* in 1989.

Although you are keeping current with musical styles, do you think that the download element has killed the art of album making?

I think we are losing a lot of things with

the age of the instant download. This generation are spoilt, essentially. One doesn't want to dwell on the past, but I remember when I was a kid and the artist that I loved would release records. Then, you would queue up all night to get them when they hit the shop, you would take them home and play them to death, you would analyse and soak up every note and every word, and there would be a sort of spiritual and physical attachment to this piece of music. That doesn't really happen too much anymore because there's so much of it and, as you quite rightly say, it is so available. It's the same with anything if you get too much of it. If you eat too much food, you get fat and ill. If you get too much money, you get lazy. It's across the board, and now you've got too much music. The recording industry is suffering too because it's not valuable anymore, people don't get remunerated to the same level that they did. Music should be on a par with a great painting or a great sculpture. We've lost the sense of rarity. The sense of anticipation has gone.

So many of the modern records are generic sounding to my ears. What do you think?

They are. It's like there are some people somewhere who have analysed what makes a hit record, how many beats per minute work and what sort of drum patterns work. I guess you're right as you do tend to get a lot of this kind of record. It's not exactly the same but it's got similar elements, because they know it works. It's very rare that you find a track or an artist that really stands out. I think audiences are a little scared of something that is unlike everything else. They've been merged into consumers; people consume music as if it was a burger. It's just the way things are.

When we started making music, the music then was a pre-eminent force for youth culture. It's not now. Music is just one of many forms of entertainment, alongside TV, video games, VR, AR and so on and so forth. It's just part of a spectrum that's enlarged beyond anything we could have known back then. Music is just a fraction of a way of diverting something in the world.

You've continued to make music with your Muscle Memory project?

I enjoy the idea of collaboration because the only instrument that I play is drums – it's not the ideal instrument to write songs with. I am always looking for interesting ways to collaborate, but the idea for *Muscle Memory* came from a couple of people, whom I'd never met, sending me a couple of pieces of instrumental music and asking if I'd be interested in turning

them into songs. I had never worked that way before – essentially it was remote collaboration. I tried it, and I really enjoyed the process and it worked really well. Having a desire to make an album, I thought that that might be an interesting way to go about it, so I expanded upon this. I'd ask people, via my website, to send me instrumental tracks that I would then convert into songs. And then I would perform the songs, little realising that I would get about 284 of them, which was crazy! But it's been great – it's been amazing.

Normally, writing is sitting opposite somebody who would play piano or play guitar, and you'd react and bounce an idea backwards and forwards till it worked. Then you'd move on to another bit. Then you'd maybe scrap it and start again. It was a real time one on one situation. But this, this was different. This was essentially being handed a drawing in black and white and saying 'Fill in all the colours. But the drawing exists, you know? This is what you are working with, pal. You can't deviate from it!' And that's a fascinating way to work!

I'd not met any of these people before and I took great care when the music came in not to investigate who they were. I only wanted to see that the music that they had sent inspired me in some way. It was only once I began to pick songs that I knew were going to work that I then made contact with them, and we would talk and begin the process at a slightly deeper level.

How many did you eventually turn into songs?

I mean to do an album, so it's probably gonna be twelve or fourteen, and I'm eleven in so far. I'm waiting for a couple of people to get back to me with some questions I have. It's taken some time because when I began the process, I had never done anything like that before. I'd never written a melody and lyrics on my own before. I'm still right in the middle of it and it's great; it's given me a new lease of musical life.

The other interesting thing is there is no one to tell me what to do. There is no one to say 'That sounds like shit so why don't you try it this way?' or 'You can't say that, try saying this.' There's none of that so I'm just doing it by instinct, which is always much better than thinking when writing music. I think it's going to be good. I'm not trying to make it sound like anything particular or specific, I am being driven by each piece that I am given. But I think it sounds reasonably valid. I think it sounds like music that should exist now as opposed to music that existed forty years ago which is always a problem with artists of my age. I guess a lot of people that come from my era tend to stick in that era musically, but I've taken on board everything that's happened since, and I am open to anything so I try and bring that to what I am doing now.

Creme and Godley - Alamy Photo Library

THE RESIDENTS

INTERVIEW WITH HOMER FLYNN

The Residents materialised during the Hippy movement in and around 1969, moving from Shreveport, Louisiana (not known for its liberal views) to California so that they could be closer to other free-thinking people. As an 'art collective,' they set out to make arthouse films as well as music unfettered by traditional structures. Due to their fascination with technology (and because musical equipment was cheaper than filmmaking equipment) they gradually became more focused on the sound side of things and are now renowned pioneers of electronic music, forerunners of the 'do it yourself' movement that became a hallmark of punk.

Taking their name from a Warner Brothers rejection letter (with no name on the application WB had addressed the letter to 'The Residents') the band has been self-publishing in the USA from their Ralph Records label since their first album *Meet the Residents* in 1974. The musical style of these albums can be split roughly into two halves: the first a deconstruction of mainstream art that produces zany and abstract versions of well-known

records; the second a series of surreal and *sui generis* narrative-based experimental albums. Both are entertaining and perplexing in equal measure.

After sixty such albums and seven major world tours, The Residents continue to transform themselves end elude definition. Perhaps best recognised as giant eyeballs wearing tuxedos, the band have employed a multitude of disguises over the years, enfolding and re-enfolding their mysterious music in enigmatic costumes. They have made an art of obfuscation, only occasionally using spokespeople to deliver their edicts. It is rumoured that some of these spokespeople may be members of the band and that some (or all) of the costumed performers seen on stage are not. The only certainty we can cling to is that the information offered by these spokespeople (in this case Homer Flynn) is unreliable, unverifiable, inconsistent, and often misleading.

They all lived in or around Shreveport in Louisiana and went to the same school. It was the late 1960s; new and exciting things were happening but most of these weren't happening in Louisiana, nice though it was. The area was very conservative but they weren't, and it was in the middle of the age of the hippy movement which they wanted to join. They headed off to California to be part of this and remained there.

Would you say that The Residents were more of an art collective than a band at the beginning?

I think that was definitely their original intention. They had actually begun to experiment with tape recordings and other projects around 1965, but they were also in tune with reality and knew that they had to make a living and had to market whatever they made just to live. Being labelled as a band gave them the opportunity to market their music to a wider audience, and they were in many respects an actual band though a very left-field one. They were always massive music fans and the music was coming from the same place it would be if they were a legitimate band, but they always felt that the description was very narrow for them, considering the ideas and ambitions and the scope of work that they undertook. For the first four years of their existence, once they had landed in California, they were experimental film makers, which was another part of their vision. But they found that it was easier, financially at least, to keep up to date with music technology than film technology.

The idea behind the mystique to the band—wearing masks and being anonymous—was this down to a clever marketing idea or was there an element of shyness about it as well?

It was actually a few years before they were brave enough to put themselves on stage, and they waited until the advent of the sampler—which also allowed them to make even more interesting tunes—before venturing out into the public. They were confident of what they could achieve in a recording studio but performing these songs on stage was very difficult as they were created on multi-track systems. It was hard to replicate these songs live on a stage, and so, masks and costumes were perhaps a shield to hide behind, for a time at least. There was definitely a bit of showmanship involved with the costumes and the hidden identities but it also allowed them to use this as a curtain to do lots of things

behind. It allowed them a certain amount of camouflage and concealment that matched their artistic vision.

On their first tour in 1982–1983 they carried twenty-two huge backdrops around with them. Lots of props; there was a sense that the music alone wouldn't carry the tour. They felt they needed a lot of smoke and mirrors to deflect away from their lack of skill with instruments. To their credit they did get over that very quickly and by the time of their next tour it was much more bare-bones and was a lot more successful, at least from a financial point of view.

The Band's signature look, the top hat-wearing eyeballs in tuxedos, where did this idea stem from?

Well, it was another of our attempts to be original and unique. We wanted not only every album to sound completely different but to look completely different too. It was part of my role as a group collaborator to take charge of the visual side (my background is in graphic design). The original idea was to have a silver globe—something like a Christmas ornament but head sized—with the same top hat and tails that you now see. It became my job to figure out how to actually create that, so I went down to LA and Hollywood and started to talk to the professional costume makers down there. Ultimately everyone told me that it wasn't possible; too hard to see out of, the wearer's breath would make it fog up, things like that. In fact, actual breathing would be an issue. So I took this advice back to the band to discuss and we had a bit of back-and-forth, and I had the idea to replace the silver globe with an eyeball. Now, this would be almost as difficult to make as the silver globe—in fact, it was a lot more difficult—but it did have a sort of a porthole in the front of it so that the person inside could see and not suffocate, as we could incorporate a mesh where the iris was placed. This would solve quite a few issues but not all of them.

It's actually a common misconception that The Residents perform in those costumes. They don't. Well, they *have*, but only for fifteen to twenty minutes at a time. It just isn't feasible to perform any longer due to the weight and the fact you cannot see your instruments properly. But the look captured the public's imagination and it became a trademark of the band.

Do you think that the mystery element of the band has ever been a handicap?

Absolutely—they had to figure out a way to market themselves. Part of the

marketing process usually involves having personalities that are charming and charismatic. On the surface of The Residents you had these faceless nobodies, which in itself can be interesting and charming, but it didn't really go very far. So that necessitated the need for them to have a spokesperson—either myself or before me Hardy Fox, and before him others—to step forward and do interviews for the band. If you don't do the interviews then magazines and newspapers aren't going to write about you or your music.

What process do the band use when making music?

They had a love of technology and they were quite prescient about how music was developing too, particularly in terms of multi-track recording. They had a sense that interesting music could be played using multi-track environments. They bought one and began to record.

In the beginning there were four in the band and it was an incredibly democratic process. As I said, in the beginning they couldn't play but they knew if they pursued this, if they followed their artistic vision, they could produce music according to their own values, not the values of the people outside of the group, including potential customers. They found this idea charming; the idea that if you pursued something long enough you would get some level of competence about whatever it was you were doing (in this case music), the idea that everyone can do anything if they set their minds to it. It was a very idealised vision and one they soon found to be unrealistic in real life. The upshot was they discovered that whilst it was true that anyone could do anything if they tried hard enough, they didn't always do it very well. So it quickly changed from an 'all for one and one for all' attitude to a more fragmented approach where they gave people tasks suited to their own skills.

They originally had a manifesto of sorts; to make every album sound completely different. Essentially, they just wanted to be unique and original. They tried to include everything over the years from brass band, big band, and obviously good old rock and roll. They also wanted to create interesting album covers, and the ideas behind the music were often driven by the covers—the two overlapped to a degree. In terms of actual music making, they were interested in most of their music evolving organically. They would experiment with different ideas until they found something interesting. Obviously, sometimes an idea would present itself from out of the blue almost fully formed as well.

The Residents at The Golden Gate Bridge

Another aspect of the band was that they were able to keep on top of the multi-track technology as it developed. They could imprint their often-primitive values (lack of skill musically) onto what was at the time quite futuristic recording equipment. It was the clash of hi-tech and lo-tech, and The Residents have always thrived in this space.

How would you say the music that the band make has changed over the years?

I'd say it has become more complex. Originally their music was made by building track-upon-track-upon-track. It was a very simple way of making music, with perhaps a couple of sounds per layering. Their skill at forming ideas and realising those ideas has developed too.

Obviously, the use of more and more sophisticated samplers has altered the way they make music. There is a world of samples available out there that is open to everyone. The band have become much better musicians, but there are samples available of even better musicians that they can use as part of their work. We use up-to-date technology, such as Digital Performer and Logic Pro on the Apple Mac, to arrange everything later. We stay up to date.

During the early 1980s synthesiser music was beginning to become mainstream. Synth-pop was appearing regularly in the charts. What did you think of this music and, as you had been using similar technology for years, did it irritate you that they were often seen as pioneers?

Well, there were plenty of examples of electronic music before the 1980s, not just The Residents, even disco-era bands that were regularly using synthesisers. Donna Summer famously teamed up with Giorgio Moroder [an early synth guru] to create

the 'I Feel Love' single in 1977. The band have always enjoyed much of Moroder's work, from the point of view of producing and arranging, and they liked to analyse how others came to their own musical conclusion.

Do the Residents have their own producer?

The Residents had always produced their own records but eventually Hardy Fox, a long-time collaborator of the band, began to pick up the duties bit-by-bit. He began developing a certain sound for the group that stemmed from electronic soundscapes. Around 1979 The Residents were also moving more and more into sample-based song-structures, particularly into songs that included world music—music with a more ethnic sound. You can especially hear this on the *Eskimo* album.

When Hardy retired at the end of 2016, he was one thing that The Residents found difficult to replace, because he had such a unique ear for the group and what it was that they were trying to achieve. Eric Feldman, who had up to that point had duties within the music framework, began to realise that he shared a lot of the sensibilities of Hardy. He then became our producer.

Would you say that mainstream music has become very predictable over time?

I would say so. I think if you look at chart music today and compare it to the previous decades, it tends to be very safe music. That sort of music has always existed, obviously, but as a subset of the bigger picture. The music charts used to be very varied; you'd have lots of different genres and styles and even age-groups all in the Top 20 at the same time in the 1960s right up to the 1990s even. Now the charts seem to be twentysomethings all singing

very similar stuff. Although you shouldn't take my views *too* seriously as I haven't listened to the charts much in about twenty or thirty years! But this is definitely my perception, yes. Something happened in the late-1980s to mid-1990s where the music industry changed from being a smaller thing full of people that were in it because they loved music to something that became big business. When you have Michael Jackson's *Thriller* selling fifty million copies, or whatever the hell it was, it becomes big business on a grand level. All of the smaller labels such as Sun Records [home of Elvis Presley and Roy Orbison and other rock and roll greats] and other smaller labels were pushed aside. Accountants and lawyers took over the role of A&R men and suddenly people were getting signed because they matched demographically what these people thought would be the biggest buying audience. Basically, they sign whatever group or artist they think will sell to this tiny section of the population, which I think has alienated a lot of the rest of us.

What *has* changed though is the technology has become so easily available, technology that is much more flexible and creative. And online platforms such as Spotify exist, so people are much more easily able to get their own music out there. The problem as always is how to market your product. So a lot of very interesting music is being made but it just doesn't get anywhere near to the charts. I subscribe to Spotify and I get introduced to new and interesting bands and songs on literally a daily basis.

Are there any bands that The Residents had wished to have worked with?

They were big fans of Captain Beefheart but they didn't get to work with him, though interestingly, Eric Feldman—who is the band's producer at this point—was actually playing with Captain Beefheart when Eric was twenty years old. He lived right down the street from him apparently. This was at the time the original Magic Band broke up, and Eric got involved with him then. Another sad footnote: The Residents have performed with the musician known as Snakefinger, whom Eric also played with before being introduced to us. It was Eric that found him after he'd had a heart attack.

What next for The Residents?

We're just gonna keep going until we are no more, I guess. It's been a fun ride though and we hope that we've brought something good to the world and entertained a few people along the way.

イケッコとツバキ

THE RESIDENTS

HAIGHT STREET ART CENTER SAN FRANCISCO CALIFORNIA

サンフランシスコ

"A SIGHT FOR SORE EYES"

JUNE 25 2022

A POSTER BY ZOLTRON FOR A JUNE 25TH 2022 PUBLIC BOOK SIGNING & ART EXHIBITION WITH HOMER FLYNN & AARON TANNER, PRESENTED BY THE HAIGHT STREET ART CENTER & AMOEBA MUSIC IN SAN FRANCISCO CALIFORNIA

INDUSTRIAL MUSIC

Most historical sources claim that the industrial music scene began in the mid-1970s, but this is not entirely accurate. Most of the key components of modern industrial music—from the electronic keys and synthesizers to the light shows, pyrotechnics, and even the subversive use of noise as 'found (sonic) art'—can be traced back at least a century earlier. In fact, the roots of what we call electronic industrial music can be found in the music halls of the 19th century.

Many historians trace rock and its offspring back to the working-class culture of the fifties, but its roots reach much further—to the world of travelling roadshows and music hall entertainers. One of the earliest known musicians to work with electronic equipment was Johann Baptist Schalkenbach, a performer whose act mainly involved using primitive electronic switching gear to control a range of acoustic devices from a sort of centralised keyboard. Some critics debate whether this use truly qualifies as electronic music, but he certainly pioneered the application of electronics in stage performance. As well as performing his own compositions, he also is said by some to have developed or inspired the acoustic special effects used by the renowned magician Maskeleyne.

In the late nineteenth century, there was a wave of new acts using similar devices, and they took advantage of the new railroad systems to tour smaller venues to perform in and thereby reach a wider audience. Both in the UK and in the USA, the country was opening up. Some performers also included cinematographic projections in their shows, not unlike the visual backdrops we see used today at live concerts.

At the dawn of the twentieth century come the first examples of electricity being used directly to generate musical tones, and the 1920s saw the landmark introduction of the theremin—the first purpose-built entirely electronic musical instrument (and still in use today). In 1934 Hammond brought out the first true electric organ. With the development of the transistor, electronic organs that used no mechanical parts to generate their waveforms had become practical. The first of these was the frequency divider organ, which uses twelve oscillators to produce one octave of chromatic scale and frequency dividers to create other notes. These latter organs were even cheaper and more portable than the Hammond, which led to the electric organ becoming a set piece of many of the great early rock bands and a popular choice for musicians even today.

In the middle of the fifties the first true synthesizer was created by RCA: the Electronic Music Synthesizer Mark I. It was an unwieldy piece of equipment, however, and the reserve of academics. It was in the mid-sixties that Bob Moog met Herbert Deutsch and was inspired to create a voltage-controlled oscillator and amplifier module with a keyboard. Not until 1967 did Mr Moog call his diverse modular system a 'synthesizer.' In 1969 Gershon Kingsley released his album *Music to Moog By*, which included the first composition of the song 'Popcorn,' later made into a hit by Hot Butter. For the first time, it was not only music nerds that were aware of the evolving new technology of the synthesizer.

In 1970 Moog released the Minimoog—the first truly portable synthesizer—and his work around this time with Wendy Carlos lit the fuse for the coming decades of dedicated synthesizer bands. Wendy released several brilliant albums, including *Switched-On Bach* in 1968, which exhibited the potential of the synth for professional musicians. The album was used as the basis for the soundtrack of

Stanley Kubrick's *Clockwork Orange* in 1971 and thereby brought the synthesizer to the attention of the public at large.

Many believe that one of the most well-recognised early electronic songs, the *Doctor Who* theme, was performed on a theremin. In fact, the song was performed by Delia Derbyshire in 1963 using a clever combination of hand-tuned oscillators and tape loops cut and spliced together in a technique known as *musique concrete*. This kind of cut-and-paste method of recording became a commonplace of industrial musicians as home studios and recording gear became more accessible.

In the early 70s Kraftwerk and Pink Floyd were arguably the best-known bands using both synthesizers and electric organs as integral elements of their musical style. Others such as Deep Purple and Emerson Lake and Palmer also made extensive use of the synthesizer and the electric organ. It was the mid-70s, though, that saw the beginnings of the modern industrial scene, with the release in 1975 of Lou Reed's critically acclaimed *Metal Machine Music* and the formation of Cabaret Voltaire and Throbbing Gristle in the UK. The deliberate use of noise and the enthusiastic violation of musical conventions were a rebirth of the music hall scene occupied a century prior by Johann Schalkenbach and his peers. A unique element of the industrial music genre, however, is the tendency of industrial musicians to cite as influences not older musicians, but artists, philosophers, novelists and revolutionaries. Many industrial artists saw their work as part of a revolutionary engagement with information as a tool of power, and one cannot easily separate the efforts of industrial music from the post-structural philosophy and radical political theory that had been informing the art world and growing in notoriety since the upheavals of May '68.

THROBBING GRISTLE

INTERVIEW WITH CHRIS CARTER

Chris Carter was a founder member and arguably lead performer of industrial band and visual arts group Throbbing Gristle. Originally an electrical engineer, Chris worked at the BBC setting up stage lighting and sound systems. While undertaking this work he began to have ideas for his own performances, which included experimental music and sounds produced using homemade electronics. Throbbing Gristle was formed in 1975 in Hackney, London by Chris, Cosey, Genesis P-Orridge, and Peter Christopherson, the latter of whom were involved in art collective COUM Transmissions.

Throbbing Gristle specialized in an abrasive and aggressive music using contorted, effects-laden distortion and lyrics yelled or moaned. Many found them difficult to watch and listen to. The performances they created were an uncomfortable but powerful experience that challenged viewers' conceptions, often using shocking film clips and photos of concentration camps and pornography to jar people out of conventional perceptions.

Floating somewhere between art rock and the most nihilist of punk, their use of DIY electronics set them apart from other bands of their type (except perhaps Cabaret Voltaire) in style when many others of the same aesthetic were using a more traditional guitar-based approach. Throbbing Gristle coined the phrase 'industrial music' following the establishment of their self-publishing record company Industrial Records. They arguably opened the gates for later bands such as Fad Gadget, Depeche Mode, Kraftwerk, and others who would follow with more melodious electronica in subsequent years.

What originally got you interested in becoming a musician? Did you have any particular groups who inspired you?

I suppose the first time I thought "I wish I could do that" was when I was 16 and I went to see Pink Floyd play at a small pub in North London. I was right up the front, and I was so entranced by the sounds they were producing on stage, the whole experience was mind blowing. I also used to go and see a lot of early Krautrock bands like Faust, Neu!,Klaus Schulze, Tangerine Dream, Kraftwerk, Amon Düül II and so on. But I was heavily influenced by unusual sounds in 1960s TV shows and radio programmes. Which, at the time I didn't know, but later discovered were mostly produced by the BBC Radiophonic Workshop.

Did you have any formal musical training?

None whatsoever, I am completely self-taught when it comes to my musical abilities. In my teens I started out by playing the bass guitar and even though I practiced quite a bit I never really connected with it as an instrument and gave up on it after 6 months or so. I guess my main instrument has become the keyboard… any old keyboard, I'm not fussed. But I'm not actually a very good keyboardist either, I don't really have the skills, the dexterity, or the chops that I should have for something I've been 'playing' for 50 years. But I do have a good ear for melody and rhythm, and I can program some decent drum patterns and bass lines.

Were you actually a part of COUM Transmissions?

Well, this is a common misconception, but I was never a member of the COUM Transmissions collective. And honestly, I didn't have any inclination to be part of it either. COUM had come from an art foundation and its modus operandi was always very art based/biased. When I met Cosey my interests and aspirations were in music, film, and technology and while I appreciated what COUM were doing it didn't appeal in the least, so I didn't get involved. Well, that is apart from my one guest appearance in the COUM film *'After Cease to Exist'* in 1977 - when it was all coming to an end and TG was becoming a reality.

Throbbing Gristle were the pioneers of Industrial Music – Were there other bands that you were aware of that were experimenting in the same way with sound?

Yes, in the 1970s there were many experimental bands around, far too many to mention. It was an exciting time back then and it wasn't all delivered to your screen or laptop in a digested daily basis (we didn't even have screens and laptops). You had to find out by word of mouth, going to gigs and record stores. A lot of it was off most people's radar, even within the world of underground music. Also, there were many different experimental strands and genres being produced simultaneously, in many different countries. The UK had thriving experimental scenes in London and Sheffield but there were pockets of similar really talented experimental musicians in France, Germany, Poland, Italy, Japan and the USA.

How were the songs created for Throbbing Gristle? Were you quite democratic, or was there a dominant leader in the group?

This is another misconception that's grown up around TG over the years but as I've said on record before TG was an experimental democratic music collective, I guess in a similar way to what COUM Transmissions had been. The difference with TG was that although we were experimental in our output, we had adopted a regular band format of musicians being fronted by a lead singer. Which obviously gives outsiders a particular impression of the group dynamic. Behind that standardised fascia the back story was very different and very democratic. Which all meant there was some significant emotional turbulence along the way.

In the early days songs mostly came into existence either by jamming in the studio, or live on stage, to one of my rhythms or sequences. Cosey or Sleazy would suggest a topic and Gen would improvise a vocal around that theme. We'd then hone and refine the songs over time. You can hear this happening over and again with songs on the TG24 tapes of live performances.

Were there any tracks that you wished you'd done differently, in hindsight?

No… I believe that's a completely pointless exercise. You've done what you've done so move on. There are songs we have produced in the distant past that I think could maybe have been mixed a

little differently but nothing that I would want to change drastically. When you are writing, recording, and mixing you get into a certain mindset and it's often a situation 'of the moment'. Those moments, those recordings are snapshots of your life, like little specific historical documents.

But there is this issue with digital music production, as opposed to working in analogue, that allows you to endlessly delay the moment of what used to be referred to as 'committing to tape'. Years ago, we used to get into a different headspace when working with tape, because at some point you have to make a pretty significant decision… is this how you want the song to 'be', for it to sound, to be played endlessly for ever and ever - with no going back. In the 1970s and 80s we couldn't afford to buy lots of reels of tape, it was expensive so 'committing to tape' became this thing, this moment of no going back. But now you can create dozens of different versions, make endless variations of the same song, different mixes and so on, for days and days. It's all too easy to get into this cycle of delaying that final commitment… *'oh let's do just one more mix, lets tweak that part one more time'*.

Are there any Industrial groups that you think have carried on where the group left off?

Not yet…

What projects are you working on now Chris?

We've done a lot of collaborations and remixes for other artists over the past few years, which is always interesting, trying out new mangling techniques and ideas with other people's material. But now Cosey and myself are focused on our own music and are both recording new solo albums.

PUNK

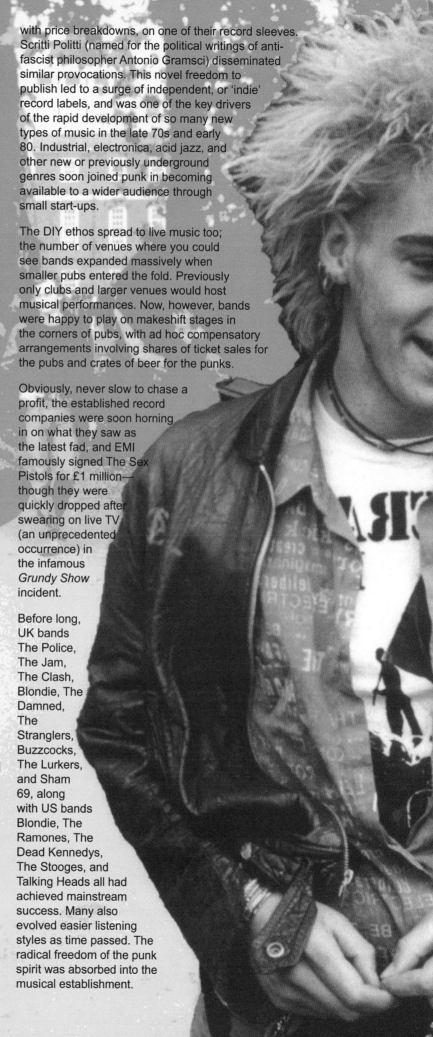

Several things combined in the late 70s to create the music and fashion phenomenon that became known as punk rock: political turmoil in the form of mass strikes and industrial action left the streets of England deep in litter; power cuts were a commonplace of everyday life; and unemployment was high and steadily rising. Amid this bleakness and misery large scale celebrations were being planned for the Queen's Silver Jubilee of 1977. These celebrations brought into stark relief the differences in living conditions between rich and poor in the UK, and out of the bitterness of this realization erupted a dissatisfied youth, angry at being forgotten by a gloating establishment that seemed unaware or unconcerned with its suffering.

Out of this miasma of resentment came The Sex Pistols. Their ripped clothing, metal studs, leather bondage gear, and spiky haircuts shocked and appalled decency. The new rock and roll that they played was loud, fast, aggressive, and explicitly political. Lead singer Johnny Rotten was especially outspoken, and his lyrics brought to many who had not already gained it an awareness of the deep divisions and dissatisfaction felt by his generation. Widespread news coverage was further incited by several publicity stunts, including being arrested while playing their hit single 'God Save the Queen' on a Thames barge. They were the new face of a youth movement that terrified (or at least annoyed) the older generation.

Malcolm McLaren, auteur, and businessman, formed the band and managed it from Vivienne Westwood's punk boutique, SEX, in Chelsea. McLaren based the Pistols loosely on The New York Dolls, whom he had informally managed. In New York an underground scene had already fermenting in the East village, fronted by Debbie Harry, Talking Heads, and The Ramones. Though not the first punk band in the UK—that honour would be retroactively bestowed on The Damned and their single 'New Rose'—the Pistols were the first to gain widespread notoriety.

Youths dressed as punks were appearing on the streets of London, and an explosion of punk bands was rocking the rest of country. Acts like The Clash, Buzzcocks, The Undertones, The Stranglers, The Lurkers, Sham 69, UK Subs, as well as early versions of The Police, The Jam, Simple Minds, and Adam and the Ants. In America they had Blondie, The Stooges, The Dead Kennedys, and Talking Heads. In punk music the quality of your playing was not material—what mattered was getting your voice heard. The complacent pop stars and bloated prog rockers were swept away on a tide of raw, exhilarating music.

Not only did the music change, a new ethos for creating music (and other things) was formed: punk DIY. Bands and listeners wanted to side-step large record labels, which to them represented the Establishment, opting instead to distribute their music directly to gig goers. With this simple but effective workaround they freed new music from a reliance on corporate distribution networks. The Desperate Bicycles famously published instructions on the basic production methods of records, complete with price breakdowns, on one of their record sleeves. Scritti Politti (named for the political writings of anti-fascist philosopher Antonio Gramsci) disseminated similar provocations. This novel freedom to publish led to a surge of independent, or 'indie' record labels, and was one of the key drivers of the rapid development of so many new types of music in the late 70s and early 80. Industrial, electronica, acid jazz, and other new or previously underground genres soon joined punk in becoming available to a wider audience through small start-ups.

The DIY ethos spread to live music too; the number of venues where you could see bands expanded massively when smaller pubs entered the fold. Previously only clubs and larger venues would host musical performances. Now, however, bands were happy to play on makeshift stages in the corners of pubs, with ad hoc compensatory arrangements involving shares of ticket sales for the pubs and crates of beer for the punks.

Obviously, never slow to chase a profit, the established record companies were soon horning in on what they saw as the latest fad, and EMI famously signed The Sex Pistols for £1 million—though they were quickly dropped after swearing on live TV (an unprecedented occurrence) in the infamous *Grundy Show* incident.

Before long, UK bands The Police, The Jam, The Clash, Blondie, The Damned, The Stranglers, Buzzcocks, The Lurkers, and Sham 69, along with US bands Blondie, The Ramones, The Dead Kennedys, The Stooges, and Talking Heads all had achieved mainstream success. Many also evolved easier listening styles as time passed. The radical freedom of the punk spirit was absorbed into the musical establishment.

THE LURKERS

INTERVIEW WITH PETE HAYNES

Pete 'Esso' Haynes is a founder member and drummer of punk band The Lurkers as well as being a playwright and author of several books. His nickname derives from the short time he spent working in an Esso petrol station.

The Lurkers emerged from the Fulham area of London in 1976. Originally a pub band, they were lacking in real direction until they discovered punk rock—particularly punk outfit The Ramones, whose music chimed with their own outlook. The joined forces of Pete Stride, Esso, Pete Edwards, Nigel Moore, and Danie Centric soon gained a local following and are notable for being the first band to sign to the legendary record label

Beggars Banquet. They recorded four Peel Sessions at the BBC between 1977 and 1979 Their first single 'Shadow' sold the entire print of five thousand records and was voted as the twelfth best track of the year by John Peel listeners.

1978 saw 'Ain't Got a Clue' reaching number 45 in the UK singles chart—their biggest hit—and the debut album *Fulham Fallout* reached 57 in the album charts. Their clout in the punk scene was enough to gain them several support slots for major acts The Jam, The Police, and Gary Numan's Tubeway Army. The Lurkers' music regularly appears in *Best of* punk compilations, and though they no longer play live they still record.

Punk apparently came from a dissatisfaction fed by a big class divide in the late 1960s and 1970s. Was this something that you witnessed?

I think there was a class divide back then for sure. A lot of my teachers were very upper-middle class and there was a disconnection between them and the kids, at least at my school. I've got to say, I think there is a much bigger class divide now, but now it's much more insidious. As an example: it was much easier to buy a house back then. A nurse married to a bus driver could easily get a foot on the property ladder, and if you could take advantage of the grammar school system you could get yourself a decent trade and join a union. Now it's almost impossible to do that.

What were your first memories of music?

I was around eight or nine years old at the time and one of the things I did because I was a bit of a manic depressive was to drum on chair seats and things like that. I actually bought a tin drum from a jumble sale for the equivalent of 1p. Then I made a group with my mate Ray Brown. We imaginatively called it The Dave Clarke Two.

Dave, my brother, was massively into music. He's the one that should have been in a band. He had a lot of health issues back then, it was awful for him. My mum used to work in the same shop as one of The Who's roadies (a bloke called Roger), who heard about Dave and suggested that Roger should take him along to see the band rehearse. My mum said he's not well enough, but Roger came round to our house with another roadie called Tony to take him over to the rehearsal room in Shepherds Bush, which wasn't far from where we lived. When Dave was there, he told Keith Moon that his brother (me) loved to drum and would drum away to 'I'm a Boy.' Keith gave him some drumsticks to pass on to me, which was nice of him.

When I met Keith years later in 1978 in a pub, he came over to me. I mentioned Dave going to watch them rehearse, and he stopped and looked at me for a while and then said 'I remember him, yeah.' And I told him it was nice of him to remember after all of his adventures with rock stars and Hollywood stars like Oliver Reed and said he was a nice person. I even reminded him about the drumsticks. He paused, and then very quietly said 'I don't suppose I could have them back, could I?'

How did The Lurkers come together?

Pete [Stride] was forming a band and asked me to come along and play the drums (this was just before punk came along). There was also Pete Edwards, 'Plug,' who was initially on vocals but turned into our roadie when Howard [Wall] joined the band. Nigel Moore began to get involved around then on bass guitar. We all knew each other from down the pub. Out of all of them I suppose I knew Pete the most, because he would talk about football a lot. He was really into off-centre music like me, too: The New York Dolls, Marc Bolan, Pink Fairies, and that sort of stuff.

We used to practice in Pete's bedroom. It was incredibly noisy. I felt sorry for this little hamster that was in a cage in the corner. Pete used to put this cloth over the cage as some sort of protection. I didn't think that was going to do much. I don't know why I never thought of asking him to just move the cage to another room or something. Mind you it lived to a good age, that hamster.

Up till then I always thought I was going to be a jazz drummer. Don't ask me why—I had no musical training at all. And I used to play this one rhythm that was a bit like a train: ter-ter-ter *tap*, ter-ter-ter *tap*. I stuck with that for a while. We used to sing songs that seemed to fit the drum beat such as 'Sweet Jane' and so on. It sounded completely shit. Eventually we started to rehearse in a school hall. After one practice session we came out and there was a bloke standing outside who said 'What the hell was that racket? That's not music, that's just noise!' and Pete said 'Actually, it's much better than it sounds.'

I think the turning point for us as a band were when we heard a Ramones album for the first time, and they weren't a million miles away from what our band were playing. Short songs with lyrics about blokes that can't get girlfriends. It was ideal, style wise, for us, and we started to see a way forward musically.

We managed to get our first gig—we were supporting Screaming Lord Sutch at a local college. We had a set together of our own songs but it was only about ten minutes long. But we played with so much energy it was knackering. After we'd been on we were packing up and he looked surprised. He said 'Is that it?' We said 'yeah,' so he said 'Well, you're going to have to play it all again then!' He was a nice bloke. He took us to one side afterwards and said he liked us. He was a local boy like us. He knew we were a bit green so he told us to be careful and that not everyone was as nice as him, and by God did we find that out later! Other bands would be bitchy or steal bits of your gear and all that stuff.

How did the songwriting work? Did you all chip in?

Peter Stride wrote 95% of everything we ever did. I wrote one or two. We could all have input about the way we played our own instruments though, obviously, but typically Peter was the driving force when it came to ideas.

Your first record deal was with Beggars Banquet; how did that come about?

We were the very first band signed to Beggars Banquet. They started off by owning three record shops: one in Fulham, one in Earl's Court, and one in Richmond. Those were the type of shops where you could take your own records in to part exchange. Now, Mike Stone was the manager of the shop in Fulham and liked what we did and saw that we needed help, so he turned the basement into a rehearsal room where we could practice. He even got a van and drove us to a few gigs. He tried to get a record deal together for us, without success, and his bosses at Beggar's Banquet tried to get us a record deal as well, also without success. Lots of people at this time still liked The Eagles and all that sort of stuff, so it was a difficult pitch for them for a band like us.

Eventually, Beggar's Banquet were persuaded by Mike that something was happening locally—a new music scene. So they took a punt and overnight they became a record publishing company. They paid £200 for us to go into a proper studio and record our first single, 'Shadow,' and figured out how to press them and print the covers, and the record managed to sell reasonably well. And both us and Beggar's Banquet were off and running.

When you began recording in a recording studio with a proper producer, did it change the way you thought about music writing?

No, not really. I wouldn't say we were proper musicians so it didn't really change us much. When we first started to work on the first album, we worked with a guy called Mick Glossop. He'd worked with Frank Zappa as a third engineer or something like that and would later work with PIL, Magazine, The Skids, and many others including Van Morrison. He was very technical and a very nice guy. He was a bit like a vicar and a social worker and a councillor all in one. He knew how to communicate with us and get us going; he knew how to get the best (and more) out of us. I think working with him lifted us as a group—one that could actually play together and in time with one another.

So the band began to take off. What happened next?

Now put yourself in this situation, right? You are a record company with a new up-and-coming band. Their first single does well. Where do you send them on tour? New York? Paris? Milan? No; you send them to the Isle of Arran! That's where they sent us—for fucking Paisley Week or something. Then we toured up and down the country and every place the record company could find for us. We had support from fucking Ivor Biggun at one gig, singing his 'hilarious' songs about wanking and trying to find his cock. The guy later became Doc Cox on *That's Life!* with Esther Ranzen. He was on the Beggar's Banquet label like us and they thought he was the funniest thing ever.

Beggars Banquet became quite big quite quickly, didn't they?

They did but they had issues early on, I suppose like any smaller publisher. What kept them alive was Gary Numan. He toured with us—this is when he was with Tubeway Army. Very nice bloke; one of the few really down-to-earth blokes I've met in the music business. I remember we were playing in the Outlook Club. It was in Doncaster, I think. They hated him and they hated us and at the end of it the DJ put on Roxy Music and Bowie and all the people got up and started dancing.

I saw Gary at the bar looking depressed, and he said 'We're doing this all wrong you know. They don't want punk. They still want fucking Bowie—look at them!' In one of my famously accurate prediction speeches, I tried to persuade him that he was wrong. He ignored me and within a few months he'd changed everything: his look, his sound, makeup, everything. And he was up on stage dressed as this automaton and sold about 400 million records.

To be fair, I've got a bit of a track record in making inaccurate music predictions. I told The Police that they were crap when I met them once after our gig at The Marquee. It was midweek and there wasn't a lot of people out to see us. At the time we weren't a name, and they certainly didn't have a big name either. They were proficient musicians though. But they were trying to jump on the punk bandwagon, in my opinion. I told them that they were too old, being around 26, and that Sting looked like a schoolteacher (turned out he was a schoolteacher). I told the drummer

they were going nowhere with a name like The Police. Not long afterwards they started to do that fake reggae-influenced stuff and sold about 400 million records.

Do you think that many of the early punk bands were targeted by groups trying to organise violence?

There was no CCTV in those days in clubs and pubs. Even travelling on the London Underground late at night was dangerous. We played literally hundreds of gigs—from tiny places to being sold out at the Lyceum. We had a large following, primarily male. Not a football crowd though, as some people would expect. It was mostly 'anoraks'. I don't know why, though we were getting attention from emerging right-wing groups such as the National Front, the League of Saint George, and the Viking Youth, who were starting to appear, especially in the London areas.

And they would just come in and beat people up, which was easy to do due to the nature of our followers, who were not fighters in any sense of the word—they

just wanted to listen to the music. They were basically a pain in the fucking arse these skin heads. Ignorant cunts. Dreadful cowards. I got into a few fights with them. I got kicked unconscious at one gig. I used to get the cymbal stand and swing that at them.

It wasn't just skinheads either. For some reason we had the most problems in shit market towns in the middle of nowhere. The local hillbillies would come out. Those places seemed to have local lads who liked nothing better than beating up people that looked a bit different. I think one of the worst gigs we did was at some leisure centre in Peterborough. We were playing and suddenly the doors at the back of the room came bursting open—these people had backed a van into the hall. Then skinheads with baseball bats jumped out and started to lash out at people. It was a horrible time.

It became a big problem for us. People would avoid coming to see our shows as we got a bit of a reputation. A couple of gigs had to be stopped after a couple of songs. It was getting too much for me at

one point. We couldn't understand it; we were in no way political ourselves.

What was it like going on Top of the Pops the first time?

We got to the studio quite early and started drinking almost immediately, so by the time we were on we were drunk. They made us do the song again and again because I was mucking about. We were the last band on, so by the time we'd finished most of the audience had buggered off.

You toured America, didn't you? How did that compare to the UK?

Well, our first album was recorded in America—in Alabama, which was great. I always wanted to go to America because I was a big fan of American writing. John Steinbeck and Raymond Chandler, they tended to write about outsiders. Even the film noir stuff showed a figure of loneliness in a busy place. And so I was very excited to be going if only for that reason. It was a weird place, and we recorded in a 'dry county' so to buy booze we had to see 'the boys,' which were basically the KKK, the Church and the police. And it was the exact same people that were behind all of those things.

So, the producer drove the band to a bar, and it was over the border in Tennessee where you could drink. I ended up in an arm-wrestling contest and a drinking contest with some rednecks. I lost the first one and won the second. They were quite friendly to us but didn't like the producer because he had a posh accent, which was interesting to me. It's supposed to be this classless society but it isn't. To me, it's a very spiteful third-world country, not that different from India but with a much bigger army. They used to go on about how even the lowest of the low could eventually become president, but we all know that is bollocks, don't we? Especially now. Lots of rich people but a lot more that can't even go and see a fucking doctor or dentist.

Do you think that the music press was quite hostile to punk bands because the press was generally made up of middle-class kids, whereas punk was a more working-class movement?

No, because most of the punk bands—particularly the big name ones such as The Clash and so on—were also middle-class kids. They were just pretending to be working-class. They were these skinny art students talking about saving society. It's just arrogant, isn't it?

I think the biggest crime from music

journalism was their treatment of Black Sabbath. When they first emerged they were a really big thing. The music press tended to have very narrow views back then because the people writing for it had no experience in life. They'd come straight from some university and they were often, as you said, very hostile towards anyone unlike them. When the first Black Sabbath album came out, one reviewer refused to listen to it and another described them as something like 'brick layers that play guitars.' The press here didn't take them seriously. In America they then became absolutely enormous, and so the press here then pretended that they'd liked them all along.

What you've got to remember is that the music journalists, particularly the *NME* cunts, are just there to sell their own careers. We had one that came down from *NME*. He came to see us play when we were in Sheffield—and this is a very good example of what that type of journalist was like. I was being polite to him and I bought him a beer. He was a bit nervy and young. We in the band were of a similar age to him but we were more grown-up cos we'd all had 'proper' jobs; I'd worked on building sites and that sort of thing, laying concrete. We'd all matured but this guy hadn't. He was like a child really, but a clever child.

We couldn't really have a decent conversation because we didn't have any common points of reference. Anyway, Howard took me to one side and told me not to talk to him. He said he'd be looking down his nose at me and he was going to take the piss out of me in the gig review later. I still felt sorry for him so I sat and talked to him about some of the other jobs that I'd had, that my dad was in the war, what my cat's name was, that sort of stuff. When the gig review was printed he was just talking about dropping acid and how he didn't know where he was, and then he fell into some free-form writing, all sort of French existentialist bollocks, you know? I used to work in an Esso garage (which is why my nickname is Esso) and he made some jibe about how I should still be working there. Nice of him.

The music that you listened to back then seemed to help define you as a character. It was an important part of your personality. But you don't seem to get this much now do you?

No, that's right. I think the 1970s and 1980s was the last time you had specific youth movements, and I think punk and so on was that last time you'd see that. It's a lot more corporate now, I think. There are still people around that like their songs, but the majority of music that people seem to listen to now is basically muzak—club anthems and stuff like that, mass produced for the masses. It's a bit like *Worker's Playtime* more than actual music, isn't it? You no longer see that two- or three-year cycle of different types of music coming in and out of fashion either, or significant clothing fashion changes (which is handy for me).

Kym Bradshaw joined the band for a while. Why do you think that didn't work out?

Well, Nigel [Moore] left the band and Kym had left The Saints, which is a band that I loved—they were so natural—and so we asked him if he'd join us. It didn't work out because he'd never worked with such a bunch of thick bozos in his life before he met us.

I think there was a presumption on our part that he liked a drink because he was Australian, but to our horror he wasn't very alcoholic. We were all very heavy drinkers. Pete almost died of alcohol poisoning on a few occasions. Howard slowly became a chronic alcoholic like his mother and grandfather were. I, on average, would be knocking back sixteen pints a day. On a good

Howard Wall, Peter Stride, Pete 'Esso' Haynes, Nigel Moore

day you could talk Kym into having a half of lager. He once had a bottle of water on stage for God's sake.

Kym's a very sensitive and kind bloke but he was always ill. He always had a head cold and he always had to sit down for some reason or another, and he was just quiet. And that's OK, you know? being quiet. But he wasn't enjoying himself.

He used to beg me to leave him alone cos I was always pissed and shouting about something or another. I'm not like that now—I was only twenty-one or twenty-two years old at the time. We never had any cross words with him but I don't think he fitted in. Anyway, Nigel came back and that made sense cos he drank a lot.

Why did Howard and Peter Stride break up the group?

What happened was that Pete thought we had gone as far as we could go playing the sort of music that we were playing, and they wanted to go in a new direction—a more rock and roll based sound—and I told them it was a huge mistake. Behind my back he became buddies with a band called The Boys, and Pete wanted to oust Nigel and me because we were not rock and roll enough. Before I knew it the band was over. Pete and Howard went off with a couple of others and made an album, and so that was the end of The Lurkers as it was then. We got back together in 1983 with a new singer called Marc and recorded what I think were some good songs, but nothing really came of it.

About twelve years ago, Pete, Nigel and myself started to record again. We don't do gigs these days but it's fun to make records again. It's nice because we know each other. I don't think I'd be able to drum with anyone else to be honest. With a new band I'd have to go through the rigmarole of having to get on with a new set of people, with all the politics and compromises that come with it. I'm not very good at that. I find most bands to be made up of egocentric twofaced wankers, to be honest. They don't seem to have any integrity, do they? They don't have any interest in other people at all.

I read your book God's Lonely Men: The Lurkers. What made you decide to write this? Did you think the time was right to tell the story?

When I was younger, I used to write poetry. I wrote a play in the early 1980s but I didn't do anything with it, and I've written a few more since. After the band had finished gigging, I decided to go to college to get a qualification. I didn't have a chip on

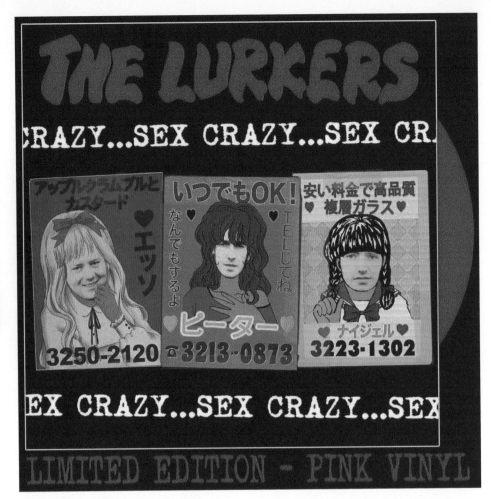

my shoulder but I did have an inferiority complex. I needed to talk to the middle-class people on their level. To do that, you've got to learn the rules of the game—that's how I saw it. So anyway, I went to Essex University and I passed the exam.

Whilst at the university, Nigel (from the band), who also went to the same university, had become involved with a theatre group, whereas I was down the pub all the time and in the darts team. So Nigel got talking about it all and took me down to this theatre where I met the director, a fella called Mark Evans. He read one of my plays that I took down there with me and he loved it and said he wanted to produce it and take it to Edinburgh, asked if I could go to the rehearsals, and I said I would. I'd never been to the theatre before, not even to watch a play, which is funny really cos I like writing them.

It got some very good reviews. I had a journalist from *The Scotsman* call me to talk about it and she asked if I had any influences besides Pinter. I didn't even know who Pinter was! But anyway, I explained this and I asked her if she could give me some names of playwrights to read, and she was kind enough to do so. The lady gave me a good write-up

but the title was something like 'Pete's a Playwright but he Don't Know It!' which I didn't particularly like; it was a bit patronising. I don't think she meant any harm though.

I then wrote a book called *Malayan Swing* in 1992/93. It's about a mentally disabled man who is forced from the group home he had lived in for years and sent out into the community. John King [who wrote *The Football Factory*, which was made into a film starring Danny Dyer] got to know me. He was a Lurkers fan and we became friends, and he has a publishing company. He published the book. That led to other people asking me to write about the band. And I obviously did, though I was a bit embarrassed because we were not a big name band and we weren't very rock and roll, and we didn't really meet anyone whose name I could drop. But most of my writing is about outsiders, and so the book is about a so-called outsider movement (punk) from an outsider's perspective (my own and the band's). And whilst most of the punk scene was completely manufactured, there is an honesty in the book.

JOHN OTWAY

John Otway is a singer-songwriter who broke out of the Aylesbury music scene (comprised at the time of himself and 'Wild' Willy Barrett) and into UK 'stardom' with an energetic rendition of his single 'Really Free' on *The Old Grey Whistle Test* culminating with him deciding to do a rather ill-advised leap onto a group of amps that consequently collapsed and leaving him briefly carrying on with obvious injuries to his nether regions, much to the amusement of the viewing public.

Far from the disaster himself and Willy had thought, this incident led to a very positive public reaction, and a subsequent record deal and a large upfront cash payment. The initial success was, however, led to an unsuccessful follow up single, that perhaps was too ambitious in scope (which included an orchestra inclusion), followed with nothing of note until 2002,

when he scored a second hit with 'Bunsen Burner.' Thanks to a combination of loyal fans (keen to give him a fiftieth birthday present) and a series of publicity stunts, this single reached number 9 in the UK singles charts.

Though John would agree that he wasn't 'an actual punk' he was marketed as one by his record company and certainly displayed all the DIY ethic and sheer determination of any dyed-in-the-wool punk. These virtues, along with his endearment to all that have met him, have secured a solid cult following for John. There are more successful bands in this book—and more talented musicians— but John's story is an important (and hilariously entertaining) one. Oh, and here's little music biz secret—he's not half as crap as he makes out.

How would you describe your childhood?

Well, I was bullied at primary school. I couldn't talk very well, I couldn't walk very well, and the kids used to beat me up, and when they did the teachers tended to join in! But I always wanted to be a musician. I started to get out of being bullied in the school playground by larking about and singing, and I became stagestruck, even without the stage. I liked being the centre of attention and just knew that being on stage was where I wanted to be. Musically, I think I was inspired by bands that were around prior to The Beatles: Cliff Richard and The Shadows, Marti Wilde, Chuck Berry, all the rock and roll greats.

How did you get hold of your first guitar?

Ah, now that was tricky. My mum gradually became aware of my musical aspirations and, knowing I wasn't particularly talented, tried to put a stop to it. She refused point-blank to let me have one. She did let me learn to play the violin though from the age of eleven, and I became quite good—I practiced for forty minutes every day. I was quite conscientious and got to a level where I could join the Aylesbury Youth Orchestra.

I had to wait till I was sixteen years old to get the guitar, and I managed to get a second-hand one from a junk shop. It cost me thirty bob and a fishing rod. I told my parents I was looking after it for someone else, but I slept with it the first night I was so terrified she would take it from me. And I think because I'd played the violin, I managed to play the guitar up to the standard I am now very, very quickly—all six chords!

When was your first attempt at songwriting?

That goes right back to the playground era. I used to just make things up as I went. Later though, I had to write my own songs because I had problems remembering the words of songs that other people had made, and I also had problems copying the music—I found the chords difficult. So it was just easier to write things for myself that I could play.

How did you get onto the stage for the first time?

Well, I was still pretty young. I went on one of those residential courses for musicians offered by the Youth Orchestra, and they used to put on these informal concert nights. People could get up on stage and do whatever they wanted to do. I did this completely over-the-top and emotional version of Peter Sarstedt's 'Where Do You Go to My Lovely?' and everyone just fell about laughing. I think that's when I started to realise that comedy could be a big part of the act. I expanded on that with other things.

How did you first come across future collaborator Wild Willy Barrett?

Actually, when I was growing up in Aylesbury he lived just up the road from where I lived. Him and his brother used to beat me up. Taking the hint, I stopped going round to their house after this happened for the twentieth time. They were a couple of years older than me. And then I didn't see him for years. Fast forward to my teenage years and I was playing the violin and guitar in folk clubs, and Willy had his own folk club by then which he would play his guitar in: The Derby Arms (also in Aylesbury). He let me do my version of 'Where Do You Go to My Lovely?' He was amused by it, and so we found each other. And we were likely to because Aylesbury wasn't really a melting pot of musicians, as you can imagine, so sooner or later we would be fated to bump into each other. We were both ambitious, but Willy had talent to go with it.

How did your music career take off so spectacularly?

I realised quite early on that with my level of talent it was going to be tricky to get a record deal. I managed to talk Willy into coming with me to a recording studio in Maidenhead, and we recorded one of my songs. It was all recorded on a Revox tape recorder, so it was a pretty basic set up. Then I decided to go the DIY route, which was popular at the time with punk bands, and found a place that could press our own records which we would then try and sell. I borrowed £100 from a friend to pay for this, and that was how my first single 'Gypsy/Misty Mountain' was born.

Now, I don't know how but John Peel the BBC DJ managed to get hold of a copy, and he was pretty well-known for giving bands (some of which went on to be huge stars) their first airplay. Anyway, my record started to get played on Radio 1. A friend of mine called me and she told me it was on the radio. Pete Townshend [of The Who] heard it and got in contact with Wild Willy's agent and offered to do a proper version of it. We did this in Olympic Studios in Barnes. It was a top-end studio and a far cry from our previous experiences. Pete ended up recording four tracks with us. On the track 'Louisa on a Horse,' Pete picked up a guitar and added my guitar parts. And I watched him play

and thought 'You know what, this guy's not bad is he?'

A funny thing happened whilst I was there. I was coming out of the studio having finished my vocals and a bloke in the corridor walked past and said 'That was good!' and I said 'Yeah it was, wasn't it mate?' This was seen by Willy from the control room, who said 'What did Mick Jagger just say to you?'

How did you get your first record deal?

It's a bit complicated. I was getting a small following because of the airtime my first single was getting—that and various publicity stunts and newsletters—and then I started to hang out at the offices of Track Records, which was the record label that The Who were under. They owned the copyright to their recording of 'Misty Mountain/Gipsy' as well as 'Louisa on a Horse.' Track Records tried to build up a London following for us, to see how we'd do. They booked us in at The Roundhouse, and in the crowd was an A&R man from Polydor, as well as the producer on The Old Grey Whistle Test. We coached in lots of fans from Aylesbury and Luton and surrounding areas with strict instructions to cheer at certain points, and it seemed to work. The A&R guy seemed very impressed.

I was trying to persuade them to put them out on record. They put out 'Louisa on a Horse,' which was a nice folky record, which they did eventually and it didn't sell well. But they wanted to put out a punk single, so they gave me and Willy enough money to record 'Really Free,' which I didn't think would be a hit, but they were insistent. So later we went away and recorded a full album instead, thinking that they would be pleased, but instead they fired us! So we put the album out on our own label, which we called Extracked, and got some pretty good reviews and airplay. Polydor though, who were the distributers for Tracks Records and The Who, thought I had potential, so they gave me and Willy enough money to record a single version of 'Really Free' with a bit more bite to it. They even helped us out with a free van as our coach kept breaking down and needed to be pushed.

You came to the attention of the public with your infamous The Old Grey Whistle Test performance. How did that come about?

The team at Polydor were trying to promote us so they got us on to two TV shows. The first one was So It Goes in Manchester, presented by Tony Wilson

[who would later create Factory Records], and the second one was a spot on The Old Grey Whistle Test. On the Whistle Test I got a bit excited whilst performing and at one point tried to do an athletic leap onto some speakers and ended up knocking them over. My legs went either side of one as it tipped and I landed squarely on my crotch as Willy looked on in absolute horror. Willy was actually completely pissed off as he'd thought I'd gone and blown it for us. Not only had I landed in a heap but I'd also managed to unplug his amp so no one could hear him, and I made him look like a prat as well. I think it was only when we were heading to the green room afterwards (separately) and started to hear everyone saying 'Wow! That was amazing!' that we started to realise that what I'd done wasn't all bad.

Did you really hurt yourself?

Oh god yeah. I was surprised I managed to get to the end of the record. I was still hurting down there a couple of days later, BUT IT WAS WORTH IT! [laughs]. Polydor, on the back of this performance, took over the album and put it into shops, and it all started there.

Polydor gave you a huge upfront payment for the time: £250,000. How did this change your life?

After the Whistle Test showing it was overnight stardom. I was getting people coming up to me in the street to talk to me. It was a big life-changing experience. It was a big sugar rush. On the back of this and the sales of 'Really Free,' which reached number 27 in the singles charts, we were given an advance of £250,000. I found out much later that they'd given

The Jam £6,000 up front, to put that into context. I think £250,000 would be about a million pounds in today's money. I rented a nice flat with some famous neighbours in Fulham and bought a Bentley, even though I hadn't passed my driving test.

Did the money help or hinder you?

I think the problem is that if you have one hit you are basically guaranteed bankruptcy. You plough the money back into your career, and it's very easy to build up an overdraft. Everything contracts quite quickly. Soon you are struggling for money again, and not for stupid reasons either. The people that got you there, the musicians that played in your band for a pittance, now expect to get paid decent money, which is fair enough, and start wanting retainers when they aren't playing—again fair enough. It's difficult (unless you are really mean) to turn around to the people that helped to get you where you are and say 'No, this is my money and I'm keeping it all for myself.' So before you know it, you're actually employing quite a large number of people, and the money disappears in no time at all.

But the single did well—it got to number 27 in the UK singles charts—and I was off to a flyer. I was on *Top of the Pops* twice and was interviewed in the music magazines. It was amazing.

Did you consider yourself punk at this time?

No, not really. Being shocking and playing badly was just coming into fashion at the right time for me. I was later tagged as a punk and Polydor marketed me as one, which I didn't particularly mind.

Retrospectively, what we did back then fitted in with the spirit of the time.

You seem to flow easily between musical genres.

Yeah, the reason for that is that it's not really me picking the genres that I play. I discovered early on that when I wrote music I had a very limited range; I tended to write around the same chords. So I like to collaborate with other musicians that sound different to the stuff I tended to create. On the *Monserrat* album, I let everyone in the band have a song and they could dictate the sound on it—it's a very eclectic way of working.

I'm a wordsmith more than a musician. What I like to do is sing a melody line and let them come up with an arrangement. I get writing periods when writing for albums and I find that most phrases don't turn into lyrics easily. I spend ages milling words because my bloody brain won't switch off. You spend eighteen months trying to get the lines right. I found that if I let lines go, they haunt you; if you release a single and there's one line that you weren't one hundred percent happy with, when you hear it later on, on the radio or whatever, it's toothachey to listen to it. So it's better to spend time getting it right before then, so you don't have to cringe continually for the next few decades.

In your early tours with Willy, there was the 'Headbutt' song where he smashed your head repeatedly into a microphone on stage. It looked like you were bleeding in some of the clips.

My relationship with Willy was based on ambition and his was the same with me,

I think. We both saw each other as a steppingstone to greater things. We had success together but could not wait to do some solo stuff ourselves. The 'Headbutt' song was written at a time when we were tied together, and I think Willy did not like me very much and he got rid of a bit of tension by grabbing me by the back of the head and at certain times in the song swinging my face into my microphone. Those were those heavy microphones from the 1970s you must remember, with the wire mesh covers. After a while, the mesh would disintegrate and some wires would stick out and be very painful to whack your head against. Our manager acted and taped a bit of sponge over the end with Gaffer Tape, in case I had a serious injury, but that microphone would mysteriously get replaced just before the song on most nights. Blood would be dripping down my face and I was in genuine pain. It used to go down very well. I think it's only recently that me and Willy started to really like each other.

You were the guest band on The Young Ones, which was obviously a classic comedy TV series of the time starring Rik Mayall and Ade Edmondson. How did that happen?

Well, my music career by then was faltering, and I tried my hand at acting. I'd decided I was a *visual artiste* by now, and I discovered the Edinburgh Fringe, which has turned into a comedy festival in recent years but was then more theatrical. Anyway, I wrote a play with a friend called Paul Bradley [who would later play Nigel Bates in *Eastenders*] and took it up there to Edinburgh to perform. Paul was big mates with Rik, who played Rik the student anarchist, and Ade, who played Vivien the heavy metal psychopath in *The Young Ones*. That was the connection. Paul had played a couple of small parts in the series, including Warlock, the hippy friend of fellow hippy Neil. Anyway, he got me onto the show. I played a song called 'Body Talk' whilst they were trying to sleep in a back alley having been evicted from their student lodgings.

You've got a very dedicated fanbase, haven't you?

Yes, and it's a great way to extend and cushion a career. A record company can pick you up and drop you without thinking about it but having a few thousand fans is a great barrier against some of life's ups and downs. They keep you going, don't they?

You were voted by the public as the seventh-best lyricist for the song 'Beware of the Flowers, Because

They'll Get You in the End, Yeah!'

Yes, it was amazing. John Lennon grabbed top spot but I beat both Bob Dylan and even The Moody Blues, who could only manage number nine on the list!

How did they get you into the charts again for your fiftieth birthday?

It was all down to a throwaway comment I made about what I wanted for my fiftieth birthday in 2002: I said I'd like a second hit single. It was a form of crowdfunding before that existed. They got my song 'Bunsen Burner' into the charts at number nine, and it was brilliant. If you hadn't already guessed, they were behind me being voted as seventh-best lyricist too! They organised that between them. It's all very amusing that you can corrupt polls in such a fashion, and what better poll to corrupt than the music charts?

We had ten-thousand fans all in on it. We released the single in three different formats to enable people to buy it three times, all of which counted towards the total sales figure for one single. We figured those thirty-thousand sales should be able to get us into the charts if all purchased on the same day, but you have got to spread the sales across the different UK regions to qualify, which means getting the stores to take them, which means persuading not only the smaller shops but the big distributers too.

The biggest problem was that Woolworths, who were responsible for forty percent of music sales and even supplied supermarkets with records, were simply not interested, which was a big blow. But this sort of worked to our advantage because the press picked up on it and it was all over the newspapers and even *News at Ten*. It became a sort of David and Goliath story, and the British love an underdog, don't they? Woolworths shot themselves in the foot when their spokeswoman announced that they decided what they were going to stock months before. So they were essentially choosing who was going to be in the charts and admitted that their own chart was a reflection of what they stocked rather than what the public actually wanted to buy. And I was later told that the poor woman was fired not long afterwards. Later, to save their reputation, they had to buy the rights to use the Doctor Fox chart for several million pounds to give them their in-store chart credibility again, and I was responsible! Anyway, the public seemed to come together to help with my ambition, and we did it! I was in the charts again, decades after the last hit single.

You toured in the USA extensively on the back of your success. Do the Americans get your act?

I think the American people do, they get the humour, but the American promoters and record companies don't. They don't understand the self-effacing stuff either. I had the idea of marketing myself as a failure over there, and they just don't understand that at all. It's against the American mentality, I think. I enjoy it over there though.

I watched Otway the Movie, which was incredibly funny but exhausting. Every time you conquered one challenge, such as getting into the charts, you set yourself another big challenge— filling the Albert Hall with fans, and then the world tour. Is there no end to your ambition?

My ambition is huge. I've always wanted to be a big international star.

You released two books about your life. Did you think it was time to tell your side of the story?

Well, the first one was written in 1988 at a very different stage in my life. My career had really hit the skids and I realised that I'd reached a point where my life couldn't get any worse. It covers the beginnings as a skinny kid, then getting the big record deal, and then the decline and ending up where I started with nothing again.

I've always liked self-effacing humour. Usually when you read a book about a musician you have a narrative where they are the heroes and the managers and record companies are these horrible pantomime villains. I thought it would be funny in my book to have the managers and record companies as the heroes and I'm the guy screwing everything up for everyone. The latest book is just about my adventures since then, and it's a jovial reflection on my career as well.

What next for you?

Well, I'm seventy this year, and I think we're just going to do something to celebrate with the band—nothing too arduous! Although you never know, *Otway the Musical* may still happen!

John Otway and Wild Willy in 1972

30

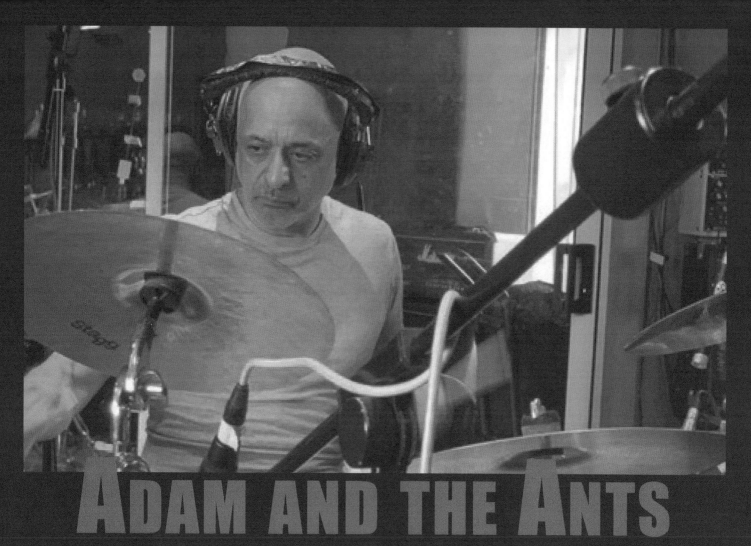

ADAM AND THE ANTS

INTERVIEW WITH DAVE BARBAROSSA

Dave Barbarrosa became the drummer of Adam and the Ants in 1977. His distinctive style—staccato, with a tribal influence—became synonymous with the ants and his next band, Bow Wow Wow. Dave has also drummed with Chiefs of Relief (created with BWW members Ashman and Gorman), Beats International, Republica (on their debut album), Chicane, Adamski, and Fine Young Cannibals among others.

Adam and the Ants were originally a punk band headed by Adam (Stuart Goddard) but with a shifting line-up that originally included Lester Square on guitar, Paul Flannagan on drums, and Andy Warren on bass. They famously played at The Roxy Club with Siouxie and the Banshees. The line-up changed again when Lester Square returned to art school and was replaced by Mark Ryan, on whose couch Dave happened to be sleeping when Paul Flannagan could not make it to a gig in Chelmsford one evening. Dave was asked to step in, greatly impressed Adam, and joined the band the same evening.

Frustrated that the band were not hitting the charts proper, the ambitious Adam hired former Sex Pistols manager and *agent provocateur* Malcolm McClaren to garner more publicity and direct a video. Malcolm then took the opportunity, however, to poach Dave, Matthew Ashman, and Leigh Gorman to form new band Bow Wow Wow with thirteen-year-old vocalist Annabella Lwin. Bow Wow Wow would have several hits, such as 'I want Candy' (9 in the UK Singles Charts) and 'Go Wild in the Country' (7). A tour of America followed and led to exhaustion and illness, particularly in the case of Matt Ashman, who was hospitalised with previously undiagnosed diabetes. This eventually led to a break up of the band.

Meanwhile, Adam's new Ant's line-up, are known for their numerous high-charting singles: 'Kings of the Wild Frontier' (2) upon rerelease in singles charts), 'Dog Eat Dog' (4), 'Antmusic' (2), 'Prince Charming' (1), 'Friend or Foe' (5), 'Stand and Deliver' (1), 'Ant Rap' (3), 'Goody Two Shoes' (1), and a number of other minor hits.

Adam Ant - 1979 Alamy Photo Library

You grew up in Stoke-Newington in the 1960s and 1970s. What was that area like around that time?

It was a vibrant, culturally mixed area. Like a lot of places back during that time period it was very run down though. Nothing like it is now, it's been gentrified to a large extent; lots of bars and coffee shops. It was probably more like Tottenham is now back then.

What were you like as a kid? And what was your home life like?

I am from a very large family. I'm of British and Mauritian descent. I grew up with five brothers and sisters in a cramped downstairs terrace flat. Again, we were no different to many other families in the area; not a lot of room, not a lot of money. I was very energetic—we all played together. I used to play football over in the park until the sun went down. It was a pretty normal upbringing for the most part.

My dad played Latin American music—it was the dance music of the late 50s-early 60s—so I absorbed a lot of rhythm as a child. There was a lot of blue beat and reggae in the neighborhood, music from different parts of the world. I liked the pop music of the day, gravitated to soul, Motown, blues rock, then glam rock. Later classical and jazz.

When did you first become aware of punk, and did you like any of the bands? Did you think that it was something that teens needed at that time?

I was only aware if it as a cultural irritant to the establishment. You couldn't hear the music on the radio, so I was unaware of the sound initially. I think the country needed to be burst wide open, socially and musically. Punk rock did that with panache.

Drums are quite expensive, which I guess is why most people learn the guitar. Why did you decide drums would be your instrument? How did you get your first set of drums?

I worked as a messenger boy in the west end when I was fifteen and saved up. It took me a long time, and I was disappointed that I couldn't afford some of the newer sets of drums. I bought a knackered set from Eddie Ryan's in Soho. I was drawn to the drums because of the order you could create from chaos and noise.

There seems to be a bit of disruption in your life prior to you joining Adam/Stuart. If you don't mind us asking,

what happened exactly? How did you become homeless?

Can't exactly, it's a bit complicated and far too long ago. But it was the usual teenage dysfunction: kicked out of school, a bit of trouble with the law. Nothing devastating. We find our way through, or we don't. Fortunately, I did. I found myself with nowhere to live, but fortunately I had the support of friends to get me through.

Before you became an Ant you were living with future band mate Mark Ryan. What did you think of the band before you joined? Mark must have been a good friend? How would you describe him?

Mark was a good friend and educator. I needed somewhere to stay, and he let me stay on his sofa. He was already a member of The Ants at the time, though I wasn't really aware of them as such. I had my drums with me and I could practice. Mark was probably the first art intellectual I ever encountered. He taught me a great deal.

How did you first meet Adam?

I'd never heard of the Ants until Mark called me and asked me if I'd stand in for their drummer at a gig that fateful night. Even though he was in the band, he didn't really talk about his band. Mark and Adam had a gig in Chelmsford and their drummer had to cancel and let them down. Mark was obviously aware that I had a drum kit and could play, and called on the phone that evening and asked if I could step in. I'd never played in front of a crowd before, but I said yes, so I was asked to have my drums outside in an hour and they would pick me up. We supported The Slits, a female punk band, who were an amazing band. It was hot, and volatile, but exhilarating.

It must have been daunting to just be asked to join an established band on stage with no practice or rehearsals.

Well it was all a bit mental back then. You just had to get your elbows out and give it everything. I didn't rehearse until after the third or fourth gig perhaps. I wasn't a schooled musician, so I had no expectations, I just loved being there.

The gigs were invariably electric: packed, beery, faggy, and sweaty. No health and safety back then. Adam always gave it everything and I did the same. Immediately after the first gig Adam asked me to join the band officially, and I obviously accepted.

What were your first impressions of

Adam once you had a chance to know him? He comes over as very focused and ambitious, with a plan. Was that the case?

Exactly right. Disciplined and focused. A brilliant artist but with the attitudes of an elite athlete. For me, he was a true leader: bold, with incredible self-belief. He knew exactly what he wanted to do.

How did working in the band work as a dynamic? Were strategies discussed, and image and so on?

There wasn't a lot of discussion. Adam was in complete control of everything, even to some extent what we wore on stage. He could play all of the instruments except the drums, which he entrusted to me. It was the same with the songwriting. We all knew where we stood.

What were Adam's musical influences? I always got a bit of a 1940s country vibe from his songs for some reason.

In his teens he was obsessed with Delta blues, the real deep stuff. He had an encyclopedic knowledge of it all. He loved Bowie, Roxy, Ian Dury, T Rex—the usual suspects—when I met first him. We all did.

How did the band get around? I'm always interested in rickety old vans and how travel was organized.

Yeah, Transits and VWs, roughing it on and in between the gear. No one complained back then; it was an honour to play gigs.

Dirk Wears White Sox is a fantastic album. What were your experiences of making the record? What was it like working with the American producer on the project? Were there any tracks that were quite difficult to get right?

It was all very exciting, as these things are. Adam is a perfectionist; his songs are his children to be nurtured and loved. The songs were as complex as the bloke that wrote them. The production is the weakness on the album in my opinion. We should have got a British producer who knew our sound.

What sort of sound do you think the producer on the album strived for?

The way we played the songs live was the way we recorded them mate, I dunno what *he* strived for—the bar, the rolled-up fiver maybe?

Malcolm McClaren, obviously famous as previously the manager of The Sex

Pistols, was hired by Adam to direct a music video and to gain the band more exposure. What was Malcolm like?

Exciting. An original thinker. A good friend to me, ultimately.

Adam always seemed to be in control, and Malcolm coming in as manager was a strange decision. Did they clash at all? They both seemed to be people with strong ideas.

Of course they clashed; look at the relationship and its outcome. They are men looking through different ends of a telescope: Adam, traditional, disciplined, pure musical talent; Malcolm, disruptive, extremely irreverent, a revolutionary.

The story goes that Malcolm introduced you to Burundi drumming, but I can hear it in earlier recordings to an extent. What influence did he have over your style of drumming?

A huge influence. He introduced me to 'world music.' Don't think it had a label back then. The ethnic drumming he introduced, plus the thudding tom-tom style of glam rock, gave me an original angle on the drums. He literally gave us records from around the world: Aboriginal, Afro, Latin, 60s surf, classical, opera. He completely overwhelmed us with different cultures and sounds and ordered us to immerse ourselves in it. It was brilliant. Adam must have also been influenced by world music, as both Bow Wow Wow and the new version of Adam and the Ants had elements of tribal drumming in their sound.

Malcolm famously 'stole' the rest of the band, yourself included, to create Bow Wow Wow. How did he sell this to you?

By saying 'You've been a side man for long enough and you can create a new sound for the drums.' We'd been with Adam for a couple of years by then and we were looking to try something interesting and new. Adam took it very well and we remained friends. He went on to be an international superstar and a multimillionaire.

Bow Wow Wow was a much more tribal sound, much faster and tighter. Was it more difficult to record in a studio than the Ant music?

BWW were never recorded properly. We didn't know when to reign it in and make it accessible. There always seemed a new horizon to get to, musically. Perhaps they were a band for the digital age, studio-wise. Who knows? But live we were pretty good.

Now that Malcolm had much more control over you as a band, what was it like wearing the costumes that Vivienne Westwood created for you? Some were quite outlandish.

I suppose it was an honour. A wild look for a wild sound? We didn't care. We had some very interesting clothing which set us apart from other bands. Malcolm and Vivienne knew what they were doing. And we became a success with several hits.

You had massive hits with Bow Wow Wow. What was touring like and how did it differ touring in the USA than the UK?

Triumphant and lawless. Unimaginable fun. Given money and absurdly praised for months and years for something most people would pay to do for one night. On that point, touring was much more rewarding in the States. They treated you like professional entertainers, not as they did over here, like scroungers with instruments.

The tour of America had to be cancelled due to Matt becoming ill with diabetes. How was this discovered and were there any warning signs? How ill was he?

We sensed something wasn't right with him for months, but we were on the road making money for the various lawyers and accountants that ran the band after

Malcom departed. He would be drinking a lot of pop. We didn't think anything of it at the time. Then he fell off the stage at the opening tour gig in New Jersey and broke his arm. He was going blind. He was diagnosed in the hospital and that was that for Bow Wow Wow. We were exhausted by the world tour by then and needed a break.

Malcolm had already left because he got bored. He has about a three- to four-year attention span to his projects. As I said, the band was exhausted at the end of touring the planet consistently for about fourteen months. It was too much. No one gave a shit.

You've been playing as a session musician for years and played with many great bands. How easy is it for you to listen to a new band and add the drums? Is there a huge fear that your styles won't gel? What's the worst thing about working as a session musician?

I have no huge fears when I'm behind the drums, but I'm not comfortable being micromanaged, so never a good session man. I've become proficient at memorising song arrangements, so no great problem learning another band's set. As I mentioned, Adam and Malcolm never did this to me. Sessioning and making your own music is chalk and cheese.

I especially like your later work with Republica. How would you say they differed from both the Ants and Bow Wow Wow, with such a lot of synths involved? Is there anything extra you need to take into consideration?

Republica gave me a little more room to express myself live, so it wasn't as constricted as other 'staff' jobs I've had. You take a hundred things into consideration when you are asked to play for people professionally. Republica was a compromise, but something I'm glad I did.

Your book Mud Sharks (a great read) is semi-autobiographical. How much is the protagonist Henry like you? Why did you decide to start writing the book?

Thank you for that. Harry. Yes, he's lived and experienced a lot of the things I have. Although not chronologically accurate, it has most of my early life documented in it. I love writing; it's another way to express myself creatively, freely. I'll have a second novel, *Mute,* out soon, fingers crossed.

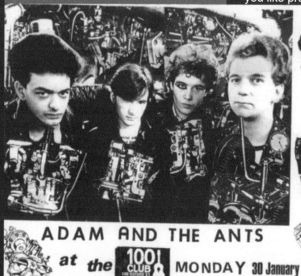

ADAM AND THE ANTS at the 1001 CLUB MONDAY 30 January

New Wave Heavy Metal

The historical context of the new wave of heavy metal is the same as that of punk rock: a large section of society was hit hard by unemployment as heavy industry began to collapse, political turmoil manifested in large-scale strikes, and there was a feeling that the country was divided into the haves and the have-nots. The surviving metal bands of the late 60s and early 70s were imputed to suffer the same malaise as their prog rock counterparts—they were (perhaps somewhat unfairly) seen as having lost touch with their fans, as stories of their extreme wealth and excesses surfaced.

Although wealth and excess are the natural preserves of the rock star, during the pronounced class divides of the late 1970s the mood began to turn, particularly in the UK.

As punk emerged, a similar scene also came out of the shadows, though not to share quite as much of the limelight. Taking elements from older bands like Deep Purple, Led Zeppelin, and Iron Butterfly, and adding the ferocity and speed of punk, a denim- and leather-clad brigade of (mostly) working-class youngsters, largely from the industrial

north of Britain, started to play their own music. The lyrics tended to have a mythological or horror content, and these worlds were often merged in the cover art.

Groups such as Iron Maiden, Judas Priest, Def Leppard, Motorhead, and Saxon enjoyed eventual success though dismissed at first by the middle-class music press of the time. It was only when American radio stations began to pick them up that sales really boomed. We chat to Saxon next, for the simple reason that they are (in part) from my hometown of Mexborough in South Yorkshire.

SAXON

INTERVIEW WITH GRAHAM OLIVER

Graham Oliver is a founder member of new wave metal band Saxon, originating in Barnsley and Mexborough in 1977 when two local bands merged so that they could fulfil their gigging commitments. Graham joined Peter 'Biff' Byford on vocals, Steve Dawson on Bass, Paul Quinn on lead guitar, and John Walker (followed by Peter Gill) on drums. They originally held the name Son of a Bitch.

They found a record deal with French company Carrere, who had spotted their potential but insisted that they changed their name to something more suitable to American audiences. And so Saxon was born.

With the backing of a large record company behind them, they were soon supporting established metal bands such as Motörhead and the Ian Gillan Band (Gillan was previously the lead singer of Deep Purple).

Their first album *Saxon* didn't attract a great deal of interest at the time, but *Wheels of Steel* delivered two chart hits—'Wheels of Steel' (20) and '747 (Strangers in the Night)' (13)—as well as hitting number 5 in the UK album charts. Further album success followed with *Strong Arm of the Law* (11 in the UK charts) and several more hit singles as well as appearances at Monsters of Rock festival and *Top of the Pops*.

When did you decide that music was a career that you wanted to pursue?

It was after seeing Jimi Hendrix live at the city hall in Sheffield as a fourteen-year-old boy. Before then I was listening to whatever was in the charts: The Who and The Stones and The Beatles, who were all hitting the Top Ten back then and were also very good. But that performance by Hendrix just blew me away, and I knew that's what I wanted to do with my life.

My dad took me to Doncaster to buy me a guitar soon afterwards. It was an Airstream 3 electric guitar by Rosetti (as a footnote, this guitar is now in Doncaster Museum). The next step was learning how to use it. I'm completely self-taught. I did try to find some books on learning how to play, but around the 1960s the only books around on the subject were flamenco or jazz based ones—both were really popular at the time—neither of which I was interested in as I wanted to be a rock musician. So I just had to wing it, really. Anyway, I practiced and practiced and became quite proficient, and this took me a few years. Eventually I left school and I worked in a factory (GEC) in Swinton in South Yorkshire and played the guitar in my spare time.

What was your first experience of being in a band?

It was a little band called The Syndicate in 1967. I did it in my spare time. Everyone else in the band wanted to play pop music but my tastes were a bit heavier. It was good practice though, and we played a few pub and club gigs. In 1969 myself and Steve Dawson met for the first time [Steve would later be part of Saxon]. We decided to create our own band called Blue Condition, named after a song by Cream, sung by Ginger Baker. I left The Syndicate and we got another bloke to join us on drums called Dave Bradley, and Steve Firth came in to do the vocals. Our first gig was in the Canal Tavern in Swinton. We got paid ten shillings for that. And then we played a lot of the local pubs in the area. The song 'Alright Now' by Free was a massive hit and me and Steve were big fans. They had an album called *Tons of Sobs* and we decided that Blue Condition was a bit naff and so changed the name to S.O.B. and then later when Punk was coming in, we changed it to Son of a Bitch (but still S.O.B. for short).

How did the merger between yourself and Coast happen?

What had happened was that we had lost our singer, Steve [Firth]. Now Coast were another band that we were familiar with; they toured the same gig circuit that we played and we liked what they were doing musically. And Coast had lost their drummer and both bands had a lot of bookings to fill, so it made sense to merge. So Biff [Byford] who was the singer with Coast and Paul [Quinn] who was a guitarist were asked by Steve [Dawson] to join us. And along with drummer Pete Gill we became a five-piece for the first time. Five likeminded people.

It was around this time that you hurt your hand really badly, didn't you?

A door slammed shut on my hand on a windy day. This led to the removal of the tip of my index finger—probably the worst one to injure too for a guitar player—my index finger on my left hand. I trapped it in a door and lost the tip. And for a while I just could not play without a lot of pain, and so I gave up trying. I even sold my guitar. I was distraught. It was friends like Paul Quinn, Tony Lommie, Bernie Marsden, and Richie Blackmore over the next couple of years who persuaded me to try and take it up again. And that took a lot of retraining as I had to learn how to play with a shorter finger.

Were you writing your own songs back then?

Yeah, myself and Steve Dawson were writing songs together. We played a full set of our own songs. In fact, 'Freeway Mad' that was on the Saxon album *Wheels of Steel* is an old S.O.B. song, written long before any involvement with Biff or Paul. 'Ann Marie' was recorded and used as a bonus track on the CD version when that became available.

You were quite a hardworking band before you made it big, weren't you?

Yes, and afterwards. As working musicians you have to put the time in to gig because that's where the money comes from, but it also allows you to hone your craft. We were playing up and down the country. A lot of the time we played working men's clubs, which was (not so much now) a preserve of the north of the country and Wales. A lot of these clubs would struggle financially and would occasionally organise rock nights as heavy metal began a revival, particularly amongst the working people in small towns and villages. One town just north of Newcastle had twenty-nine working men's clubs, and we used to gig in every one of them—places such as the Sunderland Boilermakers Club. It was a long process to get a following.

How do you think the so-called new wave of British heavy metal bands

differed from the older ones such as Led Zeppelin and Deep Purple?

When we started the band, we probably did it in the most unfashionable time to play heavy metal music, but ourselves and other heavy metal bands that were emerging were trying to do something different to the older bands such as Deep Purple. For a start we didn't play long drawn-out guitar solos or drum solos that older groups were sometimes a bit guilty of, although we loved all of the older stuff. We actually went to see Deep Purple a couple of times and we even stole some of their act to be honest. I think each generation wants to be different from the previous one.

When you were developing as a band, were you influenced at all by the punk bands coming through?

We were obviously aware of the punk bands coming through. We did a couple of gigs with The Clash before they were really big, and The Sex Pistols were around when we were touring in the early years too. Most of the punk bands that we came across were a bit raw. The punk bands that did well tended to be the ones that could play well. I think a lot of the punk bands in general lacked musicianship, which is why most of them seemed to tour down south. When you are playing in a northern town or city there is the demand that you play well. There is less money kicking about and when people in the north have paid to see someone, they expect them to be proficient with instruments. You don't want to get on stage in Bradford or Leeds without that musicianship—you'd get bottled off. We had to fashion our craft

COPYRIGHT EMI RECORDS (UK) – PHOTOGRAPHER: ADRIAN PEACOCK

playing these places, as well as Newcastle and South Wales.

In my opinion, people in London (for example) generally wanted to go to gigs to be seen with others that had the same fashion, so the actual bands could get away with not having the skills so long as they looked the part. I think punk was a fashion more than a musical genre as such, though I quite like a lot of the music. *Nevermind the Bollocks* [The Sex Pistols] is a brilliant album, but to me it's a rock album and not a punk album as such. It was quite short lived once the shock value had worn off, unlike heavy metal which seems to keep on going. Deep Purple and Led Zeppelin were around for decades, and even later bands such as Iron Maiden, Metallica, and others are still touring. But punk faded quite quickly and the bands that survived evolved into something else. One thing we probably did take from punk was the energy though.

When did you change the name to Saxon?

It was late 1978 and when we began recording for the first time, it was flagged by our record company that the name Son of a Bitch, even abbreviated to S.O.B., was something that the American public wouldn't like, and no one on radio would be comfortable saying it, so we had to think of a name for ourselves. Americans are much more conservative than the British. I honestly cannot remember if there were other names thrown into the hat, but Saxon was a brilliant name and we were happy with it.

How did the songwriting work now that you were a five-piece?

Each song was different, but me and Paul Quinn would work on the riffs. We used to practice in my council house bedroom on Dryden Road in Mexborough. The slower meatier riffs are usually mine and the faster ones are Paul's. My riffs were used on songs such as 'Power and the Glory,' 'Never Surrender,' and 'Hungry years.' We'd take these to the band rehearsals and everyone else would then chip in with their own parts, then the song would gradually emerge. It was a collective, basically.

I would never have written 'Dallas 1 PM' without Pete Gill the drummer, as an example. He was once up all night in the rehearsal room playing around with a drumbeat, and when I heard it that inspired me to come in with the guitar part, then Steve came in and started to play the bass line, which was grooving on the A string, and suddenly we had the makings of a great song. Paul came in and created a counter-rhythm to my rhythm, and then Biff had an idea for the vocals. We preferred that the singers create the lyrics because people that don't sing, when they write lyrics they tend to write poetry and not words that can be sung easily. It's subtle but it makes a big difference, and it's something I've noticed over the years. It was mainly Biff and Steve Dawson that wrote the lyrics, though Pete used to do the actual handwriting 'cos he could write a bit neater than the other two and could actually spell quite well. A hundred songs were written like that for the band.

How did your first record deal come about?

We played a gig in a club in the Northeast called the Easington Village Club, and John Verity and Dave Thomas who were part of the Sheffield Brothers' empire were there for some reason in the audience. They were impressed with what they saw and they had connections with Carrere Records in France. They were the ones that helped us to get the recording deal. They asked us for a demo record, and this was sent over to Carrere, and not long afterwards we were flying to Paris to sign the contract. Apparently, my guitar solo on 'Frozen Rainbow' on our demo record that was sent to them was the deal clincher.

How did you find working in a studio for the first time?

Well, it wasn't that much different to us because we were taking songs that we'd polished in pubs and clubs for two or three years, so all the faults and niggles had been ironed out. I think the main thing that we had to keep in mind in a studio was that you are paying by the hour, and it's expensive. You can't stop and chat about football or anything like that at the end of a song, otherwise you've just lost a hundred quid.

Did songwriting change for you change after you worked in a studio extensively?

Not for me personally. The trick is to get it down onto tape (or these days digitally) but with the speed and passion of a live performance. It can sound different to a proper live audience. Sometimes, obviously, you listen to something when you are in the studio and realise that the song would work better if you added or changed a chord in the chorus or something like that. I think that's the only difference to writing a song outside the studio; it's the immediacy of it.

Do you switch between guitars depending on what you are working on?

To a degree, yes. So I couldn't have done that guitar solo on 'Frozen Rainbow' or on 'Dallas 1 PM' on a Stratocaster, and I have to sometimes use a guitar based on finger access due to my disability, such as a twenty-two or twenty-four fret guitar. I still struggle with that.

Your first self-titled album Saxon, released in 1979, didn't do so well initially, did it? Do you think that's because the sound wasn't faithful to your live set?

Yes. Our record company asked John Verity to produce it, and he's a smashing guy, but I think the problem with it was that it was recorded not as we played live, and it didn't have that power behind it. He's talented, but there were things on the album that we wouldn't have done ourselves, things like putting backing vocals where we would not have put them. There's a lot of good stuff on the album, don't get me wrong; 'Stallions of the Highway' became a hit on the UK's alternative metal chart, and I think that helped with giving us some exposure. And our later success brought more interest in it.

Your next album in 1980, Wheels of Steel, was your 'break out' album; what did you do differently?

We co-produced this album and recorded it at The Who's recording studio. The first half of that album was made with just me, Pete Gill, and Steve Dawson, with Biff doing the vocals on his own to begin with (Paul Quinn was ill and at home up in Barnsley). So we played the Wheels of Steel title track, 'Freeway man,' and a few others. We recorded them live, basically. Paul came down later and added his parts onto it. The production by Pete Hinton isn't that great to be honest, but then Ozzy Osbourne's first albums weren't either. But they both have that spontaneity which I think you need on metal albums. Most people don't sit and analyse albums though; they just listen to enjoy them. It reached number 5 in the album charts and eventually became a Gold Disc.

'747 (Strangers in the Night)' is one of the album's highlights. How did that song come about?

We needed a few more songs for the album and so for inspiration we went to a farm on a mountain in Wales. It was owned by one of the guys from Hawkwind. Don't ask me why we chose there. But anyway . . .

I remember, it was January and freezing cold, and we were in the barn where we used to practice. We were shivering and trying to play. Paul Quinn put a great Hawkwind-style riff down, and it was brilliant but we weren't able to build on it, so we gave up and went indoors and made something for dinner and put the TV set on. We were watching one of those programmes about weird things that had happened in the past, and one was about a small electronic component that had tripped and knocked out most of New York, including Kennedy Airport. At the time a Boeing 747 was just about to land and it had to abort. We were discussing this incident and how you would feel if you were on that plane, and that's how we got

the idea for the song, and it's one of our most popular ones.

You went on Top of the Pops quite a few times, didn't you?

Four times live, and then our videos were played quite a few times too. One time when we played live on there, I think it was the first time that more than three people that had lived in Mexborough were also on the show—as far as we can be reasonably aware anyway. So there was me, Tony Capstick [who had a hit with the Hovis advert parody 'Capstick comes home'], as well as Hazel O'Connor, who used to live on Church Street in Mexborough for a while. These were filmed at the London studio, and it was very interesting to take part, particularly as it's something I'd watched on TV for years.

You've toured extensively in America with bands such as Rush, Black Sabbath, and Metallica. How different was touring there to the UK and Europe?

What's strange about it is that it's different not just state-to-state but city-to-city too. And it's only when you travel across it that you realise how vast it is. East coast we tended to play nightclubs but west coast it was stadiums. The people can be very different too.

Why did Pete Gill and Steve Dawson leave the band?

It's a bit of a long story and I don't want to talk on their behalf. My thoughts though are that our managers that we had acquired had five working-class lads, and they were paying *our* wages. This was out of the money that we were earning. And because of our working-class background we would thank them for it. It's only later when you realise 'Hold on, we should be paying them, not the other way around.' I think it's a slow realisation.

Some of the things that the management would do was a bit cynical. They turned up at the airport once when we were off to somewhere or another in America with a document for us all to sign. They said it was so that they could still pay our wages to our wives whilst we were away, and so we all thought 'Oh that's nice of them!' and 'That's a good idea' and signed it thanking them. But it was also a publishing extension agreement. We should have told them to piss off, but we were young lads and were just wanting to get on the plane and see the other side of the world. It was things like that that we started to not like.

Why did Saxon start to fall from

popularity do you think? Did you miss Pete and Steve?

Around this time MTV became amazingly popular and our record company EMI started to try to force us to be more TV-friendly. Not just the music—it was the slicker image and all that sort of thing. There is a tendency when you are in a band to listen too much to people that don't play the music: the money men. 'They sell records, they must know what they are talking about' is what usually goes through your head. We should have kept our South Yorkshire heavy metal band image instead of accepting advice and trying to promote an American-friendly image of ourselves which was like bands like Motley Crue that were then emerging.

The music changed too. You could see sales falling the minute we stopped writing songs as a collective. Once Steve Dawson and Pete Gill had left, we lost so much, because they were so important to the songwriting process. It was truly a collective, and once that started to dissipate you could tell that the music had lost something. EMI hired new producers too who didn't know anything about our band. Gary Lyons and Stephan Galfas came on board to produce the *Rock the Nation* and *Destiny* albums, but it just wasn't us. It was a radio-friendly sound but our old fans didn't like it, and we didn't benefit from gaining any new fans either.

Why did you eventually leave Saxon?

The only thing I'll say is that I wanted openness from management about certain things and it wasn't forthcoming. But I still play with my own band and Saxon continues onwards and are doing well, and I think we're both happy. My son has also followed me into music with his band Bullrush, which makes me even happier.

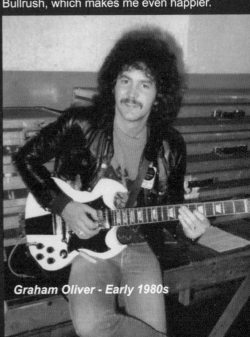

Graham Oliver - Early 1980s

SOLID BALL OF ROCK TOUR '91

PRÄSENTIERT

SAXON

SPECIAL GUEST:

HEADHUNTER

CHROMING ROSE

S A X O N
AKTUELLES ALBUM:
SOLID BALL OF ROCK

CHROMING ROSE
AKTUELLES ALBUM:
GARDEN OF EDEN

HEAD HUNTER
AKTUELLES ALBUM:
PARODY OF LIFE

MONTAG, 13. MAI 1991, 20 UHR

KÖLN · STADTHALLE MÜLHEIM

LP 211114 · CD 261114 · MC 411114

Karten bei den Vorverkaufsstellen oder telefonischer Kartenbestellservice: 0228 / 36 10 15

ELECTROLA
LP / CD / MC 796 125 · 1 / 2 / 4

LP 211151 · CD 261151 · MC 411151

GOTHIC ROCK

In the early 1980s, gothic rock rose from the ashes of punk. Many would say that gothic rock is an offshoot of punk, and for reasons not discountable. Goth hair styles and clothing are an obvious evolution of the punk look, and certain bands that were at the centre of the punk scene, such as Siouxie and the Banshees and The Damned, became prominent members of the goth movement. But gothic rock differed from punk in that it was drained of the anger and bitterness that fueled punk's political rants and lacked the compulsion to play as fastly and as furiously as possible, focusing instead on a sense of despair or exile that had nevertheless underpinned punk's affect. The power of both movements to speak to very teenage sentiments says something for their similarity.

Bauhaus and the single 'Bela Lugosi's Dead' set a tone and a theme for goth's look and sound. Bela Lugosi, who played Dracula in several black and white films, offered a perfect model for the 'traditional' goth look: black clothing, long coats that resemble cloaks, skinny trousers, tall black hairdos, pale makeup, and black eyeliner and eyebrows. With goths the vampire theme is taken up not as horror, but in the spirit of author Anne Rice's assessment of the vampire as 'a doomed romantic, cut off from society by something beyond their control.'

After the success of Bauhaus, the subgenre of goth took a huge step forward, and specialist goth nightclubs started to appear all over the UK. Often dark and crypt-like, clubs like The Bat Cave in London, run by Olli Wisdom of the house band Specimen along with Banshee Jon Klein, would lead the way. These venues brought together the remnants of a punk crowd who still stood sorely out from the mainstream of society by virtue of their taste in music and clothing, and (following the dissolution of the punk scene) needed a place to feel accepted in their strangeness.

Despite the repeated efforts of mainstream journalists to dub goth bands as doom and gloom merchants, many acts such as The Sisters of Mercy, The Damned, The Cure, and Siouxie and the Banshees would embrace a wide range of musical influences, including pop and rock-opera and even dance music, and would regularly chart with a much more upbeat sound. These bands proved that you could have a good time and *still* be a goth.

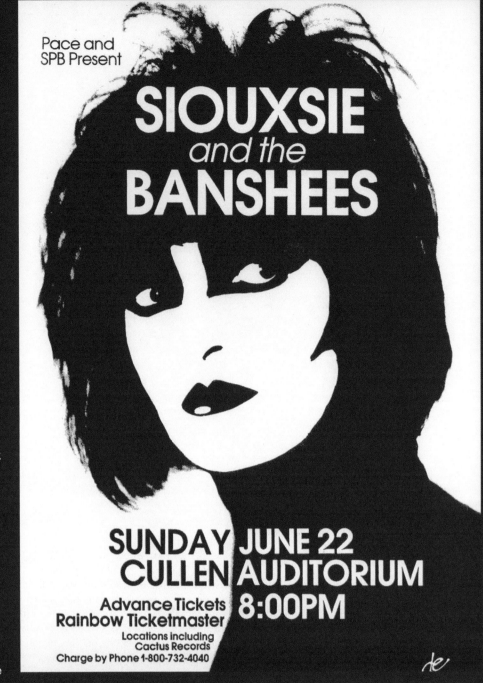

Pace and SPB Present

SIOUXSIE and the BANSHEES

SUNDAY JUNE 22 CULLEN AUDITORIUM 8:00PM

Advance Tickets
Rainbow Ticketmaster
Locations including
Cactus Records
Charge by Phone 1-800-732-4040

Photo by Circle23

BAUHAUS

INTERVIEW WITH DAVID J

David is probably best known as the bassist of both legendary gothic rock band Bauhaus and alternative rockers Love and Rockets, though he has also written and scored several plays and films and has a productive solo career. Some fruits of this latter period are the singles 'I'll Be Your Chauffeur' and 'The Day That David Bowie Died,' which reached number 4 in the UK vinyl singles charts in 2016. He continues to write and to perform.

Bauhaus were initially a post-punk band formed in 1978 from members of a Northampton art school, initially calling themselves Bauhaus 1919 in reference to the German art school and the year of its creation. Daniel Ash, the lead guitarist, formed the band with lead singer Pete Murphy, Kevin Haskins on drums, and later David J (Kevin's brother) on bass.

Using ambient noise, they developed an atmospheric soundscape to compliment the rich baritone of Murphy's voice. Their 1979 debut single 'Bela Lugosi's Dead' reached number 8 in the Indie Charts and brought in one fell swoop both what became the definitive gothic rock sound and iconography of the new genre.

At heart an experimental group, they followed up their debut *In the Flat Field* (number 1 in the independent charts) with *Mask* (number 30 in the UK album charts) in 1981, implementing a funkier sound with new instrumentation that included saxophones and keyboards. They achieved further chart success with their third outing *The Sky's Gone Out* (number 4 in the UK album charts, 1982) and their cover of David Bowie's 'Ziggy Stardust,' which reached number 15 in the singles charts.

While recording the fourth studio album, *Burning from the inside* (13 in UK charts), lead singer Murphy was regularly ill, causing some friction as the rest of the band were forced to step in to complete the album. The rift created by this difficulty would eventually split the band. Murphy eventually formed Dalis Car with Mick Karn (bassist with Japan) while Ash and Haskins formed Tones on Tail. They later rejoined David J to form Love and Rockets, who timed their emergence with that of MTV and enjoyed much mainstream success aided by well-produced music videos. Bauhaus reunited for tours in 1998, 2005, and 2008.

Bauhaus - David J, Pete Murphy,Kevin Haskins, and Daniel Ash - Alamy Photo Library

What was your childhood like in Northampton and when did you decide to become a musician?

I was mad about football; I had a George Best poster on the wall over my bed. I had dreams about being a professional footballer. And then I broke my leg really badly when I was about fourteen during a match. I also tore my cartilage, broke my ankle. A kid did a flying tackle on me during a match—both feet in the air—and came down hard. It was so bad (I found out later) that they were saying prayers for me in the school assembly. They reckoned that I'd have one leg far shorter than the other.

I was in hospital recovering in a ward with ten other blokes (I was the only kid in there), and they used to have Radio 1 playing during the day. T-Rex came on, 'Hot Love,' and I was on some sort of heavy-duty pain killers which no doubt aided the experience, but I went into some sort of trance, and I was completely transported by that music. I remember looking at rays of sunlight coming into the ward through a window and motes of dust being highlighted by those in the air. All the sounds on the ward, all the chatter and so on was muffled into this sort of nothing, and all I could hear was Marc Bolan

singing this song. I eventually came out of the reverie not wanting to be a footballer anymore and instead wanting to play music. I basically wanted to trade being George Best for being Marc Bolan. After that I joined the T-Rex fan club, the only club I've ever been a member of. Then Bowie came along, then the whole glam thing, Roxy Music . . . I went down that rabbit hole and I've never come out.

A few friends at school were similarly affected by the glam music era, and we formed what could loosely be called a band. One of the guys, Chris Day, had a guitar (the only kid at school to have one). He was teaching himself how to play. I became intrigued by this and I'd go round to his house and he'd teach me how to play songs, things like David Bowies' 'Ziggy Stardust,' and it was a revelation to me that, after a fashion, you could make your own personal versions of these recordings, often nothing really like the originals! I wasn't familiar with chords—I had no idea what a 'chord' was—but Chris showed me. And then I had proper lessons from a guy called Jim Tyson.

As for my childhood, my parents came from a very poor working-class background but owned a newsagent which became quite successful, and

they saved up to send myself and my brother off to a very minor public school in Wellingborough. I found it very draconian and left after a couple of years.

You have said in previous interviews that reggae was a big influence on you? How did this come about?

Yes, initially I used to sneak into this skinhead disco, this is when I was fourteen. We weren't supposed to be there; it was very exciting. There were a lot of Rastafarians in Northampton around that time. Once or twice a month they would have these events at an African Centre. They would have these big sound systems and they would paint everything in the colours of the Ethiopian flag. Lots of gold: women would dye their hair and the guys would wear gold suits or whatever the chosen colour was for the event. Lots of slogans by Haile Selassie painted on the walls. People would be coming in from up north and London. They would be making goat's head soup. Tons of Ganja. We'd be the only white guys in there but we were accepted very quickly. It was amazing to hear that sort of music that loud, and it was very influential for sure. I used to go down to London and buy reggae imports. Most of them featured a lot of dub. That was another big influence.

How did you go from lead guitar to bass?

Eventually I went to art school. There were a few would-be musicians, and we used to play together. Continually changing line-ups. The problem was always that we usually had about eight lead guitarists because everybody wants to be the lead guitar player. And no one wanted to play bass!

So I volunteered. I didn't mind playing bass because some of the first pure music I got into, before I identified music with personas, was reggae, and I sussed out that the bass was pretty important to reggae, and I loved the bass parts of that style of music. Not having a bass guitar at the time, I chopped off a couple of the strings on my cheap electric guitar and turned the treble down on my amp and the bass up, and that turned into my first bass guitar.

When did you take the leap from this level of playing to performing live?

Once we had a steady line up together, we played in the school hall and in a youth club. The first time we had cohesion was when my brother, who was a drummer, got together with myself and two other kids, Dave Stretton and Roger Rideout. Roger had been playing electric guitar for a while and was really good, and we formed this band called Jam—no relation to the other The Jam, obviously—and it gelled and we started to perform cover songs originally but soon started to write our own music.

After this we played in working men's clubs at the weekends. We got a hired transit van, and would drive up to Doncaster and places like that. It was great fun. We'd play in between the bingo or the comedians or the female impersonators, and that's where it all started. I was in several other bands after this one. All in the same sort of mould.

How did you meet the other members of Bauhaus?

I already knew Danel [Ash], and he knew that I'd been in a lot of bands. But I tended to be the one that organised these bands, I was always the 'band leader,' in a sort of way. I was always very driven and full of ideas.

Daniel later created his own band and I think he initially didn't want me in it—he thought I'd try and take it over. But they fired their bass player and eventually asked me if I wanted to join. I'd seen them rehearsing and they were great, I didn't hesitate.

What did the band sound like prior to you joining?

It was very minimalist, which I really liked. Everything was really stripped down. And when I saw them I immediately thought of the Bauhaus art movement which we'd learnt about at art school. When I joined the band they didn't have a name, so I mentioned my thoughts about Bauhaus, and that's what we called ourselves: 'Bauhaus 1919' because that's when this art movement began.

Do you find that when you personally write a song it's the words that come first?

It's nearly always the words. The meter of the lyrics dictate or suggest the form and rhythm of the music.

You wrote 'Bela Lugosi's Dead' as the first single. How did that come about?

There was a season of old horror films on TV around that time. Every week it was a different horror film, the classics: *Frankenstein, The Werewolf, Dracula* (with Bela Lugosi). Daniel and I had been enjoying these, and we were just on the phone together talking about them, and I said that Bela's voice with the Hungarian accent really added to the mystique of the character. He also had the perfect visage and demeanour for the role. I was really quite taken by that film.

I was working in a warehouse at the time packing and labelling boxes, and after a boring day I was pedalling home on my bike and these lyrics just started to form in my mind pretty much in sequence as you hear it. I had pockets full of these packing labels and so I started to write them all down. By the time I got home I had the full song. I wrote it all out again on a piece of paper and handed it to Peter the next day at band rehearsal.

When Pete started to sing the lyrics were they as you'd imagined them to be sung?

He sang it pretty much as it is on the actual single. I imagined it like that, yeah, but I think he sang it even better than I'd imagined.

There's quite a bit of dubbing on the single. How long did it take to create?

We booked the studio for the day and we recorded and mixed that single plus four other songs all in one take. Before we started to record it, we told the sound engineer Derek Tompkins that we wanted to put some echo on 'Bela'. We actually owned a Wem Copicat Tape Echo unit that

we wanted to use but he had an analogue one that was even better that you could use live. Daniel applied that spontaneously during recording and it came out brilliantly.

It's a very long single at over nine minutes. Did you ever get second thoughts about trying to get that song out due to potential problems with getting radio play?

Oh absolutely. When we were shopping it around a lot of the labels said it was interesting but too long. 'Can you condense it?' and all that sort of thing. But the only label that didn't say that was Small Wonder Records, which was run by Pete Stennett [the co-owner] with his wife Mari. I did worry about the length since it had been mentioned before and possibly shortening it and he said 'No, no, fuck that! You wanna keep it as it is. It's like 'Sister Ray,' the Velvet Underground track. You want to hear every note. Don't cut out a second of that song! It's perfect as it is.' And he was right.

You were very experimental—how did this work as a band writing?

We were all into that process, we loved doing that. We did a few BBC sessions and we purposely only had one or two tracks worked out in advance, and then for the other two we would just improvise on the spot, maybe not even use our instruments, just use whatever was in the studio at the time. It was very brave and audacious thinking back.

On the second album you expanded the instruments that you used to create different sounds and effects. Was any of this electronic?

Yeah: we had a WASP synthesiser, we used a Space Echo, we used a synth electronic drum pad. We were really into electronic music; I got into Can when I was at art school. We all went to see Kraftwerk at a really early gig in London in '79. I loved the band Suicide too.

I always thought that Bauhaus were not dissimilar to other experimental bands coming through that post punk period, such as JG Thirlwell and even Swans.

Completely, I mean we also liked bands such as Cabaret Voltaire, Throbbing Gristle, Fad Gadget, and Pop Group, who were all contemporary to us at the time. Also Tuxedo Moon, with whom we did a very early gig in London. We had a lot of musical influences.

During the recording of Burning from the Inside there were issues with

Pete being ill and unavailable for long periods which meant that others including yourself had to step in to do the vocals here and there. Did that put a lot of stress on the band?

We didn't *have* to, it's just that that naturally happened in the course of writing and recording. Of course when Peter did turn up he did not like it one little bit! So it was more his feelings of being usurped which caused stress.

How did you get the title for the album Burning from the Inside?

[Laughs] There's a funny story about that. They were setting up the studio for a mix—this was at Beck Recording Studios. There was a lot of nob twiddling and we wanted a break. Me and Daniel went out to the engineer/co-producer Derek Tompkins's car that was parked outside to listen to music and smoke a spliff, and we were so out of it we set fire to the carpet in the car—there was some random detritus down there too that was also on fire—it was actually on fire! And we were like 'Oh, the cars on fire.' As we were going back into the studio to tell poor Derek what we'd just done I said 'Derek, the car—it's burning from the inside!' and then Daniel said 'That could be the title of an album!' and I said *'Yes! Derek's Car is Burning from the Inside,'* so Daniel said *'No, just Burning from the Inside.'* So that's what we used. And Derek, quite understandably, wasn't too happy about his car!

I always thought that the bass is the most important part of the music making process.

I quite agree!

[Laughs] Well that forms the foundation for the rest of the music in my opinion. And yours always sounds really different to most other bands. How did you get that sound on the track 'All We Ever Wanted Was Everything'?

That's actually a cello. I'm playing a cello as I would a bass guitar, which I'd never done before. We got in a bunch of instruments that we couldn't really play. We had a harpsicord, the cello, a violin, a viola, an accordion . . . lots of weird stuff in there. They were just laying around and they were up for grabs if you wanted to give it a go.

How about that really heavy bass on 'Double Dare?'

It's just a cheap Japanese Electro-Harmonix Fuzzbox. It wasn't a pedal; it was a switch that you could turn on and off. I had to gaffer tape it to my guitar. It was a really cheap thing but it had a great sound.

Now you are regarded as the Godfathers of Goth, do you think that in many ways that first single was a bit of a millstone around your necks due to the imagery which led to the visuals of the goth movement?

Well not at first because 'goth' was a label given to bands like us later on, as I guess we didn't really label ourselves at all – possibly 'post punk if anything; we were into all sorts of musical genres. This is very evident, especially on the second album. I mean, there's funk in there, disco (twisted disco but it is still disco), dub again, avant garde, general weirdness, and some rock and roll.

Did you ever intentionally here and there push the goth image that'd been bestowed to you?

Well we dressed like that anyway; none of it was pre-planned. And sure, if you're going on stage you sort of amp up the dressing style a little bit.

Obviously after a while you guys split with Pete to do your own things— Daniel went off to create Tones on Tail with your brother Kevin, and you joined The Jazz Butcher Group. Then you three got back together again. How did Love and Rockets come into being?

Pete Murphy - Alamy Photo Library

44

Well there's a lot of erroneous information about this and it winds me up every time I see it, so, the story goes: We wanted to get back with Pete [Murphy] and so we contacted him, arranged a meeting, but Pete didn't show up, and so we thought 'Well we've nothing better to do, just the three of us here, we may as well form our own band.' That never happened! I think Daniel entertained the idea of—maybe—going back with Pete, but I was certainly not in on that conversation if it happened. I was approached by Daniel to see if I would join them, because he'd finished with Tones on Tail by then, and he wanted to form a new band and would I be interested in joining it, as a trio? I could see the potential of us three working together again, it was exciting, so I said yes. It's just a fresh band, a new venture without the difficult lead singer in the mix. It was a breeze; it was joyous being in that band.

Love and Rockets is also a comic book title, did you realise this at the time?

Yeah, that's where we got the name from—we nicked it. I'm a big comic book fan and I had some of the copies of that title on my table. We were trying to think of a name for the band and there it was right in front of us. I ran it past the other band members and they said 'Yep, that's it!' I did ask the creators of the comic books if it was OK to use it, and I got a phone call from one of the brothers, Jamie Hernandez. He said he was also thinking of using the name for a band, to which I responded 'Well I can't argue with that mate!' But he said he wanted to listen to our music to see what it was like. We only had two tracks at the time, 'Ball of Confusion' and a song called 'Inside the Outside,' so we sent those over. We got a call back and Jamie said 'Yeah OK, we like the music. You can use the name for your band. If the music had sucked that would not have been the case.' So we had their blessing, which was great.

The creation of the band coincided with MTV coming to TV with 24 hours of music. I remember accidentally stumbling upon the video for 'So Alive' one evening. I didn't' know it was you guys initially but it was a nice surprise! It was a more polished pop sound.

The MTV thing was fortunate, as was college radio which was also huge back then. I mean that particular track was probably the zenith of that side to the band, that more commercial sound. But there's a darkness to that side of our music too, there's that duality to it that makes it more intriguing.

You're quite a renaissance man, aren't you? Do you think that's a drive you have to continually try and create in new areas?

Very much so. Yes, I'm a curious fellow.

How did the playwriting happen?

Well, I had a publicist, Versa Manos, and she has a lot of ties in theatre, and there was this company in Atlanta, Georgia called Dad's Garage, a very respected theatre company, and they wanted to put on a series of short plays (eight in total) just fifteen minutes in duration and run it for a couple of weeks, and they were looking for submissions. They already had a couple of Tony award-winning playwrights onboard. Versa suggested that I give it a go and encouraged me to do it.

Well, I'd never even thought about writing a play before but I thought it would be exciting. And the old adage is 'write about what you know,' so I wrote about being nineteen in 1976 and going to see the Pistols and The Clash: punk. You also had to use one piece of music, and I used 'Anarchy in the UK.' I called it *Anarchy in the Gold Street Wimpy*. That's because that's the place we'd always end up in if we went to the pub. There was Spinadisc records next door and we would head into there to buy the latest punk single and then go to the Wimpy for a burger to soak up the booze.

Anyway, it got accepted, they flew me out to Atlanta, we had some really good actors that interpreted my words really well, and that gave me the bug. And I started to think that I wouldn't mind directing my own play. At the time I was staying with my friend Shepard Fairey and he had a screenplay sitting on his desk. It was called *Girl on Fire*; it was about Edie Sedgwick and was written by David Weisman and Paul Schrader. I read it through and was inspired to write a song about Edie. Shepard came in and asked me about what I had just written. When I told him he suggested that I phone David Weisman and tell him about it. This I did, and he invited me over to his house to play him the song. David was very enthusiastic about what I had come up with and encouraged me to write more with the idea of some kind of stage production. The seeds had been sown!

The play that finally came to fruition was called *Silver for Gold: The Odyssey of Edie Sedgwick*. The story is told in the form of Greek mythology. Edie becomes Persephone, who descends into the Underworld which is the Silver Factory in New York with Andy Warhol as Hades. I

had Bob Dylan as Orpheus. The three-headed dog Cerberus which guards the gates to the Underworld were three of Warhol's acolytes: Ondine, Chuck Wein, and Paul Morrison. There's another strange character, half man half horse, in a wheelchair. He has a horse's head and he narrates the story . . . And there's a song cycle written in the style of The Velvet Underground, all acoustic, and I sing the lyrics. And all these elements came together, and it went really well. It was originally staged at an independent theatre in Hollywood and then at the Redcat Theatre in Downtown LA which is an internationally recognised stage. I loved doing that!

What is it about Edie that first attracted you? What made you find that connection?

I first saw Edie in that famous photo of her, Andy Warhol, and Chuck Wein coming up from a New York City manhole. It was included in a newspaper article about a big Warhol exhibition in London in 1968. I was eleven and fascinated by the look of these people and Warhol's art and persona.

You tend to write about quite delicate people thrown into a media that was probably too strong for them?

This is a theme that intrigues me and I feel great empathy for these butterflies broken on the wheel of fame.

You've had quite a lot of solo success, especially recently, with songs such as 'I'll Be Your Chauffeur' and 'The Day that David Bowie Died,' which both had chart success. How do you think your songwriting has changed since your first steps with early Bauhaus?

Well, it's become a lot more personal. And because I want to sing these songs, to sing these lyrics, because I and only I have had those experiences, and I know what I'm referring to. Whereas the lyrics for Bauhaus were always about something on the outside. The inspiration could have been something from the newspaper or about some other person and situation, so it's a different way of writing, and I knew the words would be sung by Peter, and so I'd write for his voice and interpretation. But now I'm writing for myself.

大英帝国に咲いた猛毒の華

BAUHAUS

狂気の闇を切りさく戦慄のサウンド！

バウハウス

5月28日(土) 6:30 p.m. 渋谷公会堂

S ¥3,900、 A ¥3,000、 B ¥2,500

主催●文化放送 ウドー音楽事務所 協力●ワーナー・パイオニア 協賛●ブリチストンタイヤ株式会社

★都内プレイガイド及びウドー音楽事務所にて絶賛発売中

お問い合せ●☎03(205)2911 文化放送コンサート係
☎03(402)7281ウドー音楽事務所

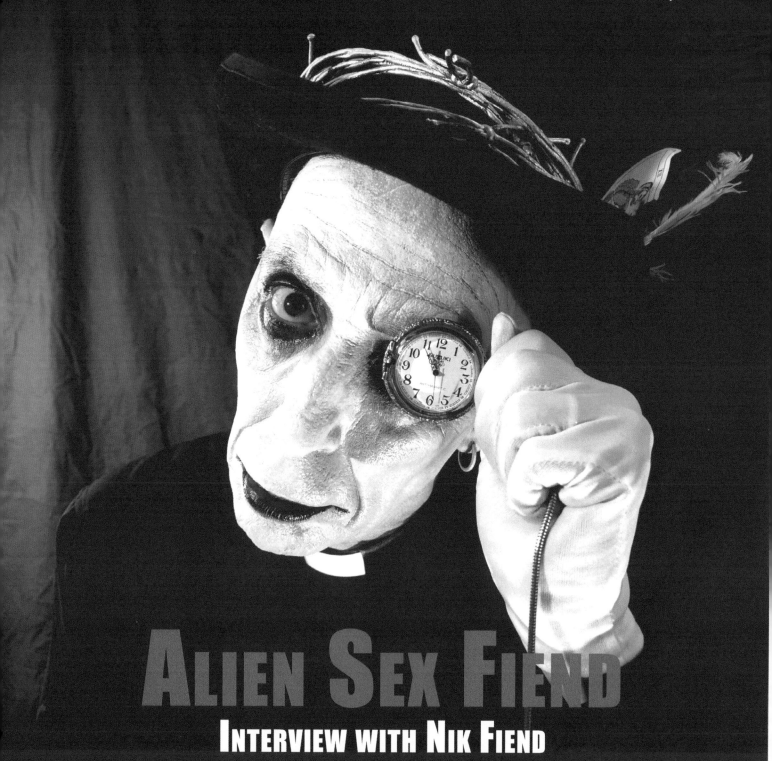

Photo credit Per-Ake: monokrom-photos.com

ALIEN SEX FIEND

INTERVIEW WITH NIK FIEND

Nik Fiend (née Wade) is the lead singer of Alien Sex Fiend and has been involved also with several casual bands, including The Earwigs and Demon Preacher. He worked at infamous original goth club The Batcave in London.

Alien Sex Fiend was formed by Nik, Mrs. Christine Fiend, Yaxi Highrizer, and Johnny Haha in 1982 and became The Batcave's house band. Though they are often and without complaint filed under 'gothic rock,' the band has an experimental approach, making liberal use of electronic equipment and studio mixing to achieve their distinctive sound. Their big break came when Youth, of Killing Joke, became producer on their debut cassette *The Lewd, the Mad, the Ugly and Old Nick*, which gained significant coverage in the music papers. In 1983 they signed to Cherry Red Records.

'Ignore the Machine' was ASF's first single, reaching number 6 in the UK Independent Singles Chart and followed soon thereafter by debut studio album *Who's Been Sleeping in My Brain* and 1984's *Acid Bath*. They released the world's first 11-inch single: 'E.S.T. Trip to the Moon.' Between 1983 and 1987 they enjoyed a constant residency in the Top 20 Indie Singles Chart, though *Maximum Security* was the only album to reach the UK Charts at number 100.

47

What first inspired you to become a musician?

I just loved music! I don't consider myself to be a 'musician' as such—I'm just me! Around 1974 I was mucking around with a couple of mates and their guitars, but it wasn't until I did some impromptu singing with another band in an East London pub that made me even start to think about doing music. Pub rock was crossing over into punk at that time and there was something in the air. It was very exciting, and it made me feel like I could take part.

You first played in Demon Preacher— your first gig must have been very terrifying.

I started Demon Preacher. I've never been terrified—I terrify the audience, not the other way around! But nervous, yes. But that's only 'cos I care, I want the audience to get the maximum, and I do too.

You played with a few more bands: Mr and Mrs Demeanor and The Earwigs . . . what happened—were you trying to find your feet and direction?

I started those bands too. There was also The Demons and No Longer Umpire. I had found my feet and direction but things kept changing, band members would leave, they'd usually get replaced but sometimes I'd feel that it was time for a change. The thing is I do lots of mad artwork as well, so I would come up with a new concept or idea all the time and I'd decide to change the band's name. We were The Earwigs for just one gig in the King's Road, which got stopped by the police. There was Hell's Kitchen for a short time just because of the name and the images it conjured up. Some line-ups lasted longer than others, some only for a week! In those days someone would turn up, play one gig then disappear never to be seen again, so it was all very loose. The important thing was being able to make a racket!

Despite the stops and starts I did get some records released back then. As Demon Preacher the first record was completely self-financed: I persuaded my boss (I was still working then) to loan me the money on the understanding that I paid it back. He was a big bloke so I wasn't going to renege on the deal—no fucking way! Also, out of respect to him, I did a 500-pressing called *North London Rising EP*, sellotaped the sleeves together myself—total punk DIY—sold them all and paid my boss back. Later I got a record deal with Small Wonder, and they released the single 'Little Miss Perfect' in 1978. It was unbelievable; finally somebody believed in me enough to finance my record. They'd put out Patrick Fitzgerald,

later did Crass, Bauhaus, etc., etc., so that was brilliant for me.

All through these times I was gaining valuable experience: doing gigs, making artwork for sleeves, being in a top recording studio, how to release a record, record contracts, what distributors do, and so on. That was all crucial stuff to learn. Later, as the punk thing was receding, I did No Longer Umpire. It was completely experimental, off the wall. We had no songs; we'd go on stage and just start playing! It was liberating and in hindsight was a precursor of where I was headed, which would be Alien Sex Fiend. ASF was a new start, a fresh canvas.

The club where The Batcave was held had many different theme nights. What attracted you to the Goth night?

A lot of the clubs back then hosted a different night each night of the week and The Gargoyle club in London's Soho hosted The Batcave club on Wednesdays. On Saturdays it hosted The Comedy Club. On a Tuesday or Thursday it would be something else. The Gargoyle was a strip club by day! Later as it became more popular the club moved to the much bigger Subway in Leicester Square, later again it was held at Gossips, then Fouberts towards the end, around 1985 I think.

There was no such thing as 'goth' back in 1982—it was a term that got used much later. Initially we were called a 'Batcave band.' Also, 'positive punk' was used to describe us along with bands like Killing Joke, Brigandage, etc. Mrs Fiend and I had read about The Batcave club in *Time Out* (the 'What's On' guide) and thought it sounded interesting in July 1982 when it first opened, but we were all busy with day jobs and in our spare time were working on Alien Sex Fiend, creating artwork, writing music, making mixtapes and hanging out, so we didn't get around to going. I sent a tape of some of our demos to *Melody Maker's* [now defunct UK weekly music paper] 'Undiscovered Bands' section where they'd review new bands. The review described Alien Sex Fiend as 'the ugliest thing in the name of music,' amongst other choice words!

But when Specimen (the band who ran The Batcave) read the review it intrigued them, and they thought we sounded like the band to play at their club. Olli, the singer, phoned up and arranged a meet-up. So that's how Mrs Fiend and I ended up going to The Batcave club for the first time. Then they gave us our first gig and it all took off from there and has never stopped.

How well did the cassette The Lewd,

the Mad, the Ugly and Old Nick do?

That was a tape of those early demos and some live tracks. I have no idea how well it sold, a mad guy used to duplicate the cassettes and sell them in Portobello Road; we never had any sales figures. But we were more than happy to get our music out there, to get it heard by as many people as possible.

You started working in The Batcave— what job did you do there?

I'd been working as a van driver delivering high-value TVs, videos, etc. and I got hijacked at knifepoint. I was put on some major tranquillisers by the doctor, and I could barely operate. Looking back I was probably suffering from PTSD, but that wasn't a thing back in the early 80s! A mate at the firm tried to cover for me but it didn't work out, so I lost that job and became unemployed. Specimen and other people who worked at the club knew me from ASF playing gigs at both The Gargoyle and the Subway versions of The Batcave. Bless them, Specimen helped me out around that time 'cos I was skint. Then they were going on tour so they asked me if I could run the creative side of the club in their absence. I oversaw the décor of the club, setting the props up and lighting, etc. and also DJing. The business side, like paying the bands and so on, was dealt with by someone else.

What inspired your look? And how did your mum react to it?

[Laughing] I haven't lived with my mum since I was about fifteen! The family had moved away from London when I was about twelve and I moved back there as soon as I possibly could, so I was free . . . It would worry me if I'd had encouraging parents! Looking back it would have probably been no good for me. Of course I'm part of my parents, but I want to do what I want to do, and having to make my own decisions about everything in my life from such an early age stood me in good stead for sorting shit out! The makeup side was a gradual addition, I realised that it helped reach people at the back of the audience, and black clothes were practical on the road.

Were your family supportive of your choice in career?

No! The opposite! [laughs] It was always 'You should get a proper job!'

Quite a few of the musicians in 'Goth Royalty' came to The Batcave: The Damned, Siouxsie Sioux, Nick Cave, and obviously yourself. Did any of the bands want to play there?

As far as I'm aware none of those bands played at The Batcave. It was a club venue; it was small, a few hundred people could get in. Even when it moved to the larger Subway in Leicester Square it would've been too small a venue for them, so I doubt that those bands would have ever been booked to play—they wouldn't have got paid enough! All those bands were well on their way by then, they were in a higher league. For us as ASF we were starting out, so playing The Batcave was fine.

But all those names did go to The Batcave, but more as a night out. Me and Nick Cave would regularly have chats—I was into what he was doing, and he would ask me if I was bothered by all the kids that would follow me around the club all night! Sex Gang Children, Marc Almond, Jimmy Pursey (Sham 69), Charlie Harper (UK Subs); all sorts of musicians would regularly hang out there.

Punk sort of fizzled out as it became a bit of a circus, and Goth took over the mantle but seemed to reach out to a separate set of disaffected youths. What do you think is the attraction of goth in general to the outsiders in society?

The imagery is good: candles, skulls, horror stuff, all that. In the early 80s you could at last get to see films like *Freaks, Plan 9 From Outer Space*, or the old Universal Bela Lugosi films, and *The Munsters* TV series—all those things got incorporated.

Anyone can get hold of some black trousers and a T-shirt, so that's easy, and then you can go as far out as you like from there! It's adaptable to everyone, there isn't a strict code or anything. It's become even broader now as well: you've got cyber goths, romantic goths, industrial goths, folky goths, all sorts. It's very flexible; a broad palette. Originally no-one really gave a fuck about clothes or haircuts, the original Batcave had all sorts of people: there was Mike with a blue Mohican, rockabillies who were Meteors or Cramps fans were into it, punks, all types. We didn't play to a select group of people dressed in black and fishnets! I always said it was about more than just a haircut and we always saw it as more of a state of mind than a uniform.

You teamed up with Youth [Martin Glover] from Killing Joke to work on music—how did all of this come to be?

Youth was a Batcave club regular. I was aware of him from Killing Joke—I was into what they were doing—so I gave him a

cassette of those demos of ours when I was DJing. Next time I saw him I asked if he'd listened to it. He said 'Yes and you're mental. I can't produce that—what do you want me to do?' So we left it there and I just got on with things. Then we did a gig at Heaven as part of a Batcave night and Youth was there. He zoomed into the dressing room afterwards going crazy saying 'Ooh the cross rhythms, I get it now! I want to produce you!' I didn't really understand what he meant back then—all that was important was that he'd said 'Yes!'

Martin went on to become a producer. When you worked together how did the dynamic work? Was Martin happier to do a lot of the studio work, or were you equally interested in this?

After we'd got signed to Cherry Red Records for a single, I'd decided on 'Ignore the Machine' for the A-side; it was a new song that had been going down well at gigs. Cherry Red were happy that we had Youth on board as the producer. Because that single did so well—it leapt to the top of the indie charts straight way—I was able to persuade Cherry Red to let us to record a follow-up album, and it was a given to use Youth again as the producer for what would be 'Who's Been Sleeping in My Brain?'

I know with other bands many producers use session people instead of the band members to play, or they impose their own style on a band, but that's never been the case with us. We had written the songs already, even in a basic form. In some cases we'd been playing the songs live so we knew how they should sound, so all Youth (and anyone else subsequently) needed to do was to make sure that the songs were captured on tape. We played live in the studio with very minimum overdubbing—we didn't have the studio time to mess about very much!

How did the record deal you signed with Cherry Red Records come about, and did you have any other offers on the table?

I knew Phil Langham, singer with The Dark, a North London punk band. He'd been given a new label by Cherry Red called Anagram in 1983, and he was getting bands to do one-off singles. He'd already checked us out and so he asked me if we'd be interested in a such a deal. We said yes straight away; they were an independent label and that suited us better than dealing with a major label deal. I was never interested in going that route.

How were your experiences with them? Did you try to change you at

all, or did you have freedom to do as you liked?

We had a few arguments over the years. Initially they wanted to have 'Ignore the Machine' edited down in length, but we and Youth said no, and that was the end of the argument! We were lucky to be able to go outside the usual rules and regulations, that is, having to demo every tune for the record company to hear first for approval before recording. We didn't have any of that. Luckily the first album *Who's Been Sleeping in My Brain* was successful or we probably wouldn't have been able to make a second one! I don't think they really knew what was going on—all they knew was that the records were selling very well and kept hitting the top of the independent charts!

Bottom line, we recorded stuff and Cherry Red/Anagram put it out whether they liked it or not, 'cos they wanted their money back! [laughs] When we started to break into Europe and the US and elsewhere and it was a much bigger concern, I would go and have a chat with the boss, Iain McNay, and we'd have a to and fro. We'd agree a budget for the next project and that would be that.

A funny illustration of this is the famous 11-inch single 'EST (Trip to The Moon).' As well as a 7-inch, Iain wanted a 12-inch single. I really wanted to do another 10-inch (like 'R.I.P.') so we discussed it a bit, then I said 'How about a compromise?' He looked at me: 'Like what?' and I said 'What about an 11-inch?' He looked puzzled for a moment then said 'Hmm, I don't know if that's possible, let me check.' It turned out that yes it was possible—you press a 12-inch then cut off 1 inch all the way around! Job done! Result! [laughs] You couldn't make it up!

What is the most interesting part of the song-making process for you?

It's all interesting to me; we don't work in an orthodox fashion, to the dismay of some engineers. The whole process is interesting from the initial spark of an idea—whether that's a beat, a sample, a riff, a keyboard sound—through to coming up with lyrics, Mrs Fiend and I swapping ideas, or her finding some mad sounds which add another dimension to what's happening. I play guitar now too. There's a sense of purpose in creating a new track. It won't be perfect; what's important is to capture the essence of something, the original spark. I want to step off the planet for a while—that's the point. Sometimes we'll just sit and listen to the playback, not do anything or add anything, just listen. Sometimes that's enlightening. All the way through to final mixes, deciding which mix

ALIEN SEX FIEND
AFTER CONCERT PARTY AND ART SHOW
WEDNESDAY JUNE 10   HELTER SKELTER

is best and so on. All of it fascinates me, it always has.

You were one of the first bands to play with tape loops and had a lot of influences from industrial music. Did groups such as Throbbing Gristle or Cabaret Voltaire have any influence on you?

Not Throbbing Gristle, but we liked some of Cabaret Voltaire, along with a lot of other bands. Back then you didn't know how songs were recorded, and we didn't dissect anything or analyse what we liked, we just experimented and went our own way. That was what they were doing—we might like it but we didn't want to be them or sound like them, we were doing our thing. There was loads of good music around back then, I would say bands like Velvet Underground and Suicide were bigger influences than Cabaret Voltaire.

You had a much rockier and heavier sound than many other Goth bands, many of which were starting to sound quite pop orientated. Were you a little bit disappointed in the likes of Siouxsie and Co. who seemed to be going more mainstream?

That didn't bother me at all, it did not come into my thinking. We were so involved in what we were doing ourselves I wasn't looking at other groups. They'd do what they did and good luck to 'em, but I'm gonna get up and do my thing! With a name like Alien Sex Fiend there's no way it's gonna be on *Top of The Pops* or daytime Radio One, whatever we do! So that kind of stopped us from being mainstream. I just wasn't interested in the mainstream; the music I'm into is still underground, obscure. That was my ambition (if I ever had one): to be in a weird, underground band that sold cassettes in Portobello Road! The fact that we got way, way further than that is a constant amazement to me!

You made a lot of brilliant music and were a trendsetter in many ways. Do you think that music journalists often didn't give you enough credit?

Thank you—wow! It was a good thing that they didn't give us too much credit, like overindulgent parents going 'Oh he's a genius.' there's only one way to go from that: falling flat on your face! The fact that some journalists in the early days didn't get us meant that we were underdogs, so it was win-win as far as I was concerned. 'The ugliest thing in the name of music,' what a great line! 'Velvet Underground on Mandrax,' again another great quote. If we hadn't really believed in what we

were doing such things might have put us off, but far from it! The main thing was we got a reaction, and a strong one. Like Marmite, love it or hate it, that's it. I prefer that to sitting on the fence. We have had journalists apologise to us since, saying they didn't get it at first but then did, which was cool of them to admit that. As we said on the last album *Possessed,* 'This is music to comfort the disturbed and disturb the comfortable!'

If you could change one thing about your career, what would it be?

To have been able to clone myself—then I could have done even more! [laughs] But no, I wouldn't change anything, even the bad bits. You learn something from those times; the hard way can sometimes be the best way to learn!

How do you think goth music is doing now, and do you think its image has changed over time?

I ain't got a f'ing clue! There are hundreds of people pontificating daily about what is and what isn't goth—they've all got opinions. There are arguments about whether it all started at The Batcave or in northern clubs etc. etc. I'm not really interested in those sorts of debates. As I said before, when we started out there was no such genre. Now it pops up all over the place. Some people don't think we're goth because we have a sense of humour or because we paint from quite a big palette. We understand we're not everyone's cup of tea—I'd be more worried if everyone liked us!

The main thing is that it still hasn't gone away. Along with reggae, heavy metal, it's got to be one of the longest-running movements I think. Each new generation adds their take on it, which is what keeps it alive really

Speaking of which, I personally think that music companies now are too safe and don't take risks with new bands making different types of music. Do you think that is true?

Probably, it's hard to know reasonings behind it because we're busy getting on with our thing, we're not part of the music biz to that extent or involved. But there are always people with initiative and there are certainly more outlets now online, like Bandcamp and so on, but I don't know how difficult it is to get a career going off the back of that. Of course, it's tough now 'cos of the covid pandemic and venues are having problems etc. etc.

Record companies would often sign bands

then try to change them. I don't know if they're still doing that, I don't see the point of that at all. If they'd tried it with me then there's no point in me doing music because unless I can do what I want to do, it's not going to work. You are unique, so why try and change that? They'd get producers in to change the band's sound, all of that went on. There are a lot of nightmare stories out there. The bottom line is if you believe in what you're doing, stick to your guns, persevere, figure out a way around whatever problem it is; that's all we ever did. Oh, and keep your fingers crossed!

You're still going strong—how do you keep your enthusiasm up and do you think you'll ever retire?

As of December 1st 2022 we've hit the 40th anniversary of Alien Sex Fiend's first gig. 40 years, I can't believe it, it's amazing! I have no idea how that's happened really. The problem is that you can't retire from yourself, can you! [laughs] That's the catch! For me, I need a balance; I love rock 'n' roll but also spending some time in nature these days. I've seen too many people go too one-sided and want to be something they're not. 'I want to be rich' or 'I want to be famous' are too shallow an ambition. 'Famous' is not how I think, and money has never been my motivation. If that's what you're after I wouldn't get into music!

Not every day is funny and positive, but sometimes when you're a bit down having an outlet like art or music is much better for you than getting a prescription from the doctors. Even in bad times I've always had—even in the back of my mind—a thought about 'Oh that new song or new set of lyrics, I wonder . . .' As I've said to other people, I don't need a therapist—I've got my art and music, thank fuck.

Nik Fiend live at The Lyceum, London in 1983

SYNTH AND ELECTRONICA

Electronic music has been around as early as the 1950s, and even earlier if you take into account experiments in the Victorian era. These were primitive and often used the manipulation of white noise by oscillators. The Moog and Mini-Moog were electronic keyboards that featured different 'voices', but music still had to be produced manually.

In 1979 the Fairlight CMI was introduced. This audio workstation —which was the first to incorporate a digital synthesizer, sampler, and sequencer—cost as much as a small house, and as such it was only available to established and wealthy musicians. Peter Gabriel [formally of Genesis] championed the relatively portable device and introduced it to popular singer songwriter Kate Bush. Their music showcased the potential of the device, and soon it became the development tool of choice to those that could afford it. It enabled musicians to use built in samples or to record their own -

and then manipulate them by the changing of speed, pitch, and so on, and incorporate them into a piece of music digitally. It was the first-time musicians could create a list of sounds, etc to be played in a certain sequence (hence the term 'sequencer').

Some of the built-in samples would be heard in songs released for years afterwards—prime among them the 'orchestral stab,' or ORCH5 as it was labelled - a second long sample from a classical piece of music (from Stavinsky's Firebird Suite) that was a particular favourite of musicians during the 1980s, and appeared on Kate Bush's album The Dreaming, Duran Duran's 'A View to a Kill', as well as The Art of Noise single 'Close (to the Edit)', before becoming a bit of a cliché.

The key breakthrough lay in the more advanced sequencers that followed the CMI. These machines introduced the software-enabled control of multiple

external instruments, allowing artists to orchestrate music with exact timing. This advance meant that song producing was not only easier, but segments of songs could also be reused and elements such as drums could be pre-programmed to begin at specific junctures.

The first records produced using these techniques were often quite simplistic, with an overtly electronic sound. This electronic emphasis became the signature of what was then labelled 'electronica', and groups such as Kraftwerk would bring it to a wider audience. Orchestral Manoeuvres in the Dark (OMD), Fad Gadget, The Normal (AKA Daniel Miller - later boss of Mute records), Depeche Mode, Buggles, Bruce Woolley and Thomas Dolby would also lay the groundwork for emerging bands like The Human League, Heaven 17, Soft Cell, Blancmange, and others. The early 1980s was dominated by synthpop, before the sound became more sophisticated and merged with mainstream pop.

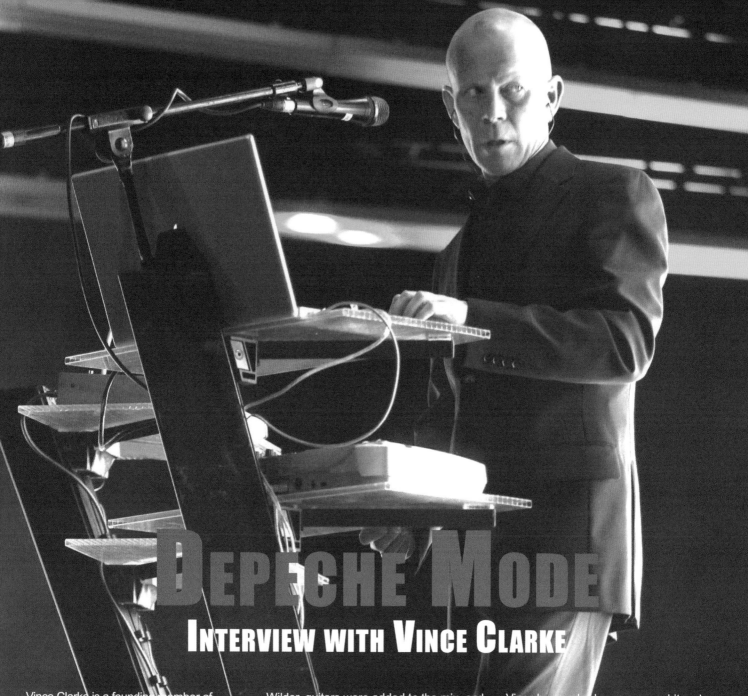

DEPECHE MODE
INTERVIEW WITH VINCE CLARKE

Vince Clarke is a founding member of Yazoo, The Assembly, Erasure, and most famously Depeche Mode with whom he pioneered electronic music in the late 70s and early 80s. He and his bandmates of the original line-up hail from Basildon, Essex.

Formed of Andy Fletcher, Vince, Martin Gore, and later Dave Gahan as lead singer, Depeche Mode became one of the most successful bands of all time, with a total of fifty-four singles in the UK charts as well as seventeen Top 10 albums, starting with 1981's *Speak and Spell*. Among the many hits are 'Dreaming of Me' (57), 'New Life' (11), 'Just Can't Get Enough' (8), 'Get the Balance Right' (13), and 'Everything Counts' (6).

Vince left the band after *Speak and Spell* and the single 'Just Can't Get Enough.' He was eventually replaced with Alan

Wilder, guitars were added to the mix, and commercial success boomed with stadium gigs being sold out worldwide. Staggering successes were also in store for Vince and singer Alison Moyet, however, as their new band Yazoo (Yaz in the US) soared even higher than Depeche Mode during this period. Yazoo's hits included 'Only You' (2), 'Situation' (20), 'Don't Go' (3), 'The Other Side of Love' (13), and 'Nobody's Diary' (3) as well as albums *Upstairs at Eric's* (number 2 in the charts) and *You and Me Both* (number 1).

Alison departed for a fruitful solo career and Vince started working with vocalists on one-off singles under the moniker "The Assembly". This project began and ended with Feargal Sharkey (The Undertones) on the single 'Never Never' (5), however, and was discontinued due to complex contract issues.

Vince by now had a name as a hit maker and lived up to this with his next band Erasure alongside vocalist Andy Bell. After the slow start of 'Who Needs Love Like That' (55 in UK charts), 'Heavenly Action' (100) and 'Oh L'amour' (85) the band broke through with 'Sometimes' (2), 'It Doesn't Have to Be' (12), and 'Victim of Love' (7). Impressively, the next eleven singles Erasure released all charted in the top 15 (and often the top 5), though their only number 1 single was 1991's 'Lay All Your Love on Me.' Success continued with the next seven singles breaking into the top 20 of UK Singles Charts, and four consecutive number 1 albums from 1988 to 1994. They continue to perform and record and are one of the most successful pop duos of all time.

Martin Gore, Andy Fletcher, Dave Gahan, and Vince Clarke

How would you describe yourself as a schoolboy and your early life?

I was very small and very introverted. I knew exactly where the school bullies used to hang out and I'd generally avoid those places. I was a pretty normal kid, I guess. I collected stamps and built Meccano.

We moved from Woodford to Basildon when I was very young. Basildon was one of eight new towns that were built to create accommodation for people after World War II, and I later heard that Basildon had a bit of a reputation for being rough when I was growing up in the late 1970s. I suppose looking back it was, but it's only when you move away that you realise—it's just normal when you don't know any different. Though saying that I don't think I had any major problems myself.

It was quite a normal family really. We weren't particularly musical but we were all fans of music. My parents loved Frank Sinatra but none of us could play instruments or performed, at least then. I was a huge fan of *Top of the Pops* (though I suppose everyone was at the time) but I didn't really aspire to be on the show at all. I did learn to play the piano and violin at school but to be honest it was just a means of getting out of maths classes which I hated.

I think my music interests began to perk up a bit as I got a bit older and I eventually began to learn how to play the guitar in the school guitar club. I suppose it was the guitar club that really set me off with the entire being in a band idea. Stick a bunch of musicians, even young ones, together and those ideas seem to formulate in their minds. A couple of my mates formed a one-gig band with me called Three's

Company, with which we entered a local talent contest. I think we did a couple of versions of 'Streets of London,' originally sung by Ralph McTell of course. Me and one of my mates were playing guitar and we had a girl doing the singing. This was my first exploration into performing.

I liked all types of music, and still do, but I suppose I veered towards folk music to a degree, and in particular Simon and Garfunkel. I'm primarily known for my synth music and I think I first became aware of the style of synth music that is probably better described now as electronica when I saw Gary Numan on *Top of the Pops*. I think that performance opened a lot of people's eyes. Shortly after this, I remember 'The Model' by Kraftwerk made a huge impression upon me too. But having said that, I was more interested in bands such as The Cure.

How did Depeche Mode come about?

Well, me and Andy Fletcher knew each other; we both went to the same Boys' Brigade group. He was in the school guitar club with me. He was playing bass guitar and I was playing guitar and doing some really terrible singing. We started to make music together. We were just kids so we had to practice in my bedroom with a drum machine that we had somehow acquired. Martin Gore happened to live around the corner from me and we found out he had a synthesiser and so he sort of joined the band. We called our band various names but eventually settled on Composition of Sound.

After a while we also realised that it was much easier, on a technical basis, to make music if we all had synthesisers—after watching Martin for a few sessions. So me and Fletch individually saved up to buy our own. The thing that did finally prompt

the change from our traditional band line up was an OMD [Orchestral Manoeuvres in the Dark] single called 'Electricity.' And whilst the A-side was excellent, the B-side called 'Almost,' which was quite folky and similar to the stuff I'd been listening to in my bedroom (but obviously created with synthesisers), really caught my attention. And we thought 'You know, we could do that.'

I wasn't comfortable being the front man (some things never change) and so we held auditions for a singer in one of the local school halls. Dave Gahan was one of the ones that came along, and sang 'The Price of Love,' and we thought 'Wow, he's good,' and that's how Dave joined us. I think we changed the band's name to Depeche Mode around this time. We didn't really know what it meant but it sounded good.

We had our first gig at one of our local schools—you could hire a hall out. I remembered we had this crappy PA and invited all of our friends along. This gave us confidence to seek out other gigs and we began to play locally in a few pubs.

How did you write songs together?

It was quite well organised. We could all shout out ideas and it was quite experimental in the beginning because we were just starting out. We all had our own roles: Fletch played bass synth, Martin played all of the complicated bits, and I played the easy stuff. Dave obviously sang and we put him in charge of the drum machine as well.

Quite a few electronic bands were emerging from North London and Essex around this time—why do you think that was?

New town boredom, I think. There wasn't much to do in Basildon, we didn't even have a cinema! I think people needed something to do. It wasn't just electronic music though; all sorts of bands were emerging. But electronic bands were definitely on the increase, probably due to the price of electronics slowly dropping.

How did Fad Gadget enter the picture?

A lot of people think that Frank Tovey [aka Fad Gadget] took us under his wing, so to speak, but what actually happened was that we got our first London gigs in the East End at a place in Canning Town. We were the sort of resident support band in a pub that had a small stage area. Fad Gadget played there one night and Daniel Miller, who ran Mute Records, came to see him and saw us too purely by accident.

Something must have clicked in his head as he later came backstage (or 'the toilets' as it was often called) and basically asked us if we would like to make a single for his record company. We said 'Yes please!'

What was the first musical issue you found when the entire band (bar Dave) were all using synths?

When we're all performing live—as in on a stage—it's important that the timing is exact, and I started to get really obsessed with it. Daniel Miller, who was himself interested in synths and had performed under the moniker The Normal, introduced us all to sequencers. I think in the evolution of electronica the sequencer was the most important cog in the entire process. It was a revolution, as they link up every part of a record and do so with exact timing. You could programme something that you could never in a million years play. If you listen to Kraftwerk, it *is* almost machine music. Synthesisers just made life so much easier. After seeing Daniel's set up [the ARP 2600] I went straight out and bought my own.

You were offered the chance to contribute a single on the Some Bizarre electronic music sampler by Stevo Pearce, which also included tracks by Soft Cell, The Normal, The The and Blancmange. How did all of that come about?

If memory serves me correctly, I think we were offered that slot on the album by Stevo round about the same time as Mute Records and Daniel Miller were showing interest in signing us. Stevo was very excited by the emerging electronic bands and would later sign a lot of them for his Some Bizarre record label. He wanted to showcase these bands to a bigger audience and thought this was the best way to do it. It was an important album, maybe not for ourselves but for electronic music in general. A lot of the bands that were on the album began to get record label interest and went on to have a lot of hits. We chose the single 'Photographic' simply because it was something that we'd played a lot on stage and something we thought we could reproduce in the studio. Daniel Miller produced it for us.

How did you get to grips with using the technology? Did you ever have a computer as a kid?

No, I think my generation missed out on those. The nearest thing I ever used to a computer was the Language Lab at school—the ones where you could listen to pre-set recordings with your headphones on. We had one of those

Licensed courtesy of BMG Rights Management (UK) Ltd

at school for French and German. But I think programming my first sequencer was the first time I'd ever really messed with technology, and I found that when I wasn't messing with it, I was thinking of what I would do next time I was.

Did your equipment have many pre-sets?

The early synthesisers didn't have any built-in pre-sets [sound effects] and were often quite unpredictable. It was one of the main attractions for me really as you didn't know what was going to come out of the speakers most of the time and you could accidentally make some really interesting sounds. It's true even now; I have a collection of old or oldish synthesisers because the happy accidents are so exciting to find.

The way I write music is to sit down and write melodies, add a bass line or something, and then I'll have an idea to add a sound that in my mind is a trumpet but it'll usually come out sounding like something completely different. Then I'll think 'Oh, that sounds quite interesting,' and take it from there. And that's basically been my entire life: lots of happy accidents. I try and sound as different as possible—people keep telling me that everything I do sounds the same though!

[laughs]. I wouldn't do it otherwise, to be honest. I couldn't go to work every day knowing what I was going to end up with at the end of it. It's the unknown that keeps it interesting.

Once you had the extra technology at your fingertips, did you have a greater interest in how others were using theirs? Did you listen to any particular bands that you admired to see if you could figure out what they were specifically doing?

Not really, although I was always curious as to how other bands recreate their music live (I still am). If there's something really clever that I listen to then I'll try to analyse it, but I rarely obsess about things like that.

What was your own musical set up at this time?

I used a Roland MC4 which triggered a Pro-One, RSF Kobol, and a Roland Juno 60. The MC4 takes a while to learn; there's just a single numerical display and all the information (CV, gate and step time) is entered one number at a time. It made a lot more things possible. If I had an idea in my head, it could be programmed and triggered without the need for me to learn and play the part. This is extremely useful if you're a crap keyboard player like myself. Eventually I upgraded to UMI with the BBC Micro—this enabled me to trigger 16 synths simultaneously.

Fame seemed to come quite suddenly for you all—were you surprised by this?

We were all shocked. Our first singles both got into the charts, 'Dreaming of Me' at about 57 in the UK, I think, and 'New Life' just outside the Top Ten. We thought we were so lucky. None of us even had a car back then and we were still using trains and the London Underground to get to gigs, carrying all of our equipment! We even went on *Top of the Pops* and had to use public transport to get to the TV Studio. 'Just Can't Get Enough,' our next single, was our first Top Ten hit. Then obviously the album *Speak and Spell* did really well. It was strange for sure, and we were suddenly in the limelight.

Your decision to leave the band so suddenly was quite a shock to the music world. Why did you leave Depeche Mode and start Yazoo?

I can't really remember to be honest—musical differences. I still listen to them and like what they've done. I think it was just time to go in my own direction, which is obviously where Yazoo began. I needed a singer because I don't like being at the front of the stage. I advertised for one in *Melody Maker* and Alison Moyet replied, and that's how we got together.

Yazoo had a very different sound to Depeche Mode. Was this something you aimed for?

I wasn't purposefully avoiding any particular style. I think that Depeche Mode's style was changing anyway now that Alan Wilder had joined. I was just writing and playing around with electronics as I would usually do. I think music and bands evolve, sometimes even over a short amount of time, especially if they are just starting out. Alison had a very different voice, a more traditional bluesy voice, so we were going to sound differently.

Do you ever regret not doing more music with Alison?

No, the time was right to move on, I think. We did a tour together many years afterwards but that was because Erasure had a break and Alison wanted to tour to perform live songs from Yazoo's second album *You and Me Both*.

You've sort of stuck with the formula of lone singer and keyboardist since then, and Erasure has lasted for years. Why do you think this arrangement

suits you the best?

I am a bit of a control freak. Not so much now, perhaps, but definitely back then. The thing about synthesisers is that you *can* do everything yourself; it's not like you have to hang around waiting for a drummer to turn up or for a guitarist to turn up and not be hung over. So yes, I do like the ability to write and perform all of the music myself and then have someone turn up and sing the actual song part.

The music press seemed to be very hostile towards electronic bands in the early 1980s. How did you feel about that?

Well, I don't think the music press took that type of music seriously then to be honest, but then we didn't take the music press seriously either. I got the impression that many music journalists thought that anything to do with electronics was somehow cheating and the equipment was doing a lot of the work for you, which was obviously not the case.

How does song writing work between yourself and Andy Bell in Erasure, and what do you think was the biggest change in yourself musically over the years since you formed the partnership?

I think I now have a greater understanding of how music works—of songs—a greater understanding of how to write a song or a melody that evokes some kind of emotion. I didn't really understand that or was interested in that when I first started to make music, but now I have that skill to an extent.

When Andy and I are messing about with ideas something will just click and we both immediately know that there's something there. With me it's usually about resolve. A song can be nice and happy and everything but there needs to be an emotional twist in it, either by changing the sound you are using or with the lyrics, or perhaps because of the way the chord structure changes which will then change the melody. This will sort of rub you up the wrong way but then you move the structure back to being happy again and this creates the resolve. It's almost physical thing. I think once you have that in a song, you know you have a fairly decent one. And by that I mean a song that people will listen to more than once! [laughs]

Do you think that modern music relies too much on samples?

I don't think it's really about what's there waiting to be used, its more to do with *how* they use them. If someone can find a way to make a fantastic sound from something that's been used a million times before then that's cool, you know? I think it's quite easy though to fall into the trap of using something because you've heard it before and it sounds good. And I do it myself; I'll use a loop or something and then after a while think 'OK, I'll make my own version of that to make it different.' I typically write digitally using pre-sets just for speed but then replace all the sounds later using analogue sounds. I'm not necessarily trying to replicate the previous sounds but it does give me a starting point to work from. And again, due to the inherent unpredictability of the analogue synths, something quite different will usually emerge anyway.

Do you think that older synths had a warmer sound that digital ones?

Ah, the old warmer sounds question! Yes, of course I do. I keep my old analogue synths around for this reason and I even prefer the sound from vinyl records. What I found interesting recently—I read this somewhere—apparently humans cannot possibly accurately discern between, say, a vinyl recording and a well recorded CD. Our ears just can't do it. But I still think that you can!

What do you think will be the next big step in electronic music?

I think it's already happened really. I think it's the growth in these little boutique companies that are making their own EuroRack modules that create their own effects, and that these can all be strung together to make different sounds. I find that very fascinating. And how lots of little companies are starting up to add more.

So where do you see yourself going from here?

I still want to make a record with Paul Simon if I ever get the chance, an electronic one. And I think that working with the composer Philip Glass would be interesting because he creates music that sounds like synthesiser music but isn't. Until then I'll keep trying to make the perfect pop song!

LENE LOVICH

Born in Detroit, Michigan, Lene Lovich (known then as Lili-Marlene) moved to Hull, England when she was in her teens. She and Les Chappell met at school, and they would go on to be life partners as well as musical collaborators.

After trying a few local bands and projects without meeting much success Lene decided to seek the help of London DJ and author Charlie Gillett, who was well known for helping aspiring artists—notably Ian Dury with Kilburn and the High Roads as well as Dire Straits. Charlie ran a radio show called *Honky Tonk*. Charlie suggested that Lene make a demo, which he then took to Stiff Records and won a record deal.

Lene and Les shot to prominence in 1979 when their hit single 'Lucky Number' stormed the charts, reaching number 3. The band hung around the Top 40 over the next few years, notably with their second big hit 'New Toy' (written by Thomas Dolby) which reached 19 in the Singles Chart in 1981.

Lene has since worked with various other artists including Nina Hagen, Hawkwind, and The Residents and has also worked on live stage plays and other projects. She now continues to tour with The Lene Lovich Band.

You were originally from Detroit—how did you compare Hull in the UK to the USA?

I came to the UK to stay when I was thirteen. I'd visited a few times when I was growing up so it wasn't unknown to me. I was happy to arrive in Hull; it was an escape from my monster father and more peaceful than my rough neighbourhood in Detroit.

What were your first musical influences?

When I was young we had a record player but very few records. The two I heard most were Tchaikovsky's 'Marche Slave' and 'Molasses' by Spike Jones. As I got older I listened to lots of music on the radio. Any kind of music appealed to me but I was always drawn to distinctive voices and unusual sounds. I thought the records produced by Joe Meek were fascinating; the instrumentals made pictures in my mind. And I was amazed by The Beatles' *Sgt. Pepper* album and anything by Jimi Hendrix, The Doors, and Frank Zappa. I think the first record I bought was probably *'House of the Rising Sun'* by The Animals.

How did you meet your lifelong partner and musical collaborator Les Chappell?

I met Les Chappell at school. There was a natural attraction, and he was learning to play the guitar—I'm sure that was something that brought us together. When I was little I would write songs as a distraction from my sometimes hurtful life. I discovered how powerful imagination can be; it can be a refuge from the craziness around you. But you have to learn how to handle it, because it can make you crazy too.

Do you think your earlier stints as a busker helped your stage confidence later?

While Les and I were students at art school in London we got a student grant from the government, but it was never enough to live on. We used to busk in the subway at Tottenham Court Road for an hour before classes, catching the crowds going to work. I liked busking because the sound in the subway was great and there was always a constant flow of people. Sometimes they would stop and listen. Even if we didn't make much money, it was a chance to practice in public and it was good to feel wanted. In the beginning there was a happy atmosphere, even the police smiled as they told us to move on. But eventually the atmosphere changed and it wasn't fun anymore.

Did you want to be a conventional artist?

Yes, well, I always wanted to be an artist or a doctor. I did not have a stable enough home life or good advice at school to get the right exam results for university, so it seemed more possible to try art school. It was a huge excitement when I got accepted at a London art school, and after a year Les came too. But unfortunately, I found the reality was disappointing. I wanted to make art driven by my imagination, but this was not appreciated. It became obvious that you had to do the art like the tutors to be taken seriously, and you had to be able to justify everything verbally. I didn't have the skills to defend myself, so I spent a lot of time wandering around London, teaching myself how to draw. I gradually became confident enough to start making the ideas I saw in my head. Most of my ideas became sculptures. That's when I started plaiting my hair and wrapping it in scarves to avoid the dust from plaster and cement. That's where that look came from. It was just my normal dress.

How did the band come about?

Well, Les and I continued playing music while we were at art school and formed a band with our student friends. It was very casual, mostly busking with the occasional pub gig, but it was more positive and a lot more fun than the art world. After art school Les and I tried to make a living by joining other people's bands. He was a great rhythm guitarist and was drawn to danceable soul music. I tried to learn the guitar, and although I managed a few chords it always felt awkward. When my beautiful pink guitar was stolen from the rehearsal room, I never got another. I went for saxophone instead!

The London pub rock scene in the 70s was amazing. Bands could play somewhere any night of the week and the atmosphere was great. But the bands we were in did not last. I took a job with a British band working in hotels and clubs in Europe. We were on stage five hours a night playing all kinds of music, and I learned a lot.

I returned to London looking for work but did not find any. When listening to Charlie Gillet's radio show *Honky Tonk* I decided to advertise myself on his regular slot where musicians and bands could make contact. No one replied. So I wrote to Charlie and asked for help. He was kind enough to give me a chance, and Les too. Charlie and his friend and business partner Gordon Nelki were gathering an odd mix of performers to form a band.

Rehearsals seemed to go well. It was not until we recorded a demo that it became obvious it wasn't going to work. So Charlie and Gordon divided us into compatible groups. Les and I were presented to Stiff Records. Luckily for us, Nick Lowe and Elvis Costello had just left and they were looking for new artists. Thanks to Charlie and Gordon we were signed to Stiff.

What was it like working with Stiff Records?

It was a really happy time for us in the early days. Some of the other artists needed more help than me and Les, so we had total creative freedom. Everyone who worked at Stiff was talented and so dedicated. It was easy to communicate. If you had an idea or a problem, you could just go in and find someone to help.

'Lucky Number' is such a catchy tune—how did you go about writing this?

'Lucky Number' was created by trial and error and trusting our imagination. Every song Les and I wrote was instinctive—they evolved. It was a unique time. Finally, I was able to release my creative energy and be my natural self. It was a huge surprise when it became a hit and we went on *Top of the Pops* and other shows. It was an amazing experience.

The problem with this sort of success though, is that it generates a lot of pressure to keep the hits coming. But though the later singles didn't do as well, we were playing a lot of live gigs and had a lot of fans. We obviously had a quite successful single with 'New Toy' that was presented to us by Thomas [Dolby] who was playing with us that the time. He went on to be very successful in his own right.

Why did you give it all up?

Les and I had two children, and you prioritise different things. We always did intend to return to touring, and we did eventually after a number of years. We are still very creative and had been working on various things in between the band stuff. Musical theatre and other projects. We kept busy!

I heard you were a firm believer in reincarnation?

Yes, I've been able to watch myself reappear in an endless succession of other artists, from Hazel O'Connor and Toni Basil to Cyndi Lauper and most recently Gwen Stefani, who has mimicked my voice and kooky hairdo.

HEAVEN 17

INTERVIEW WITH MARTYN WARE

Martyn Ware is an electronic music pioneer who, along with Ian Craig Marsh and Phil Oakey, was a founding member of The Human League. Both Marsh and Ware were ousted by The Human League's management and subsequently formed the British Electric Foundation—the project which would spawn Heaven 17. The Human League would of course go on to be one of the most successful bands of the 80s.

The two recorded their first cassette-only album *Music for Stowaways* under the B.E.F moniker, joined by new lead vocalist Glenn Gregory. When the three became Heaven 17 success at first seemed out of reach, with none of their singles making the much desired Top 40. However, the debut album *Penthouse and Pavement*, with its anti-yuppie agenda, caught the imagination of the buying public and reached 14 in the UK charts. This was followed by *The Luxury Gap*, which reached number 4 and featured hit

singles 'Let Me Go' (41), 'Temptation' (2), 'Crushed by the Wheels of Industry' (17), and 'Come Live with Me' (5).

Heaven 17 are also renowned producers, helping to relaunch Tina Turner's career with 'Let's Stay Together' (for which they also provided backing vocals). Other notable projects include their appearance on the Band Aid record 'Do They Know it's Christmas?' as well as several production stints for other groups.

What was your childhood like, growing up, and what sort of music were you listening to?

I lived in Walkley, towards Upperthorpe in Sheffield, just off Weston Street, down from where the Arts Tower now is. Until I was about eight, I grew up in an old-fashioned council house: two-up two-down, outside toilet, three other siblings living there until I was a bit older. It was proper poor. My dad worked in a steelworks and my mum was a housewife.

Then we moved to another council house, which we thought was super luxurious, in Burngreave. Everybody said 'Aren't they grim, those council houses?' but believe me, compared to where we were living previously, it was absolute luxury; central heating, indoor toilet, that sort of thing. After that, the family ended up in Broomhall Flats in Sheffield, which is where I spent most of my teenage years.

I had two older sisters who were really into 60s pop and Motown. I was listening to Radio Luxembourg under the bedsheets at night—this was before Radio 1. Radio Luxembourg was a major part of my musical development, listening to things like The Beach Boys and much more interesting music than anything put out by the BBC, who weren't yet catering to younger music fans.

As soon as I started going to secondary school (I went to King 'Ted's' in Sheffield) I began mixing with other people my age and expanding my own musical taste. The first record I ever purchased was Deep Purple's 'In Rock.' The blossoming of my real love of music, I suppose, was the prog rock bands. I'm a big fan of King Crimson, Emerson, Lake and Palmer, Van de Graaf Generator, and those kinds of groups. I've always loved pop music too. I always had incredibly eclectic tastes.

Then I moved onto my second phase. I was always interested in anything that had any kind of electronic basis to it or sounded different, to me it was the sound of the future. Even things like 'Good Vibrations' with the use of the theremin and the *Doctor Who* theme tune—the BBC Sound Effects department was breaking new ground with electronic music and effects. I was attracted to anything that had a kind of futuristic element to it. King Crimson's use of the mellotron sounded very much like a science fiction soundtrack to me.

This coincided with my interest in actual science fiction. It was an exciting time for science and the Space Race was in full swing, a particular moment in time when

myself and my peers were all growing up through an 'in the gutter looking at the stars' kind of thing, hoping that the unimaginable year of 2000 would be this fantastic place where everybody would fly around in flying saucers and jetpacks. You have got to imagine that at that point, anything seemed possible because there were men walking on the moon.

Anyway, all that futurism led to an appreciation of futuristic-sounding music. Groups such as Kraftwerk began to emerge and, much more interesting to me at the time, so called kraut rock—all mixed up with glam rock, which was still a big thing at the time. And artists such as Bowie, Brian Eno, and others were experimenting with new ways to make music. Giorgio Moroder also played quite a big part in my musical appreciation. He was working with electronic music, but you couldn't tell (usually) from his records. They just sounded like incredibly sophisticatedly produced 'normal' records.

Myself and a few others who I knew were friends with members of the band Cabaret Voltaire, who were one of the first groups to really experiment with the idea of making music without instruments. Chris Watson, who formed the band, had a background in electronics—he had worked as a telephone engineer. I suppose at the time that sort of knowledge was important because this was before the era of cheap off-the-shelf products. The band were experimenting with sampling and tape loops and the like.

Hanging around with Chris and the other band members was interesting. They had not yet received a lot of media coverage but we loved their attitude, which we found really liberating. Every year the band had a big garden party at their parent's house. The one absolutely epiphanic moment for me was when they got this 3K rig in the back garden (God knows how they got away with it, it was so loud), and they were playing things like Can and Neu! I had previously heard some early Kraftwerk and I found it a bit wet. It was a bit like flimsy Tangerine Dreamy, drifty hippy stuff and I was not that mad about it, but they put on 'Trans-Europe Express' at high volume with big bass and it completely blew my mind. I thought 'I want to do this.' That was the moment where I thought 'I don't know if I can do it but if I could do anything this is the kind of music I'd like to create.'

Now that you had decided to make music, what was your plan?

I bought a guitar with one of my first wage packets. I bought a Gibson SG copy for 30 quid, second-hand. I tried learning guitar

but it hurt my fingers, so I did not fancy that. I do not know why I bought the guitar, I think it was sort of ingrained into people that guitars—then at least—were the thing you had to buy, almost as a default. But it soon occurred to me that I was never very keen on the idea of learning traditional written music and doing scales and all that bollocks. I'm not really interested. I never had any musical training, never had keyboard training, never had any lessons or anything; I was never interested.

I was really more interested in the sound of things and that was another great inspiration from Cabaret Voltaire. Again, their attitude was 'just make something,' and it was this entirely different appreciation of sound and music that influenced me. As soon as the entry-level affordable synths came out, which was fortuitously around about that time, I jumped on it. I've still got the synth—it was a Roland System 100.

How did this lead to forming a band or playing live?

Well, I was part of this thing called Meat Whistle in Sheffield, which was a creative arts youth club in the Holly buildings round the back of the City Hall. That was where I first met Glenn Gregory and Ian Marsh (who later joined me in Heaven 17) and a load of my long-term friends. There were about fifty or sixty of us. A safe environment to make up imaginary bands and perform for your friends and try things out, it was a kind of experimental thing, sort of semi-serious. It was just fun.

Then we started getting a little bit more serious when myself and Ian Marsh separately started working fulltime as computer operators, and started going 'We can't do this forever, it's going to drive us mad. So we got a lot more serious about creating a band and making music. We formed a band called The Future along with Adi Newton, who would later form another group called Clock DVA.

I found that putting everything onto audio tape was a good way to work. Traditionally, a band would sit in a rehearsal room and jam until something decent began to happen, and only then would they begin the process of recording it. But I didn't like the idea of that; I wanted to control the process. It also gave me the option of using something that I'd created previously, that had perhaps happened by accident.

Punk had emerged around this time in the late 1970s. Were you influenced by that movement at all?

The interesting thing was that we saw ourselves as more punk than punk because we were actually doing something radically different. Though generally we saw punk as having the same sort of ethos as electronic bands, the entire not needing to be virtuoso musicians to make sounds part, we also saw it as a continuation of what had gone before, musically. We were punks for about three weeks but soon got bored with it because we thought it's the same old-same old, and we wanted to be the future.

To avoid repeating the past, how did you go about trying to be different?

The only way we could break free of the past way of doing things was if we set ourselves a manifesto, which was 'no guitars and no songs about love.' Well, not overtly about love. We weren't allowed to use the word 'love' for example. We created some demos and hauled them around the record companies. They all said 'This is terrible,' apart from Virgin and Island Records who showed some interest and said 'Go away and write some tunes,' by which they meant write some pop tunes. Anyway, we did just that. I've always had an ear for melody and found that I could quite easily create simple tunes that sounded good. Ian also had this talent.

We needed to change things around a bit. We now had a few tunes but discovered

that Adi, who was our front man, couldn't actually sing that well. And that's when I remembered my best mate from school, Phil Oakey! Phil looked the part but we had no idea if he could sing. We gave him the backing track to 'Being Boiled,' which me and Ian had just written, and said 'Could you try and write some lyrics to this and sing something on the top of it?' He came back with the words and a tape recording and it all led from there— that was our first proper song. We also changed the name of the band to The Human League at this point.

I played 'Being Boiled' to my friend Paul Fowler from Sheffield and he sent it to Bob Last, who ran a tiny record label in Edinburgh called Fast Records. He loved it! When he got in touch with us, I said 'You can't be serious, nobody's going to want to listen to this, it's too mad!' but he had faith in us. He put it out as a single—next thing we know the DJ John Peel's playing it on his late-night BBC 1 radio program. It then sold five thousand copies by word of mouth and we suddenly had a few record companies showing interest in signing us. One of those companies was Virgin—they were our preferred choice. That's where we ended up, though EMI and Fiction Records were also interested.

We began playing lots of live gigs and we went up and down the country, sometimes supporting other more established bands, such as Siouxsie and the Banshees. It was

all great experience and we started to feel like we were 'proper' musicians and were gaining a following.

Apparently, David Bowie was in the audience one night listening to The Human League and he was quoted as saying 'I've just seen the future of pop music.'

Yes, very nice of him to say so. He was right, really, in a way. There's a better story to that, actually: unbeknown to us, a month earlier we played a sold-out gig at the original Marquee Club in Soho, which to this day is the hottest gig we have ever performed. It was so hot and sweaty that the synths wouldn't stay in tune. It was really terrible—I mean, it was fun and kind of punky, but it was problematic. Anyway, we perform *that* gig, and on that night David Bowie and Iggy Pop turned up at the door and got turned away by the bouncers because it was full. Fortunately, he returned to a later gig down at a shithole pub in Earl's Court which I can't remember the name of now. He just walked into the dressing room unannounced after the gig.

You left the Human League not long after this time?

It was a little while after. As I said, we were gigging and creating new songs. I just turned up at our studio one day and our manager was there and said 'We're throwing you out of the band, Martyn,'

Glenn and Martyn

became one of the most popular types of music in the early 1980s. What did you think of other bands or artists, such as Gary Numan and Thomas Dolby?

Well, with Gary Numan I thought his records sounded great. I loved them. After that I was completely pissed off, as you can imagine, because we'd been flogging our arses around touring with Siouxsie and the Banshees and The Stranglers and all sorts of people, trying to build up an audience for synthesiser music. What does Gary Numan do? His first Gary Numan record goes straight to number one. With a fucking reel-to-reel tape recorder on stage (the idea nicked from our stage show by the way) and a bunch of guys behind keyboards. I just thought—I felt like we were being ripped off a bit. It sounded a bit like a pastiche of what we were trying to do.

Thomas Dolby is a good friend of ours. He's performed with us. He came from a more traditional musical place; he could have been a jazz player.

What do you think happened to electronica music? Why do you think it went out of favour?

Nothing, it's still there but it's just not new anymore. It got merged into the general music making process and I guess over time music producers have learnt how to incorporate the technology without it sounding overt. And that's a good thing in many ways.

Some of the older bands haven't evolved. Let me give you an example… I love Kraftwerk and I've seen them several times. It's a fantastic pony but it's a one-trick pony. They managed to make a fifty-year career out of it. I think they found a niche and they're absolutely flogging that horse to death. They've been touring the same show now, more or less, for the last few decades? Don't you think you'd get bored? I know it's earning plenty of money but I just don't see the point because they don't even do that much on stage. They might as well be replying to their emails. I'm not criticising them—they are providing entertainment to a lot of people around the world. But the irony is in the late 70s they did a few gigs where they had robots on stage instead of them. They could definitely do that now, couldn't they?

Heaven 17 have survived for a long time, haven't they?

We were one of the most successful bands from the 1980s. We got dropped by Virgin but we never split up, it never

just like that. I remember saying 'Why?' Of course, I was gobsmacked—I had no warning! It turned out in the fullness of time that it was all contrived by our management and the record company to try and get two bands for the price of one. Ian Marsh also left, leaving just Phil. We had no idea what they were going to do with just a front man left, but it was not our concern.

So then you formed Heaven 17?

I hadn't given up on the idea of a band. Myself and Ian formed Heaven 17 and the first thing I did was ring up Glenn Gregory to sing for us. We'd been friends before I met Phil Oakey. Had Glenn not moved down to London to find his fame and fortune as a photographer about three months before we formed The Human League, he would have been the singer in that band. His career in photography had not worked out and he was back in Sheffield—the timing was perfect.

We sat down and had a look at the situation: 'How can we make this different and better than The Human League?' The key to it all was finding John Wilson, a bass player. He was a genius. So we had to hastily rethink our stance on not using guitars so we could get John's input.

Having thrown away our original 'rules' we could now have used real drums too if we wanted, but we preferred the sound of the new drum machines. They sounded more futuristic and I could program them as well, so even better!

You had almost immediate success. Did the way you produced the records change much from your time with The Human League?

Yes, to begin with. We wrote 'Let me go,' 'Temptation,' and 'Come Live with Me' on a kind of Neanderthal version of a digital audio workstation. Again, the limitations made you do things in a different way because you only had a set number of sounds. You had to focus on the actual impact of the chordal sequences and melodies because the sounds weren't very impressive. In a lot of ways were still writing like we had before, though now that we were signed to a major label we moved into multitrack territory. But we still preferred to write with a limited palette. We wrote the whole of the demos for the album *The Luxury Gap* on an Akai keyboard with a port-a-studio built in. We've always been big fans of a restricted palette. It makes you more creative.

Electronica and synth music soon

ended. In fact, we've been touring nonstop for the last twenty years. We've released loads of albums as well; it's never really stopped. We took a hiatus for a while, while I did my production work with people like Terence Trent D'Arby and Erasure and Tina Turner. We're still alive and kicking.

How do you find working with other bands?

I'm not super keen on working with actual bands, there's always too much politics involved. You know, perhaps the drummer hates the fucking guitarist and there's cliques and all that stuff. I can't be doing with it. I decided quite early on just to work with solo artists and put together musicians around them and do the more traditional interpretation of what a producer should do, more like the 60s version of a producer. I'm more of an auteur type.

What did you bring to the Tina Turner sound that was different?

A respect for the original and perhaps a soul context that she could've had, which she kind of turned her back on for a bit. She saw being rock and roll as being more future-facing than soul because she grew up with soul. When I first saw her she didn't have a record contract. I said to her, 'You've got to nail your legacy as being one of the greatest soul singers that ever lived.'

What do you think of the way the music industry is today?

Broken—at least for the actual musicians. The problem started in the late 80s when the marketing people started taking over and interfering with the creative process. They thought they knew better than the artists and started to decide the type of songs that needed to be created. They were only interested in sales and were trying to find a formula for success, which meant analysing the safest songs to create. Fast forward that over thirty years, you end up with a much-reduced gene pool and a much narrower ecosystem of ideas.

A&R departments don't really exist anymore in the major labels, it's all metrics and demographics and profit-and-loss projections. There are very few companies that run on gut instinct anymore. You know, the days in the 70s and 80s when there was a kind of buzz about a band, every A&R man from every record company would turn up. They'd get into a bidding war and all of a sudden there was a vibe about this amazing new band. That shit happens less and less now—it's all how many followers have you got on

Early Human League - Philip Adrian Wright, Ian Craig Marsh, Martin Fry, Phil Oakey - Alamy Photo Library

Twitter and YouTube. I'm not even being cynical; it's how they actually do it. They sit in an office all day analysing what the existing market is for these fans. If some non-entity played something on the guitar on *Celebrity Big Brother*, for example, that person would stand more chance of getting signed to a record label than the most talented individuals making music full-time.

I must say that I worked with Simon Cowell before *Pop Idol* and before he was on television. He basically used to say he was one of the vanguards of that new marketing. That's all it is, it's a manufacturing of music. Basically, the way *Pop Idol* works is they'd sign up someone on the cheapest possible terms and then mould them into something that they thought the public wanted, based on an incremental difference from something that'd already made a load of money. That's why you end up where you end up. I personally despise it.

Do you think that modern distribution methods have had a hand in killing music and turning it into something less valuable than we used to perceive?

The biggest problem—and I said this fifteen years ago—the biggest problem about the digital proliferation of music is

the artistic de-conceptualisation of the music. We started with CDs and the idea of random access and then, of course, streaming just killed the perceived value of music stone dead. Let me explain: I've got a vivid memory of my daughter when she was eight. I'd bought her an iPod and she'd got a load of recordings of mine on there. I put my record collection in a folder called 'Dad's songs' or whatever. She was playing it to her friends on a little speaker. I was listening to what they were playing. They would literally play ten seconds of a song then move on to something else. It's the ultimate decontextualisation. They didn't know who it was a lot of the time, they didn't care who it was or when it was made, what the artwork looked like, what the original artistic intention was. I'm not being judgmental, it's just a sad denudation of meaning.

There's a positive side. A good thing in terms of being a consumer is you can listen to anything you want, anytime you want. It's a Library of Alexandria of music at your disposal in your pocket.

What next for Martyn Ware?

I still love creating music, obviously, and there are many, many more contexts in which music can be used now so, yes. I can't imagine anything worse than retirement, to be honest.

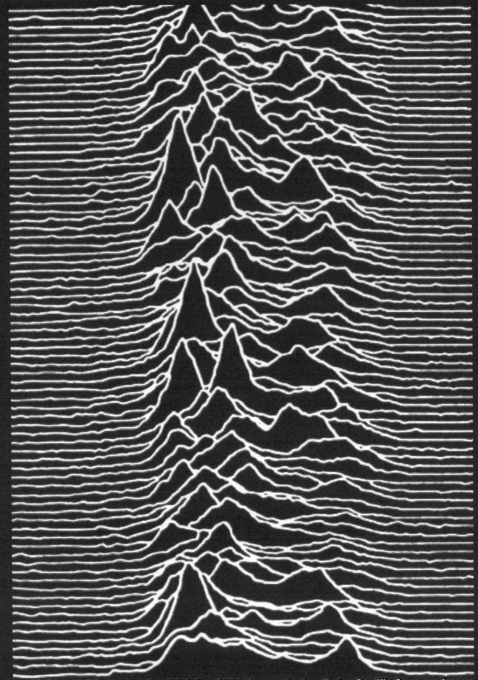

Unknown Pleasures Joy Division 1979 Cover design Peter Saville from an image sourced by Bernard Sumner

POST-PUNK

Punk was a fantastic event. It gave the complacent music industry a much-needed shakeup and let loose a wave of creativity, issuing music that demanded new and independent labels as its vehicle—labels with the brazenness to rupture the profit-minded, risk-averse publishers of yesterday. Punk existed to break the rules, but before long (and somewhat inevitably) punks, punk bands, and in particular journalists writing about punk were forming their own rubrics that constricted what a punk was and what sort of music they listened to.

By the late 1970s punk had become something of a carnival act. Established punk bands struggling to stay in the roving eye of the public were going to greater and greater lengths to shock, to entertain, and to outdo their rivals. Some bands losing patience with this posturing removed to a certain distance and reinvented themselves as more serious musicians. Bands like Wire were actively flouting punk conventions, and the release of their album *Pink Flag* would be definitive of the post-punk sound.

At the same time, Howard Devoto left Buzzcocks (under goodwill) and began to experiment with different approaches to music with new band Magazine. With others the evolution was simply a new intermixing of influences: The Clash and The Police tapped into reggae, The Jam looked to the music of The Who and led a mod revival, while Simple Minds, Blondie, and the Talking Heads branched into subgenres of pop.

MAGAZINE
INTERVIEW WITH BARRY ADAMSON

Barry Adamson is an internationally renowned bass player who has been involved with some truly legendary bands in his long and illustrious career, first joining post-punk band Magazine at its inception, then helping pioneering electronica band Visage with the release of their first hit singles before becoming a founder member of Nick Cave and the Bad Seeds. He is a respected solo artist in his own right. He has also remixed

singles for Depeche Mode, produced film soundtracks, and written a brilliant book entitled *Up Above the City, Down Beneath the Stars*.

Magazine was founded by Howard Devoto in 1977 upon leaving Buzzcocks. Singer Devoto was joined by John McGeogh on guitar, Dave Formula (eventually) on keyboards, and Martin Jackson on drums before Barry auditioned to be the final part of the jigsaw.

Their first album *Real Life* (1978) was met with universal acclaim and reached 29 in the Albums Chart as well as producing their hit single 'Shot by Both Sides' (peaking just under the UK Top 40). Further singles success eluded the band, though following album *Secondhand Daylight* (1979) reached 38 on the Chart, *The Correct Use of Soap* managed 28, and *Magic, Murder and the Weather* found 39.

You grew up in Manchester during the height of punk. How would you describe the time?

The mean streets of Moss Side at that time, from the 1960s to the mid-to-late 1970s, were a pretty black and white world. It was a time of austerity, but you could see that the people that lived there were very attached to music—everyone seemed to have a radio on. It would also be pounding out of local working men's clubs and strip joints. My earliest memories of songs are from bands such as The Hollies and The Mindbenders and, of course later, 10cc, all which people tend to forget were Manchester groups.

Punk was soon arriving on the scene and to a youngster it sounded exhilarating and fresh. We then had The Buzzcocks and Slaughter and the Dogs playing locally. And obviously on a national level there were many others coming through from different areas—The Sex Pistols, The Clash, The Damned—and I wanted to be part of it (I originally wanted to be an architect). One of the attractions of wanting to be involved in that world was that there was an immediacy to the music. You didn't need to spend years studying musical theory or practicing an instrument to be in a punk band.

How did you get hold of your first instrument?

Well, my parents bought me an acoustic guitar, but I couldn't grasp the technique that well to be honest. I could pick a few tunes out on it but it was proving difficult. But I muddled along for a while. I was fortunate because I had a friend and he was really into music. I went to his house one day and he seemed to have everything, an Aladdin's cave of instruments: drums, guitars, the lot, including a bass guitar with only two strings, which he gave me. This was more my thing.

How did you get your first big break with Magazine?

Well, I knew that Howard [Devoto] had left Buzzcocks. Buzzcocks were huge at the time and especially well known in the Manchester area, so it was big news. This world of music was still a mystery to me though and it felt at the time that these bands were all in some sort of exclusive club that we were not privy to. So I was very surprised to see an advert requesting the services of new recruits for Howard's new band. I was in the Virgin record shop to buy the extra strings for my new guitar and saw the advert in the window. I wrote the number down but I was too nervous to

get in touch at first. I was living in a shared flat at the time and my flatmates gradually talked me into it. I called him up and he asked me to go over the next morning to audition.

So obviously I was not very skilled, having only owned the bass for a couple of days. But I stayed up all night (having put the new strings on) to practice. I'd managed to get together something to show him. No melodies or anything like that but just something that I could play, some rhythms. And the next day I went to see him. It was a Sunday morning. Howard let me in and we sat in his front room. He played me one of the songs that he had already written for the new band, called 'The Light Pours Out of Me.' When I heard it I realised that what it needed was a sort of pumping one note bass. So, I played it and that basically got me into the band.

Did you find the bass easier to play than the acoustic guitar?

I seemed to take to that more easily once I'd repaired it. I had in my mind all these great Motown records from the 1960s with great bass lines, and I could approximate them quite easily. That's how the bass became the instrument of choice for me.

How were you introduced to the other band members?

Well, I went to the first rehearsal and met everyone for the first time. Well, almost everyone. Howard was there but John McGeoch, the guitarist, was away (I think he was at Uni and taking his final exams?). Martin Jackson, the drummer, was there—actually, we met at *his* house. And there was vague talk of a keyboard player coming in at some point. We were just sort of messing about really, it was a slow coming together. After a while we started to rehearse properly. We soon hired a proper rehearsal room and began to meet down there. We had a few songs nearing completion, which included the first hit 'Shot by Both Sides' as well as 'Motorcade' and 'The Light Pours Out of Me.'

Was it quite daunting to join the band, due to your inexperience?

I didn't see it that way. I was so excited and I felt accepted by them on a personal level, and of course the whole punk ethos is based around the DIY element. There didn't seem to be anything to be afraid of and everything to gain, and I felt quite propelled by it. I was trying to soak up as much as I could from the experience.

How did the song-writing work in the band? Were you all involved?

In the beginning, not really. It was Howard's band and he had written a few songs already with John [McGeoch] and that sort of continued along the lines of the Lennon and McCartney partnership. But later we all had some input. On 'Motorcade,' for example, the song had quite a dramatic intro and we were all suggesting chord sequences and trying new things. Your ideas might not be used there and then but they would be remembered and maybe would be used on something else later.

When you first started to record in studios which part of the process surprised you the most?

I think if I'm honest it was the immediacy of it all. Things are recorded and you can immediately hear how not only your own instrument sounds but also how it gels with the rest of the song, and it can often be quite surprising. It's different to when you are rehearsing. And it's funny that you should ask me that because it still surprises me to this day. I was working on something recently and I thought I'd messed something up but when I listened back to it, I thought 'That's great!' Whilst it doesn't happen too often, the happy accidents can make a nice embellishment to a track. Or you can listen to something off the beat and realise that's how it should have been all along.

Do you switch between several guitars to get certain sounds?

Yes I do, actually. The other day I swapped out a short scale 1950s bass to work on something with a full-scale Fender because I knew the sound was more solid and right for that piece. Sometimes I'll use a semi-acoustic guitar with a whammy bar to create some interesting noises. Sometimes just using a Telecaster is the way to go. It's a bit like painting a picture. You need to use the right brush and the right tone and colours.

'Shot by Both Sides' was a big hit and Magazine's first single in 1978. Were you surprised by the immediate success?

I was surprised it wasn't a *bigger* hit to be honest. We were surrounded by bands in Manchester, such as The Fall and Joy Division, who were all having a lot of success, and we thought we were on the same level as they were. There was a feeling of massive disappointment from everyone in the band. But it was great to play on *Top of the Pops*. We were still young and we were telling our families about it—it was incredibly exciting. Back in those days the programme was

MAGAZINE

WED 29 NOV

MOUNTFORD HALL LIVERPOOL UNIVERSITY

Tickets: in advance £1.50   at door £1.75

TICKETS from STUDENTS UNION · ERICS · PROBE

Doors open 8.00 pm.

Special Guests
NEO

That type of music wasn't really my thing and it was more of an interest to Dave [Formula] and John [McGeoch], who asked me to come along. I was able to give some input as Visage were just in their embryonic stage then. I had some ideas to bring to the table for their first single 'Tar.' I played bass guitar on that song and John played saxophone. Dave was obviously on synths. It was a strange consortium of people that worked on that track and they were all there to create a hit. What struck me was meeting Midge Ure for the first time. He was so focused and obviously ambitious. I knew of his work from The Rich Kids. He'd go on to international stardom later with Ultravox and his work on the Band Aid single, and I wasn't surprised.

'Tar' defined the eventual style and sound of Visage. I have a writing credit on the single but didn't want to be a full band member. But I did play on three other singles, 'The Anvil,' 'The Damned Don't Cry' and 'Night Train,' as a session musician.

In 1982 you became a founding member of Nick Cave and the Bad Seeds. How did that come about?

Well, as you will know Nick is an Aussie, but he was over in the UK. I had heard of Nick and his previous band The Birthday Party. Someone had played me 'Mr. Clarinet' which I thought was astonishing. I went to see them a few times in London. A couple of years later they managed to mislay their bass player for a while and, as seems to be a constant theme in my life, I was asked to step in for a few gigs. I became friends with Nick and we hung out together and went to a lot of parties. A little while later they went over to Germany, having found their original bassist again to tour again, but something happened, and the band imploded whilst they were over there—I think it all finally fell apart in Berlin—and this was the genesis of where The Bad Seeds would emerge. By now I'd left Magazine and was mainly getting involved in session work, so I was asked to go over and join the band as a full member.

How did the Bad Seeds differ from your previous bands?

It was very different. It was a lot more experimental, much more visceral. They had a very strange approach to the song writing process; it was a lot more organic. I'd learnt a lot about playing music since my inception in the industry with Magazine, but with The Bad Seeds it was almost a deconstruction of what I had learnt, because that is what was

a British institution and it was a family ritual to sit down and watch it together, so it was a huge thing for us. It gave us a lot of recognition. I wished I could have been cooler about it and nonchalant, but I wasn't—I was telling all my mates to watch it. And it was amazing to see myself on this show that I'd been watching since I'd been a little kid. What was funny was, I was in the canteen at the BBC studios before filming and I saw the cast of *Blake's 7* in there. They were just eating their dinner dressed in their space costumes.

Pete Shelley from Buzzcocks had helped Howard to write 'Shot by Both Sides,' so he must have been on good terms with him still, after he had left the band?

Yes, there was a lot of friendship between not only Buzzcocks and our band but others in the area. We didn't see ourselves as in competition with each other. When Magazine had a bit of down-time, Pete needed a bass player to help with a tour and I was available to step in. It was just for around six shows.

What was Pete like to work with?

It was a very different dynamic. The speed of the music was so fast and so frenetic. I really had to get my chops together. He was laid back and friendly enough. I was just there to lend a hand, so I didn't really have a say in anything band related or in terms of how the music was played.

You were getting quite well known now as a bass player—how did your brief stint with Visage happen in 1979?

Well, that was just me helping out again.

needed. But I suppose I only had the mental tools to do that because I had learnt to approach music from different perspectives and differing angles. I'd been lucky enough to work with some very skilled and talented musicians and that helped me during this time.

You were maturing as a musician by this point. What were you learning about yourself?

I think it was during my time with the band that, mentally, I was moving away from the bass and into music with a broader brushstroke. I was starting to see how the process of song writing, playing, and final execution worked as a whole, if you see what I mean. I started to write my own songs and dabbled with other instruments: a bit of piano, a bit of organ, a bit of lead guitar. I started to think about the music I wanted to make and what was going to take me forward as a musician.

Was this the beginning of your ideas for imaginary soundtracks?

Yes. I wasn't in a good place being in the band anymore and I had the urge to expand, but I wasn't sure where to go with it. But then fortuitously I was given a cassette of various parts of film soundtracks, a great mixture of them—everything from Mancini to Quincy Jones and Morricone—and I started to listen to them, but I started to listen to them as though they were one album, and an idea began to form. Films are comprised of different scenes and scenarios, some are happy, some are sad, some contain violence—perhaps I could construct an album full of these filmic ideas.

And I did just that. I was also working on music for a 'film' I had entitled 'The Man with the Golden Arm.' I released that as a single (as a statement really about where I was now, musically) and an album, *Moss Side Story,* and I started to get commissions after those. They were sort of a calling card. That was the idea anyway.

Was this leading to the creation of an actual film?

Well, I'm not a film maker and I thought that films were out of reach for me. I was more interested in the listener inventing their own film by absorbing the music, and that intrigued me. Also, I think at the time at least, the idea of doing a 'soundtrack' like this was quite leftfield.

When did all of this lead to soundtrack commissions?

When I left the Bad Seeds I had signed

MAGAZINE TOUR DATES

JULY 1ST.	**BIRMINGHAM**	BARBARELLA'S
JULY 2ND.	**REDCAR**	COATHAM BOWL
JULY 3RD.	**EDINBURGH**	TIFFANYS
JULY 5TH.	**BRADFORD**	ST. GEORGE'S HALL
JULY 6TH.	**COVENTRY**	LOCARNO
JULY 7TH.	**MANCHESTER**	RUSSELL CLUB
JULY 8TH.	**LIVERPOOL**	ERIC'S
JULY 9TH.	**SHEFFIELD**	TOP RANK
JULY 10TH.	**DONCASTER**	OUTLOOK
JULY 12TH.	**TORQUAY**	TOWN HALL
JULY 13TH.	**PLYMOUTH**	METRO
JULY 14TH.	**BRISTOL**	COLSTON HALL
JULY 15TH.	**AYLESBURY**	FRIARS
JULY 16TH.	**CANTERBURY**	ODEON

EVERY MINUTE COUNTS IN REAL LIFE
FIRST ALBUM BY MAGAZINE
Out now on Virgin Records V2100

a recording agreement with my record company and they were on the look out for a film connection for the music I wanted to make. David Jarman, who was at the time an up-and-coming director, came to the record company looking for something he could use on his latest project and was played some of the things I'd been working on. He was quite taken and I was asked to write some new pieces to be used on his 1987 film *The Last of England.* That was the beginning of it.

Is this where David Lynch entered the scene?

He heard *Moss Side Story* and got in touch through my record company. Then he gave me a call. He explained that the film *Lost Highway* was a film of two halves and only the first half had been scored. So

this would work perfectly, as it was a film with two distinct moods.

I've worked on many film scores now, including *The Beach* in 2000. I like to try different things, so I didn't want to focus on films completely, but I do find them very enjoyable to work on.

When you remix another band's records, such as Depeche Mode's 'Useless,' how do you approach doing so?

I think you have to listen to the original recording… Something inspires you and then you take it off in that direction. Sometimes it's easy, sometimes not so easy, but you have to use that as a starting point. It's important I think to not come in with ideas at the beginning, as then you force the song into a direction that it might not want to go. I can sometimes complete a remix in an afternoon. I tend to get focused, like a dog with a bone, and I can't leave it alone until it's done.

Do you think that the experience of working across the divide as a remixer or producer has altered the way that you make your own original music?

Absolutely, and in fact it seems to be every time you enter a studio you pick up something new that you can then apply to your own music—a new consideration, even if it is someone else's idea. You can store it for later.

I won an award recently for 'innovative production,' an award that people such as Giorgio Moroder had won previously, and I'm quite proud of that. And I think that what helped me to get to where I am was the lack of conventional training, and this is true of others that I admire too. Figuring something out from scratch from the very beginning leads you to new and original paths, whereas sitting in a classroom and being told how to do something guides you in a certain direction, one where many others have trodden before.

I keep hearing phrases such as 'renaissance man' when people describe you, and I can see why, as you have turned your hand to lots of things.

To me all the things I do are part of a whole; they are all art of one type or another. I started off wanting to be an architect (as I mentioned) before I was introduced to punk, and I sort of became one in a roundabout way. You have to think about how to construct things in music and any art, from the ground up, to give it a framework.

You teach as a Professor of Digital Arts at a University in Manchester. What is it that you try to pass on to your students from your own experiences?

I think it boils down to not only the not having rules, which can be difficult in a classroom setting, but also willing them to become their version of Renaissance Man or Woman—and by that, I mean multi-disciplinary. I try to get the students interested in painting, films, drawing, sculpture, as well as music. It's all part of a similar sensibility, I feel. I always say to my students: don't just do one thing. If you want to be a guitarist, be a producer too. If you want to be a producer, be a drummer too. You can do what you like really, but don't focus just on the one thing, as this gives you a greater perspective, even if it's just messing about.

Do you think that the amount of variety in the music charts these days compared to the 1970s and 1980s is down to anything in particular?

I agree that the music these days, in the charts at least, is very homogenised. I think it is mainly the fault of reality shows where people are taught that there are only a few ways to make music, and how to sing in a certain way. When you look back at, say, the 1970s and see bands such as Slade and how fantastic and exciting they were, they wouldn't exist today. The vocals were so rough, the sound was so messy, but the songs were as catchy as anything. You could say the same about T. Rex and many other bands. Not only were they very different but most of their songs were different from each other too. If they went on *X Factor* or whatever now they'd not last a second. There is a lot of good music out there if you go looking for it, but certainly the stuff that gets into the charts, it's very similar sounding.

You authored a book about your experiences?

I wrote *Up Above the City, Down Beneath the Stars,* which covers my earliest years, through Magazine, The Bad Seeds, and right up to working solo, and I wrote it intentionally in a film noir style. It's quite dark in places, with the odd shaft of light. It's a culturally cinematic odyssey through a character's life. I just happen to be that character. It's not an easy read but, from what I hear, it is invigorating.

Do you think you'll ever retire?

Naar, I've only just got started!

Magazine in 1979 - Alamy Photo Library

Colin Newman
by Malka Spigel

WIRE

INTERVIEW WITH COLIN NEWMAN

Colin Newman has been the lead guitarist and one of the principal songwriters of Wire since the band's creation. He is an authority on musical history and has released several albums under his own name.

Wire was originally composed of Colin (vocals, guitar), Bruce Gilbert (guitar), Graham Lewis (vocals and bass) and Robert Grey (drums). They were all intent on experimentation, which moved them away from their fast and frenetic punk in their first incarnation, to a wide range of musical styles. Their debut album *Pink Flag* broke away from the norms that had established themselves in punk music and as such is seen as a landmark of the post-punk genre.

Wire's habit for bucking trends resulted in music that can sound very accessible and they did see commercial success with some albums and singles. 'Outdoor Miner' reached 51 in the UK Singles Chart in 1978. 'Our Swimmer' reached the UK Independent Singles Chart (13) along with 'Crazy about Love' (28), 'Ahead' (2), 'Kidney Bongos' (8), and 'Silk Skin Paws' (5). 'Eardrum Buzz' reached the UK Singles Chart in 1989 at number 68, and 'In Vivo' reached 11 in the Indie Singles Chart the same year.

Wire remain a band celebrated by journalists and adored by musicians and are cited as an influence by many alternative groups today.

You originally attended art school. What was your motivation for doing this?

So I could be in a band! [Laughs]. Well, all of the musicians that I'd admired at that point had gone to art school before they went into a band: The Beatles; I can't remember if Bowie had?; Brian Ferry. People that did interesting things with music tended to have gone to art school first.

And why did you want to be in a band?

It was the only thing I could possibly think of doing. I had an overpowering fascination with music, to the point that I would literally feel ill if I was listening to music I didn't like. I'm talking about my life at between seven and ten years old. I would have such strong opinions about music I must have been seen as highly pretentious. I used to think that anything by The Beatles or anything released on Motown was perfect; there was nothing I could do to improve them. As for many other songs? they could definitely do with my help to make them better.

Music was the only thing I was interested in as a kid. My parents were not musical, there were no musical instruments in the house. My introduction to music came about when my uncle gave me a Dansette record player when I was about six years old (or around that age). It came with a pile of singles, each of which was a terrible as the others. But that record player became my companion. I used to have it in my bedroom, as I grew up and bought my own music. I would lay sideways on the bed and immerse myself in the music by putting my head as close as possible to the speaker. I don't know if you remember the Dansette record players at all, Shaun? They were all treble with the lid up and a bit of bass with the lid down, but not a lot. I'd also managed to get a guitar along the way, and I was learning to play.

What sort of band did you want to create?

A good one! [Laughs]. I didn't have any particular ideas; I didn't really understand music as such. I didn't understand musical movements, I didn't even really understand what the different types of guitars were for many years. But one of the things punk gave us was an understanding that you could now, if you wanted to, make something—be it music or noise or whatever—and you didn't need to be a virtuoso anymore. And it would get attention if you were any good or it appealed to others in some way.

When did you become aware of punk?

WIRE
CHAIRS MISSING

STEREO
POST PUNK PIONEERS
1978 BLEW NOTE

COLIN NEWMAN
BRUCE GILBERT
GRAHAM LEWIS
ROBERT GOTOBED

Right from the beginning. At this point in around 1974 I had an encyclopaedic knowledge of music, and it was already being predicted that something along the lines of punk would eventually appear. I became a punk along with my mate Desmond long before most people did. We even had our own punk band (though we never played in front of anyone). We were aware of bands such as The New York Dolls and other exotic groups that were hitting the scene in America. This was in 1975, before The Sex Pistols made all this sort of thing popular in the UK of course. Desmond and I got our hair cut short and wore skinny jeans. People just didn't do that sort of thing back then—even bank managers had hair that was collar-length. It was not acceptable to have short hair. People thought we were convicts.

Did you think that music needed a bit of a shake up around that time?

I sort of understand the general feeling behind that idea, but I could never understand how new music coming along would suddenly make older music less relevant. Prog rock is often cited as a sort of final straw situation that broke the back of the music industry, and though I was personally not interested in the later stages of that type of music, I was a mad King Crimson fan.

I first came across King Crimson on one of those Island Records samplers that they used to put out. I used to love those; it's

also how I discovered Nick Drake, Nirvana (the original one), and many others. I probably went to see King Crimson more than any other band around this time. What I loved about them was that they were so focused and serious about making music. There's a technical excellence combined with these really unusual arrangements that was just unbelievable.

So how did Wire come together?

I can only give you my version of events. I was living with a girl in North London. It was quite an idyllic situation really; she was friends with my best mate Desmond and they shared an apartment and I moved in with her, so I had my best friend and girlfriend living under the same roof. That lasted for a year, and we had a lot of fun. Then she decided she'd had enough of me, and we had that dreaded conversation about 'Can't we just be friends?' which roughly translates to 'You're out on your ear.' So, I had to find somewhere to live and I had to move out fast.

I was at art school by now and I had some friends that I was on the course with. Some of those also wanted to get their own place, and so we rented a house together. This was in 1976. This opened up a few more social situations for me, and I think it was the very first weekend after I'd moved in I went to a party and I got talking to some people who were discussing setting up a band for the end-of-term event, and they asked if I wanted

to be in it. Well, I was full of swagger and told them I could sing and also play the guitar. This band became Overload, that also had Bruce Gilbert (who was later in Wire) and a guy called George Gil as the nucleus. The band did one gig, without a drummer. It was rubbish. After, we used to practice in my bedroom in a house in North Watford, three of us on guitars using one amp. We were playing George Gill's songs which I never liked much.

The upshot though was that if we were going to carry on as a band, we needed to go in a different direction. We began working on these one-chord sort of long drones, which wasn't much musically, but at least it wasn't George's songs. We needed to expand the personnel. Bruce said he knew a bass player, Graham Lewis; I knew a drummer, Robert Grey. We became a five-piece, but the 'formal' songs were still George's.

Then fate took a hand. George broke his leg whilst trying to steal an amp at somebody else's gig. He ended up in hospital for a few weeks and we carried on rehearsing without him and discovered we sounded much better when he wasn't there, even when we were playing his songs. By the time he'd healed and came back, I think mentally as a band we'd moved on, and he was already ejected, though it took us a couple of months to actually kick him out. We changed the name of the band to Wire around this time.

How did you go about writing your own songs?

I think it was the ever practical me that decided that we couldn't really play George's songs any more if George wasn't in the band and that we'd better start writing our own. I said I could write music and Graham said he could write lyrics.

How precious was Graham about the lyrics, and did you have problems fitting them to the music you were creating?

I'm quite good at stuffing words into my music willy-nilly, to whichever structure I've decided to use. So whilst I didn't change the actual lyrics to accommodate the song, I did take a few arbitrary decisions and perhaps took some liberties. If the lyrics coincided with where I'd decided to put the chorus, for example, then whatever was in the lyrics at that point was suddenly the chorus.

I was very conscious when writing songs for Wire that I had an inkling of what I didn't want the songs to be like. I'd never been interested or excited by rock and roll music, you know? The three-chord blues progression, all that sort of stuff just seemed overdone. It had been done a billion times over and I couldn't see the point in going in that direction. I mean, why would I be repeating that? So what I tried to do was a "different kind of trick". For songs on *Pink Flag*, our first album, I wanted to do things differently. I wanted punk to have ended and what we were to be whatever came after punk. The term post punk, though obvious, hadn't yet been coined. On some songs I'd use two chords; a first chord and then a second which was exactly the wrong chord to use—those sorts of devices. And I used influences that were not considered cool. The funny thing about punk was that it was supposed to have this freedom element to it, but by 1977, as a genre, there was already this litany of rules and things that you had to be to be considered a punk or a punk band. So we purposefully went against the norms.

I think we identified with the American punk scene much more that the UK one, which didn't really produce that many classic albums if you look at it objectively. The Americans always thought that the UK scene was more of a fashion thing, style over substance, and we were closer to The Ramones than anything happening here. 'Lowdown' as a song was played slow because the punk diktat was that everything had to be played fast. It involved taking other musical forms and warping them. It wasn't some sort of stance against the music industry as it stood or anything like that; it was just wanting to have fun writing things. What became obvious after a while with Wire was that it's not about how brilliant the musicians in a band are, the important thing is how they play together as an ensemble.

How much would a song change from early forms through to being released for sale?

I'm a rhythm guitarist, so basically when I write the rhythm is in-built after the genesis of the song, and that rarely changes. Generally speaking, the structure will stay the same throughout as well. Once I've written a song, I'll describe it to the other guys and then it's up to them to interpret that—I'd never dream of actually telling them how to play something. I'd tell them what the chords are, obviously, but they should pick up the rest from the rhythm.

The Roxy Live WC2 album got you a lot of attention.

Well, we played live at The Roxy a few times, along with a lot of other punk

bands. By now we were playing a lot of gigs all over London. We were at this time considered to be punk, but maybe a little different to other bands.

They recorded the whole of 2 nights of a 'punk festival' there which turned into an album. The person sat there recording everything was Mike Thorne, who later produced Wire's first 3 albums.

Those recordings basically became our first set of demos. Mike was not only a record producer; he was also A&R and he was pretty keen to get us signed up from the off. EMI put up the money for us to record better demos, and they signed us based on the demo recordings eventually.

Some of that set you can hear on the *Live at The Roxy /CBCG* album (which pinkflag released in around 2004 - Wire's full set from each night of that "punk festival") actually ended up on *Pink Flag,* and this wasn't too long after we'd kicked out George. We'd only been a four-piece for about a month and a bit. We tended to move quickly as a band and with song writing. By the time *Pink Flag* had been released, our live set was mainly new songs written after Pink Flag.

Mike contributed keyboards on the first three albums, didn't he?

Yes, he played keyboards on those albums. You can't hear them so much on *Pink Flag* though. You can hear them a lot more on *Chairs Missing* and *154.*

Did Mike have any influence at all over the song writing?

No.

As your albums progressed, as a band you seemed to experiment more and became more ambitious. What do you think are the biggest differences, say between the Pink Flag and Chairs Missing?

I think when we recorded *Pink Flag* there was an idea in our mind that we wanted to get away from punk, though there were still a lot of punk elements to it. By the time we had moved on to the second album, British punk was well and truly over. By the time the Sex Pistols had come to an end the entire thing had become a bit of a comedy circus.

Despite all the funny ideas that we occasionally had; we were still only really concerned with writing good music. We progressed; we grew up. The idea that the second album would be different to the first is not that weird. Journalists made a big thing about it and our rapid progression and all that, but go back to the 1960s; you had mod bands that became hippy bands, you know? It's just what bands did and probably continue to do.

What do you think the essence of Wire's unique sound is?

As a band we tried to be as different on each song as we could and so I hope we don't have one! I think lots of bands would be content to stick with the sound on whatever hit album they have first, but it's

WIRE

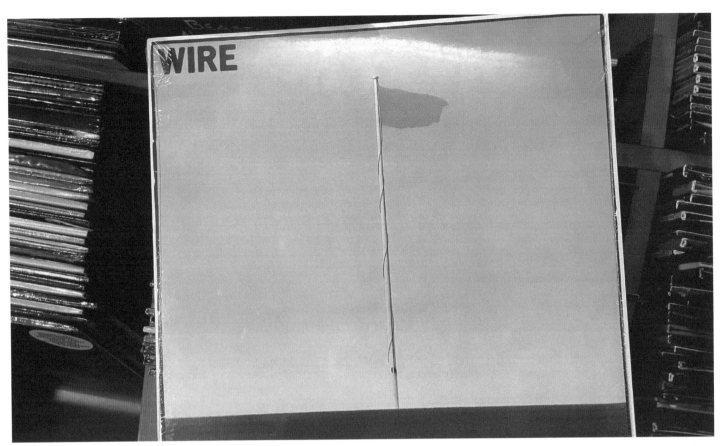

not in Wire's DNA to be like that. I do think though that both myself and Graham have very distinctive voices and delivery—Rob's drumming is quite distinctive too—so we no doubt do have a particular sound just for these reasons.

How much freedom did EMI give you, musically?

We just did what the fuck we wanted [laughs]. To be quite honest, I think they tried to say something at various points. I don't think we took any notice of anything they said, ever. Mike Thorne was EMI's occasional mouthpiece, and I remember him coming into one of the sessions for *154* and saying 'I've just been in a meeting and EMI would like this album to be a series of singles.' We just looked at him blankly. That was the end of the discussion.

The band took a bit of a hiatus from each other around 1981 after the first three albums. Do you think that you all just needed a break from each other for a bit?

That's a bit of a complex story. The internal politics of all bands can be difficult. It can be kind of gruesome the way people can start to see things, and differing attitudes start to appear. I would say that the simple way to sum it up would be that if there are more reasons to keep doing something than not doing something then it tends

to go on. And similarly, if there are more reasons to not do something than to do something then it stops.

You recorded three solo albums after this which were excellent. How did you like working alone?

Well, I wasn't alone—it was myself and Robert Grey, the drummer from Wire. Basically, Graham Lewis and Bruce [Gilbert] just told us down the pub one night that they wanted to do new things..... That left Robert and me. We worked on the *A-Z* album, which was a lot of songs that would have gone on the next Wire album had that come to pass at that time.

After the band came back together in around 1985 you had another sound, with electronic elements. How did the new low-priced synthesisers affect the way you made music?

By the time that *Ideal Copy* had been recorded I'd already been working with sequencing. It was kind of a revelation. I started with Steinberg music programs — the Pro 16 and Pro 24 which were pattern based - they were similar to programming a drum machine. Around 1990 Steinberg brought out Cubase. That was the big step forward as it looked more like the way you might visualise a tape machine in some way. It was the first time we had a tool where you could edit music on a timeline. You could see the different instrument

tracks and see where they came in and out again. These days I work on Pro Tools. It's audio rather than MIDI but works in a similar way.

Do you think you've changed the way you've approached songwriting since the early days?

It depends on what it is specifically; it's the same and it's different. A song is a song is a song. Again, technology helps, but the actual art of writing songs doesn't really change. I perhaps collaborate more with others than I used to, particularly with Malka who is a very talented musician.

As a guitar player has your style changed over time?

I started with an acoustic guitar, and I usually chose guitars on how good they look. That first one was an Ovation Breadwinner, which sounded bloody awful but looked fantastic. It's all about the effects for me though. Clean amp but try to dirty it up with the effects pedals. MXR did the best ones in the 70's, but on recordings you can use lots of different types.

Would you ever retire?

What for? I run all of the business around Wire as a company. We own our own back catalogue now, which contributes a considerable though not life-changing income. I suppose I'll keep going until I decide not to.

EXPERIMENTAL AND NO WAVE

Another movement emerging from the punk scene in the early 1980s, originally in New York, no wave shared the same DIY ideals of punk but was much richer musically. The name is a minor satire of the new wave genre that was developing around the same time.

It is not easy to classify no wave as a style. It has links to the slightly earlier art rock and bands such as The Velvet Underground, as well as electronic music—particularly bands like Suicide and Dog Face Man—though it should not be confused with industrial music. It differs from more established musical genres by its rejection of the trappings of rock and traditional song structures and, more importantly, by virtue of its avant-garde experimentation, playing in a diverse range of styles. It is not unusual to find classical, jazz, disco, and world music influences in no wave songs, all enriching the mood and texture of the music, which features are often (though not exclusively) the focus of the songwriting. The eschewing of structure in favour of texture can lend it an abrasive quality at times.

No wave bands tend to be long-lived, with a huge mixture of musical output delivered over several decades. Among the better-known bands are JG Thirlwell's various projects, The The, Lydia Lunch, and Swans.

FOETUS

INTERVIEW WITH JG THIRLWELL

J G Thirlwell has been a powerful creative source for decades, releasing material that encompasses rock, contemporary classical, noise, soundtracks, jazz, and much more. Originally from Melbourne, Australia, he briefly studied fine art there before being inspired to make his own music by the explosion of punk in 1977. After moving to London to be closer to the centre of the action in 1978, he worked in a record store and joined short lived post-punk band pragVEC. It was after this experience that he decided, following a handful of releases, that he preferred to work alone due to the level of control he could have over the final recording. He was working in a record store, and it was here that he first met Steve Stapleton of Nurse with Wound. This eventually led to his Foetus projects, which were a number

of albums each with 'Foetus' in the title of the band, under different iterations: Scraping Foetus off the Wheel, You've Got Foetus on Your Breath, Foetus Under Glass et al.

As a respected musical force, he was soon asked to work on projects with Nurse with Wound, Marc Almond, The The, Nick Cave and the Bad Seeds, as well as (much later) collaborations with Faith No More, Nine Inch Nails, Swans, Front 242, Pantera, and Thurston Moore of Sonic Youth. Now residing in New York, Jim has steered himself towards a more classical approach, using large ensembles to create very ambitious work. He also creates the soundtracks to the animated shows *Archer* and *Venture Bros*, and other multimedia projects.

You were born and brought up in Melbourne, Australia. What was the music scene like in Australia at this time, and when did you decide you wanted to work in music?

Well, I was obsessive about music, even from an early age. First of all, when I was younger you couldn't tear me away from the radio, and then as I grew a little older I'd begun to buy records, which led to an extensive record collection. The first band I ever saw was The Monkees when I was very young.

I think it's the case with people from a lot of 'smaller' countries such as Australia that you may think you are culturally inferior to bigger countries. Apparently this is known as the 'cultural cringe,' and that was the case with myself, especially towards countries such as the UK and the USA, which were the source of most of the music I was listening to. This stayed with me until punk rock came along, and then we had bands such as The Boys Next Door, and suddenly we had Australian bands that were quite exciting.

The first of my musical revelations came in the 1970s, just prior to punk, and I began to realise that I wanted to become a musician. I was still at school, and so I began to learn how to play various instruments in music clubs actually at the school, but I found it difficult because I had problems sight reading scores. Then punk came along and democratised the entire process. This taught me that you didn't necessarily have to be a virtuoso to be in a band, so I taught myself bass guitar and then moved to London. This was in 1978.

How did moving to London change your musical outlook?

It was in London that I bought myself my first synthesizer (a Wasp). After that I bought a Korg MS-20, and soon after that I started to make tapes of my own compositions. My other inspiration was the ethos of punk. I think punk was important in many ways because the ethos was all about avoiding the usual classical music training, and for perhaps the first time people were discovering ways of making new sounds. People were using their instruments as sound generators instead of pure tools of music. Punk caused a fracturing of the music scene in many ways, although actual punk music was still tied to the past, being the classic three-chord rock and roll. But it was the knock-on effect that it brought that was important.

Some of the first bands I saw in London were Throbbing Gristle, This Heat, Joy Division, and Essential Logic. Independent labels such as Rough Trade began to sign some of these groups and give them distribution. Mute Records were also starting to put out early synth music too—Fad Gadget, Depeche Mode—as was Some Bizarre Records, who had just released their Some Bizarre album that introduced a lot of synth bands to the world: Depeche Mode, Blancmange, Soft Cell etc.

When did you begin making your own music?

I was in a band for a short while [pragVEC, which mutated into Spec Records], but that experience made me realise that when it came to music making I preferred not to work in a democratic environment. This would be a problem when making music of course, because I would have to play all the instruments myself, and I wasn't a very good instrumentalist. But I wanted something where I could either stand or fall on what would be my own individual statements. Because I worked in this way, the actual studio and the technology became a very large part of the creation process. I'd been experimenting with my own compositions for a while of course, and it was a mixture of being exposed to bands with a lot of the DIY ethos firsthand, coupled with working in a London record store, that was giving me the confidence to self-publish my own albums under the name Foetus.

It was around this time that I had also met Steve Stapleton who had his own experimental band, Nurse with Wound. He came into the store one day and picked up one of his own albums and asked me about it, and (having listened to it) I told him about it, and he seemed impressed that I had actually heard it. Then he said he was the guy on the record. Steve was a big influence on me. He would every Friday go to an eight-track studio in Shepherd's Bush called IPS. He might not actually go in with any specific ideas, but he would still go and experiment and try to create something. He wouldn't always take instruments with him—he might try and make a tape loop from banging a chair or clattering some objects that he'd brought in with him, perhaps playing it backwards or slowing it down, manipulating it in some way. By the time he'd finished with it the source material was unrecognisable. I thought that this was such a liberating approach to making music. I work differently to Steve in my approach as I tend to enter a studio with a definite conclusion in mind. I tend not to experiment and then see how things evolve, on purpose at least. Although, because I am layering tracks, what I end up with isn't always one hundred percent

the way I originally envisioned it.

Were there any other, perhaps obscure musical influences affecting you at this time?

I was beginning to listen to modern twentieth century classical music. This too was revelatory to me, and it was also instructive about how people came to musical conclusions in different ways. I was reading the writings of Cage and Stockhausen and applying them to my own work. Minimalism was evolving and Steve Reich had a huge impact on me, as did Phillip Glass.

How long does it generally take you to finalise a composition in your head before you enter a studio?

I find the creation process quite random; sometimes I could be walking around with an idea for years before I think of a way to implement it, and other times it's instantaneous.

How did the DIY punk scene at the time change the way you approached distribution?

The means of distribution was always important to me. It was less because I thought that people would try to control the style of music I was playing—because I didn't think that was going to happen—but I liked the democratising aspect to punk, and self-distribution appealed to me on this level.

I think there was still a bit of a mystery about the music industry before punk. When networks of independent record labels began to appear and people realised that anyone could do it, this mystery was taken away. There were bands like The Desperate Bicycles and Scritti Politti that were early pioneers of self-distribution. Scritti Politti even had a cost-breakdown of one of their singles on the actual record sleeve: how much it cost them to press, how they pressed it, who distributed it. This was one of the reasons I set up my Self Immolation label to distribute my own work.

I noticed that you don't use images of yourself on record covers—was this a general shyness or was it something else?

I was trying to create a mystique around the music. I didn't want it to be a 'cult of personality' thing either, as I was the sole artist. The first single under the name Foetus under Glass, I put a few made up names on the credits. This not only made it a 'third-person' thing for me, but again it gave it a mystique. I created various pseudonyms; if I guested in a record, I

would use their name on the credits. This approach also meant that I could take the records to the BBC or *NME* [*New Musical Express*] in my lunch break and pretend to be a sort of corporate representative of Self Immolation Records. I also took a bit of inspiration from The Residents too, that I was a big fan of. They famously hide their identities but in a much more extreme way, with masked performances. Eventually, because I was inventing things about the band continually and feeding them to the press, I was finding it hard to keep up with it all, and finally came out of the closet, so to speak.

How did you find marketing your music to the press? Did you take to it well?

Yes. I was a little bit shocked to discover that I could type out a press release and hand it in to *NME* at their offices, and it would appear almost verbatim in their publication the following week. I remember one of the press releases where I listed several people as band members (all made up), one of which was Clint Ruin, who I slowly added to a number of other projects over time, and journalists began to believe he was a real person! I was trying to keep a certain look to the album covers that I was designing and illustrating myself. Every one of them had the red, white, and black (with shades of grey) coloration. Obviously, these were cheaper to print with a reduced palette, but it created conceptual throughlines for my albums too. I also named the albums in a stylised way, with single syllable four letter words: *Deaf, Hole, Gash, Soak,* etc.

Although you do prefer to work on your own, you have had guest vocalists on your albums and have worked with other bands on their own projects.

With Foetus I have collaborated with others very occasionally, if I felt that we needed something different that I wasn't able to contribute. I have done some work with Matt Johnson of The The. I was introduced to him at a party hosted by Cherry Red Records, and I was familiar with his work, having seen him live quite a few times. His album Burning Blue Soul was a completely different animal to the live act—it was just himself in a studio, much in the same way that I worked—and we really hit it off. We're still very good friends. He asked me to work on Soul Mining, which I did under another persona of Frank Want. We work in different ways when it comes to composing; Matt composes on instruments whereas I compose in my head. I helped out in the studio. I've collaborated on live shows with other musicians—too many to mention here—and I've created quite a few remixes for various groups.

You decided to sign with Some Bizarre record label?

Signing with Some Bizarre gave me access to twenty-four-track studios and greater promotion.

I noticed that a lot of your contemporaries moved to New York around the same time (people such as Matt Johnson). Why was that?

I personally moved over to New York as I did a show with Lydia Lunch, Nick Cave, and Marc Almond under the name Immaculate Consumptive. That was in 1983 and that was in New York, and I just fell in love with it. I'd been in London for five years by then and I guess I needed a change.

Everything was the exact opposite of London; everything was centralised in New York—and by that I mean centralised in what is known as the East Village. Everything was East Village-centric. There were probably people living there that never went north of 14th street or south of Houston. It was a 24-hour city and you could actually walk everywhere as well. London is sprawling and quite difficult to get around without changing between buses and tubes a lot. At one point I was living in Hackney in northeast London but worked in Acton. If you know London, you'll know that even though these neighborhoods aren't far from the centre of London, getting between them takes a long time. It would be the same when you went to see gigs; the tube system would close down around midnight, leaving you stranded.

There was also a different vibe; New York was a lot more relaxed. I knew about some of the music that was happening here too—Sonic Youth and Swans were beginning to gig, as an example. I met a lot of people I liked as soon as I got here, and I just decided to stay. I was also in a relationship with Lydia Lunch, so it was an easy choice. I was by now signed with Some Bizarre and I had a good working relationship with them, and I found myself jetting back and forth for a while. I've lived here most of my life now—it's been thirty-nine years!

Is there any type of music you haven't done yet?

I have worked with large ensembles and chamber ensembles, but I haven't worked with full orchestras yet, though I have produced music that sounds like one. I want to do something like that on the next Foetus album—use a full symphony orchestra. I've never worked with a full choir either. I'd like to do some choral work. It's all about time management for me. I need to plan my time correctly to make sure that I can cram all of my ambitions into my life. I do get up very early every day and stay up very late, mostly because I see a lot of live bands late at night, to be honest. I also have to factor quite a bit of procrastination into my time as well!

How do you go about writing music for classically trained musicians, since you are not classically trained yourself?

I am a little trained now, actually self-taught. I still can't sight read when I play music but I can look at a score and follow it. I listen to a lot of contemporary classical music, and I always try and figure out how they are voicing things and how I can do something similar if I like a certain piece. When I write my own scores I use Logic Pro and create templates; so I'll have violin 1, violin 2, viola, and write cells. So once all of these are done I then have to go into a scoring page and put them all together. This generates a score, but not a very elegant one, so then I may collaborate with someone else to put it in a scoring program like Sibelius which adds the expression I was trying to make.

Often the things I have in my head won't translate well to the actual instruments that the musicians are playing; my work often has big leaps between notes or difficult double-stops which aren't very comfortable to play, and so they will suggest something else that is close to what I originally wanted but more practical to play.

You seem to be on a never-ending quest to discover everything about music.

I came into music ass-backwards. I often find that it has taken me twenty years to discover something musically that I could have learnt in the first six months if I'd just gone to a conservatory in the first place all those years ago. I do get to the conclusion that I wanted, though, and I enjoy discovering things my own way. There's always something new to find, and that's what keeps me going.

JG Thirlwell in 2007

Michael Gira -
© William Lacalmontie

SWANS

INTERVIEW WITH MICHAEL GIRA

Michael Gira is a multi-instrumentalist who founded and is the lead singer of Swans. His childhood in California was foreshortened by an unstable homelife and punctuated by numerous arrests for petty crimes. At age fourteen he was shipped to Germany on his father's orders and told to straighten up and fly right, to which he responded by leaving and hitchhiking across Europe alone. He was eventually imprisoned in Israel for selling hashish, flown back to Germany by his father and

returned to the USA to attend art college.

Michael formed Swans in New York in 1982, at which time the rest of the lineup fluctuated. They were noted for the incredible aggression of their droning riffs and the bleak lyrics, often fixating on sex, death, and oppression. Their music was seen as an extreme form of anti-commercialism, teeming with a resentment that alienated their listeners. Incredibly loud volumes at gigs would often empty

venues, sometimes following police intervention.

It came therefore as a surprise when the band added female vocalist Jarboe to the lineup and looked to soften up some with their poppy version of 'Love Will Tear Us Apart' in 1988 (reaching 17 in the Independent Singles Chart). They returned to their nihilistic roots for a couple of years before reemerging with a more sophisticated and melodic sound

Can you remember much about your family life as a child?

Well, I think the earliest memories were from about the age of five or six. Musically, my parents used to play a lot of soundtracks: *South Pacific* and so on. I can also remember listening to the Disney movie *Brer Rabbit* being narrated on an album. I think these soundtrack albums actually heavily influenced me and the way that I later made music, the way I sculpted sound later on.

Having been born in 1954, the first bands that made an impression upon me would have been in the 1960s—I still hunger for the sensuality of it. One would have been The Doors. I know that most of Jim Morrison's poetry was bad, but when sung that didn't matter at all. For that matter, if you look at bands such as The Beatles and Led Zeppelin their words often aren't very good, but again it doesn't matter. The Doors had a singular effect on me but not really a musical influence on me, mostly because when I was listening to them I had no idea I wanted to become a musician.

Another California group, The Mothers of Invention, were to me very a powerful statement about modern American society. They are very sardonic of course. I was a teenager, and you could say that I liked most of the great bands from the 1960s, but I think I also had a great affinity with Pink Floyd, though I lost interest in them when they became this sort of stadium act.

Did you have a stable home life?

No [laughs]. I was having issues at home as my parents had divorced. My mother was ill and not much of a presence in our lives, and I was left to look after my younger brother. I was getting into low-level trouble with the police. It was decided that I would live with my father in Europe for a while. My father was a businessman and he took me over to Germany just to give me a fresh start. He was a disciplinarian, and at that time I was not open to the idea of discipline.

He gave me an ultimatum that I could either go to a school in Switzerland for the children of business executives or go and work as an apprentice in a factory in Germany, which I chose and worked at for around ten to twelve months. I think the factory owner was related to my Dad's German wife or something. I think my dad thought that I would work there and after a while say 'I can't take this' and then go to the Swiss school that he wanted me to go to, but I didn't. So in the end he sat me down and told me that I *would* be going

to this school whether I liked it or not. So I ran away.

I wasn't sure where I was going. I found myself at a music festival in Belgium in 1969, and I saw Pink Floyd at that time (I was on acid of course). It blew me away. Other bands at the festival were The Soft Machine, The Chicago Art Ensemble also played, an early version of Yes . . . We were a bunch of hippies in the dirt tripping and listening to psychedelic music, free-form jazz, and so on. I still didn't know I was going to be a musician at that point.

I hitchhiked around Europe and found myself moving east and ended up in Istanbul. I managed to raise money to get a plane from there to Israel. I lived in Israel for about a year, doing anything really to make ends meet. I was arrested and spent a few months in an adult prison for selling hashish, which wasn't a pleasant experience.

How did you get back to America?

When I came out of prison I asked my father for some money and then flew back to California and went to art college. I was training to be a visual artist, and I did at the time think that that would be the thing I was going to pursue for the rest of my life. But as I progressed in art school I began

to develop an antipathy for the art world. I was coming to view art as being akin to deciding to become a lawyer or similar. When punk came along, it seemed a lot more relevant to modern life—it was more immediate. I just thought 'This is it' and I started a band in LA [The Little Cripples], which didn't last long, and later moved to New York.

I started another band called Circus Mort, which was another failure. I'd started to play bass at this time—before then I was just singing. Bass is easy to play if you don't care if you aren't good at it. I was just trying to make something happen on it. Together with a drummer I was just making rhythms, and I was gathering people together and just . . . made sound. I would get a second bass player and a lead guitarist and try to direct them, which was difficult as I have no musical training. I would have to describe what it was that I wanted.

From there sprang Swans. The music we were making at that time was instrument-led, and because we weren't using synthesisers but had the same aggressive sound as industrial music, we were often described as post-industrial or no wave, but we didn't really identify with any of these titles—or any titles come to that. I

guess 'experimental' covers it. We would get on stage and we'd often try new songs out on the audience before we'd had a chance to rehearse them properly. The joy for us was that the song could change as we were playing it, and being in the middle of it all when that happened was something magical. It was often the case that the music was playing *us*. It was a lot like freeform jazz in many respects. We were once described as the loudest band in the world. Some audiences would disappear—literally run away. It wasn't for everyone, and sometimes it would work and sometimes not, but we were getting good reviews in the music press and we began to get more and more gigs.

How would you describe your music? Some would describe it as hypnotic rhythms?

We would play as a band and see if we could find a good groove and then stick with it. It always seemed silly to me to even change chords if what you were playing was good. We just hammered it out until it was spent and then did something else. Again, we don't give ourselves labels—it's purely about making music and hoping that it sounds good.

I first came across your music,

particularly your early albums, in the very late 1980s via friends. They told me that they were pretty inaccessible, but I got them straight away. What were you trying to achieve on those records, such as Filth, Cop, and Greed?

They probably *are* inaccessible to most people, probably still are. I have been asked if I was trying to deconstruct music, but that's something that a critic would do. I came out of the punk scene and I was just trying to make shit happen, to make a sound and to have an excuse to scream. But later on, the sort of thudding and thumping and the heavy downbeat began to become constraining. It could become a cartoon if repeated too much. My musical palette began to expand quite a bit after those albums, and different sounds began to enter in. Ever since the album *Children of God* [1987] I began to think of my music as soundtracks without a film, and I've continued that quest up until this very day. I saw an album as not just a collection of songs, but a unified thing that created a world into which people could escape for a while, and this preoccupied me for some time.

Your music style has changed over the years. Originally it was quite

an aggressive sound, but it later mellowed into a more recognisable style of music that mainstream listeners could identify with. Would you say that the female vocalist Jarboe who joined the band in 1985 was a catalyst for this?

It came about I guess because of the need to not be musically boring to yourself. It's the need to challenge yourself and to find new ways to work. The need to hang onto something is death, basically.

What usually happens is that I work within a band for a while, or a group of people, and after a while the music becomes predictable, and so I discard it, but I find things in that past iteration that are fruitful to draw upon, and move forward with that aspect. I discarded Swans for a while to work solo [in 1997] and headed in a much more acoustic direction. I realised I needed people around me to perform some tasks musically and to knock ideas around with, and so I formed a band called Angels of Light. I later revived Swans with a changed line up.

In regard to Jarboe, she was a fantastic resource, and of course we were deeply connected personally. She is a very talented singer and keyboardist. She was originally from New Orleans and her family had convinced her to train as a jazz vocalist at a young age. She had a much greater musical knowledge than I possessed. So yes, I would say she was pivotal to Swans for some time.

Were you picking up any non-musical influences that steered your music?

I was reading a lot of Jean Genet [French criminal and vagabond-turned-writer who wrote lyrically about whores, thieves, and people on the edge of society], especially his *Our Lady of the Flowers* and *The Thief's Journal*. I was reading a lot of Marquis de Sade too. I think I need to explain that I didn't gravitate towards that subject matter, particularly with de Sade, but I liked the fact that what they wrote about was outside of the accepted societal norms of their periods, and both of them forged a life on their own, following their own standards. Later I was reading all of the classics; things like Hemmingway.

Would you say that any eastern philosophies have been an influence on your work at all?

In the last five years certainly, from I would guess 2015. I wouldn't call myself a Buddhist, but if there was any sort of spiritual practice that attracts me then that would be it. I'm kind of fascinated by the

SWANS

white light from the mouth of infinity.

mental conundrums of Zen Buddhism and the unsolvable paradoxes that it proposes and the mental uncertainty that you are faced with when you grapple with these paradoxes. I think the truth lies in that sense of uncertainty.

The cover of 'Love will Tear Us Apart' [Joy Division] was a big departure from your usual style. It was very pop orientated.

That wasn't the original intention. I hated it. I basically gradually got sucked into it; it just sort of came out that way. I originally envisioned it as having this very eerie, misty, foggy sound. This would suit Jarboe's voice completely—the type of sound you might associate with the very old recordings of 'The Little Drummer Boy,' not orchestral, but one that was melancholy and where the sounds are shifting together, mournful sounding. But somehow drum machines got involved, which lead to everything else having to be strictly timed. The vocals in particular are stiff. I just lost all connection with it. Whatever. It isn't something I'm ashamed of, it's just something I did along the way. I've made a lot of mistakes, as do most people. It gave us a lot of attention, both good and bad. It did end up getting us signed to a major label [Uni Records, an offshoot of MCA], which was another huge mistake. That only lasted for one record

though, and we then managed to get out of the deal, so . . .

What happened with the record company? Did they attempt to mould you in any way?

Well, they had an external producer who obviously wanted a say in how we make music, and we hit it off personally, but the aesthetic wasn't there, or at least our joint aesthetics weren't as aligned as they should have been, in my view. I did actually enjoy the process at the time, and the album that came out of that, *The Burning World*, has some excellent songs on it. I just didn't think the *sound* was good. This is integral to how I work as an artist. When we left the record label it gave me the impetus to strike out on our own with our Young God label, which was a good thing.

Did you find it difficult to operate your own record label? Did you have to learn any new skills?

Well, I had people help me with a lot of the office work—the accounts and other such things. I had previous experience in business as when I first moved to New York I supported myself by working in construction. At that time I would price my own jobs and reap either a loss or profit at the end of the job—based on material,

labour, things like that—so I did have some experience. I just transposed the one on top of the other, so the mystery of running a record label became a very similar thing; how much does this cost? how many should we order? That sort of thing. When we began signing others to the label, we had a strict 50/50 split in profits and tried to make the enterprise as little like a typical record label as possible. We had a lot of help from Mute Records and Some Bizarre in the UK—that helped us to market over there.

What was your criteria for signing other bands? Did they have to have the same ethos as yourself?

They had to be talented of course—we had to like their music—and they had to be individual. That was the main thing, individuality. They didn't have to sound like us or have a certain commercial appeal particularly.

So, what next musically?

I've always worked from a 'soundtrack without a film' point of view, and I'd love to create one for an actual film. I occasionally get asked, but nothing has suited so far. I aim to be more connected to that world and see what comes about. I've also written some short stories in *The Consumer* and *The Egg*.

Michael Gira Live - Alamy Photo Library

MOD REVIVAL

Towards the end of the 1970s a so-called Mod Revival occurred, centered mostly around a single band: The Jam. Paul Weller, the principal songwriter, took clear influence from The Who, The Kinks, Small Faces, and occasionally The Beatles, but he also captured much of the energy and social commentary of the fading punk scene. The band's emergence coincided with the 1979 hit film *Quadrophenia*, and other bands such as The Lambrettas, The Chords, Secret Affair, and Purple Hearts also sprung up.

THE VAPORS

INTERVIEW WITH DAVID FENTON

David Fenton was the founder member of The Vapors, who formed in Guildford, Surrey in 1978. The band's initially fluid line-up eventually stabilised with David on lead vocals and rhythm guitar, Edward Bazalgette on lead guitar, and Steve Smith on bass guitar with Howard Smith providing drums. After gaining a following in their local area, The Vapors' big break came when Bruce Foxton of The Jam happened to see them in The Three Lions pub in Farncombe and offered them a few gigs as The Jam's support. He and

John Weller (father of Paul) also offered to manage them.

The first single 'Prisoners' didn't sell well, but breakthrough hit 'Turning Japanese' caught the attention of the buying public amid schoolground rumours that the lyrics referred to the facial expression of an onanist in climax. This additional interest, in addition to the brilliance of the single, brought it to number 3 in the UK charts in 1980, number 1 in Australia, and generally high chart positions across the English-

speaking world, where much laughter in playgrounds also abounded. 'Turning Japanese' is now considered an iconic 1980s song.

The band's next two singles, whilst performing admirably, didn't do as well. The band cited indifference and a lack of support from their record label and eventually disbanded in 1982. After a considerable hiatus, The Vapors re-emerged in 2016 and began performing gigs for their loyal fanbase once again.

DEBUT ALBUM THE VAPORS NEW CLEAR DAYS

DAVID FENTON - GUITAR and LEAD VOCALS

HOWARD SMITH - DRUMS

STEVE SMITH - BASS GUITAR and VOCALS

EDWARD BAZALGETTE - LEAD GUITAR

ALBUM INCLUDES HIT SINGLE 'TURNING JAPANESE' BP334

What was your childhood like?

I'd say I had a happy childhood. My parents were great, I had a younger brother and we got on fine. Also had an elder brother who looked after us a bit. My dad was a headmaster though, and he made sure we did our homework and were good at our own school.

It was entirely different then. I grew up in the 50's and even having a car was something of a luxury, as were TV sets. I used to go to bed with a radio and listen to the pirate stations at night. Whatever was playing, I liked the English stuff: The Kinks, The Who, Small Faces, particularly, The Beatles, Rolling Stones. You know, the usual. I watched bands on Top of the Pops, thinking 'I can do that!'

When I was about 10, I was on holiday down in Bournemouth with my parents and my younger brother, and we got the offer of being taken either to a funfair or along the high street where The Beatles were playing. We went to see The Beatles, and that really clinched the music thing for me. All those screaming girls! That was 1963. The screaming was louder than the amplifiers on stage. I got my first guitar

not long afterwards, a second hand acoustic. I started making up chords and working out how to tune it.

What were your first forays into music?

I was around 17 years old, and by now I was pretty good at playing. I was playing in folk clubs, acoustically, by myself. I was quite influenced by people like Roy Harper and the other famous acoustic guitarists, as I couldn't afford to buy an amp! I couldn't afford a car either, so I had to gig locally and with little equipment.

How did the Vapors come about?

The Vapors were my first proper band. I think you can only achieve so much playing on your own, and eventually I managed to save up enough for additional equipment such as amps and a car to get around. But you really need to play in a band if you want to get anywhere.

The band goes way back into the mid-70's. A lot of the members from the first incarnation were friends I knew from school, and a lot of them left to go to various universities once they got to that sort of age. I had to get new people in. The line-up of The Vapors that signed the record deal really was the result of the various other bands in Guildford that had fallen apart about the same time I was trying to put a new line-up together. It was fortuitous timing really.

How did you organise the song writing in the band?

I would be the one to get the ideas usually, but everyone could join in. It was quite casual and open to ideas from anyone. Obviously, everyone has their own specialist instrument, everyone has got their own bits to play, and ideas about how to do it. If the song had not got a certain feel to it and didn't feel right to me, we

could discuss it. It was democratic up to a certain point, but as they were usually my songs, I would sometimes have to make a decision. But everyone had their chance to input their own ideas.

Once we had a few songs, we started to get local gigs, and practiced, and got quite tight as a band.

I believe the first Vapors gig (with the initial line-up of me on lead vocals and rhythm guitar, Steve Hedges on bass, Mike Jordan on drums and Rob Kemp on lead guitar) was at Lakers Hotel in Redhill, Surrey in February 1978. The support band was a 3-piece from Horley called The Cure! Our first gig with the final line-up of me, Ed, Steve and Howard was a lunchtime gig at Godalming College, on 15th May 1978.

Initially we hired a transit van from friends who also helped us with the PA and backline. Once we started touring properly the PA and backline went in the artic (articulated lorry) and we bought a yellow Ford Cortina estate (which we called the banana) for the band to get about in.

We had to call around to get our own gigs, and again, friends helped us with this. Then eventually Cowbell Agency signed us up, and they arranged the gigs for us.

The Vapors were famously spotted by Bruce Foxton from The Jam.

We'd been gigging for a while, and he just happened to be in a pub that we were playing in. It was called the Three Lions (nicknamed 'Scratchers' for some reason), which is near Guildford. A typical gig at the time, just a couple of people at the bar and about 20 people there altogether.

Our bass player Steve [Smith] noticed Bruce and spoke to him afterwards at the bar. He was with his dad, John Foxton, who managed The Jam. Bruce said he loved the gig, he liked the band, he liked the songs too, and did we want to do a couple of nights supporting the main band on The Jam's Setting Sun tour? We obviously accepted; It was unbelievable. After a couple of beers, Bruce and John also offered to manage us too, and we couldn't believe our luck, and accepted that offer as well.

After we had played a few gigs with The Jam, we began to attract attention, and John and Bruce got us offers of record deals, one from Polydor, which was the label The Jam were on, and [one from] United Artists, which is the label we eventually went with.

Did either John or Bruce attempt to

change you musically at all?

No, not at all. Bruce would make comments on whether he liked certain things or not, but no, he didn't make us change anything, and nor did John. We could be ourselves, and it was pretty much business as usual for us, musically.

What surprised you about recording in a studio for the first time?

While it was an eye opener (or ear opener) to work in a professional studio in the late 70s and learn how to manipulate sound and make a record, it was nothing like the surprise of working for the first time in a digital studio with Steve Levine on our third album, Together. It's just amazing what the new technology can do now, and especially in correcting mistakes, by retuning notes or voices, copying good takes to replace fluffed ones, and moving parts in time or changing the speed without affecting the pitch. Previously, a mistake meant rerecording that part – not anymore!

Do you think that experience of recording in a studio changed the way you approached writing songs at all?

Yes. It certainly taught us a lot about how to get the results we wanted and what worked and what didn't. It also gave us the opportunity to write in the studio by building parts and experimenting. 'Spiders' on the Magnets album was 'built' in the studio from a guitar riff and effects loop, the recording being done even before the lyrics were finished.

I got to know of the band through the second single 'Turning Japanese' – that was such a big hit!

It was amazing, I couldn't believe it – from writing the song in my flat in Guildford to hearing it on the radio. I started the song in the flat where I lived, and it was coming back at me from the other side of the world. It just made the whole world seem a lot smaller. It's a fantastic feeling.

It got to Number 3 in the UK. It went to number one in the charts in Australia, too. It only got to thirty-six in America, but that led to us doing a tour of Australia and then the USA, where we did maybe half a dozen dates on the East and West Coasts and all of those sold out. First day was Whisky a Go Go, Los Angeles. It was brilliant.

I don't think we failed to sell out any gigs in America, unlike England. I think we had a bigger fan-base in America than we did here.

You've been asked this a hundred time, but was 'Turning Japanese' about wanking?

No, it wasn't. It's just a love song. It wasn't until we got to America that the Yanks thought it was an English phrase meaning wanking. It wasn't an English phrase meaning wanking. If anything, the Americans made it an English phrase about wanking and quite liked the joke and the visuals that go with it.

When you do interview sessions for the record company, they would get a lot of journalists in all at once when you release a new single, and a new one would come in every 15 minutes or every half hour, and they'd be asking the same questions over and over and over again, and you'd spend four or five hours basically repeating yourself. We'd always get asked this question at the height of our fame, and so just to make the interviews a bit more interesting, we used to say, 'Yes it is' or 'No it's not.' It kept the interest in the record up there, at least for a while. It does get very boring doing interview after interview.

Was the song based on your own personal heartache?

It's based loosely on my own experience of many broken hearts suffered as a teenager. Often, all I have left of the relationship is a photo. That's often the case.

What was it like going on Top of the Pops? It must have been quite strange?

It was. It was a TV show that not only I had watched all those years before, but pretty much everyone I knew watched it as well. It felt like a validation of sorts, and you knew that people that you knew were more than likely tuning in.

What many people at the time didn't know was that bands on the show had to mime. The studio wasn't big enough to put a proper gig on, and there's no room for amps and all the cables that you usually have laying around. You're supposed to re-record the actual single in the studio before you are on stage, but nobody ever did. You're just miming along to your single. The funny thing was the BBC film crews did two or three takes because they weren't happy with the camera angles or whatever, but the editing of the film footage was a bit lax and what you saw on camera didn't match the music. One of the clips that they left in was when Howard [Smith] dropped his drumstick and embarrassedly walked around his drum kit to pick it up, but the drums are still heard to be playing in the background!

The sound of The Vapor's albums changed between New Clear Days and Magnets. It seemed a bit heavier sounding on Magnets.

Yes, the difference between the first album and the second album was a different producer, I think. The record company kept pushing for a really clean AM radio sound. I think we relented on the first album as we wanted to keep the record company happy, and just assumed that they knew better than us. Dave Tickle, on the second album, went for a more raucous sound because that's what we asked for and that's what we wanted, something a bit more rock and roll than the dried out clean version of our sound that Vic Coppersmith had produced on the first album. We were more confident about making decisions such as that.

I'm not arguing the validity of the first album's sound, because it still stands up and it still sounds good, but we always preferred to sound as close to our live sound as possible. If you ever listen to our John Peel session, that's the sort of sound that we aimed for.

'News at Ten' was a great single. It seems to be a reflection of getting older – what inspired it?

That song is basically a reflection on myself and my old man and our different attitudes to life. In the song, he's telling me I'll end up like him, sitting in the house and watching telly in the evenings, and I'm saying, 'no way, I want something more exciting.' Unfortunately, he was right, so apart from gig nights I'm usually found in front of the telly.

Lyrically, has a band influenced how you write?

Although I grew up on The Beatles and they were the first band I saw live and therefore a first influence, my main writing and lyrical influence was always Bowie. I probably wouldn't have been so keen to follow a music career if it hadn't been for Hunky Dory and 'The Man who Sold the World.' And I may not have written 'Turning Japanese' if it hadn't been for Devo!

Lyrically, I have always loved Leonard Cohen, but then he was a real poet. So, there's a few influences, but there are probably loads more. How long have you got?

What were your experiences with your record company?

Mixed views. We were signed to United Artists, and it was very friendly to begin with, great people and they liked what we were doing, and we liked the way they worked. It was a great little label with about a dozen acts on it: there were The Buzzcocks, The Stranglers, Gang of Four, Dr Feelgood and a handful of other similar bands. There was an open-door policy… you could go and talk to the managing director without an appointment. Within about six months of signing though, EMI bought out United Artists, and we got inherited by an enormous conglomerate. It was more like joining the civil service. All the previous people we dealt with were made redundant. We didn't know anyone at EMI, nobody there had signed us; they'd inherited us. They didn't much like us, they were far too busy with Duran Duran, Kate Bush, and all these important artists. It went from absolutely brilliant to absolutely terrible overnight.

The follow up single to 'Turning Japanese' was 'News at Ten'. It got to number 44 in the UK charts. It would have been much higher placed in my opinion, but there was a TV strike, and so Top of the Pops wasn't on TV just at that moment in time. But difficulties began round about then, and our own management were on the other side of the world, touring with The Jam and out of contact with us, which didn't help. John was in France when we were in New York. It was just awkward. Eventually both Bruce and John told us that they wanted to stop managing us. They had too much work to do with The Jam, who were by then one of the biggest bands in the world.

We soldiered on for a while and released a few more singles, but we didn't think that we were being supported. We had no fans in the record company and just felt as though we were being side-lined.

The real last straw was having a meeting with the A&R head, who came down to the studio where we were rehearsing to listen to what would have been our seventh single. He watched us for a while and listened to what we were playing, and he said 'yes, fine,' then he took us all for a drink and a sandwich afterwards, and it was all brilliant. He seemed happy and was patting us on the back and all that and we thought the record company had finally come round and liked us again. But then he went back to the office straight afterwards and cancelled the actual recording sessions without telling us. Why couldn't he have told us to our faces?

I left the band, and that was the end of it. I just felt I was fighting everything uphill.

How did the other band members react to you leaving?

You'd have to ask them. Obviously, we were all pretty pissed off, but having lost our record company support… Ultimately it was simpler to walk away from the car-crash than to try and put everything back together again with no-one to help.

What happened after that, what did you do?

I was a qualified Solicitor, pre-dating our record deal. I wanted to give the band a chance, and when we had a record deal, I thought I'd give the music a try for a while. So afterwards I had another career option. I became a full-time solicitor, concentrating on legal disputes in the music industry. In 1999, I joined the Musicians' Union as their in-house solicitor.

I also kept my hand in with some Live sound engineering, managing other bands, and I did a bit of record production. I had various other bands myself that I didn't front, but which I wrote for. I wanted to be involved with

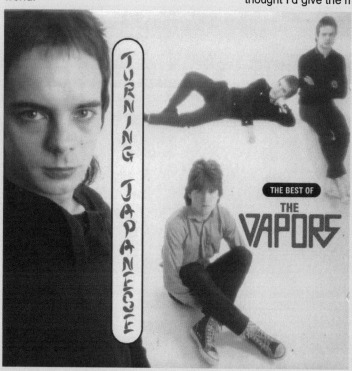

music, but I was sick of the limelight. But it was nice to try new things and be positive about things again after being stuck in what felt like a bad relationship for so long.

Do you prefer sound engineering though, or working in a band?

I prefer being in a band because I don't have all those worries that a sound engineer has. I just do my bit on stage or in the recording studio and I know it isn't going to sound too bad because the amps are all set up the way I want them to – there shouldn't be too many mistakes for the sound engineer to correct later. It's nervous for both parties, really. Getting the best sound, you can for a band when you may not have heard them before is hard, it's always tricky.

What do you think of the way that the music industry has evolved?

I prefer the old way, frankly. At that time, it was 50p to get into a gig and the album cost five quid or ten quid. Now it's the complete reverse. It's £40 or £50 to go and see the band, and more or less they give the music away for nothing. I think that's wrong. Anyway, can't help that. That's the way it is now.

Do you think that mainstream music is a lot more formulaic now?

That's how it's ended up. I think X Factor and programs like that have done a disservice to the music industry, really. Young people now think the way to get anywhere in the world of music is to be a glorified karaoke singer. They won't bother to learn instruments and think everything is about the image and being famous in general. I think Simon Cowell and the others have just made themselves a lot of money, and the actual artists that he promotes typically have very short careers and poor contracts, so even they don't really benefit. They get their 15 minutes of fame, and then they're on the scrapheap, opening nightclubs in small provincial towns.

Have The Vapors reformed in recent years?

Yes. We eventually got the Vapors back together in the last few years, since 2016, and really enjoyed performing again now that we don't have other jobs to worry about and we can relax and enjoy playing once again. We get big crowds. It's fun again.

BRIEF HISTORY OF SKA

The true roots of Ska are to be found in the colonial origins of Caribbean culture, which is to say in the very dawn of the slave trade in the Americas. It began with Spain's extermination of most of the aboriginal population of Jamaica and the slow replacement of said population with imported black slaves from Africa. In 1655 Jamaica passed into British hands and the replacement process continued. During this long period of oppression slaves were allowed to maintain certain cultural practices, including drumming and the singing of tribal songs. Similar allowances were also being made to the north in the newly formed port city of New Orleans, where black inhabitants were on occasion permitted to perform in the town square. This activity was the origin of a range of American and Caribbean musical traditions, including early jazz music. The high volume of trade between the ports of Jamaica and New Orleans ensured the exchange of culture and music as well, beginning a long tradition of shared styles between the two areas.

When Britain banned slavery in 1834 there was a natural surge in and revival of various African and Caribbean cultural and musical traditions in Jamaica. Many aspects of traditional African folk music from different regions, like clapping, stomping, percussive breathing techniques, and the improvisation of melodies started to make their way into contemporary Jamaican music. In the early twentieth century many people were moving to the bigger cities, and this concentration of activity stimulated the

development and performance of local music by wandering street musicians. This is where we get both the calypso and mento genres of Jamaican music. There was a blending of African traditional music and the European quadrille musical style, as well as the adoption by native Jamaicans of various European musical instruments, which played a large role in the process.

Thanks to the twin technologies of record players and early radio entertainment, by the dawn of World War II American big band music was already showing clear influences from calypso, and Jamaican music was equally being inspired by early jazz and blues trends. At this stage records and radios were often outside the reach of working-class Jamaicans, but many of the Jamaicans who travelled into the U.S. to perform seasonal farm labour would then come back with the highly sought-after big band, R&B, and jazz records. It is stated in some anecdotal sources that during World War II American soldiers used records to barter for cannabis or prostitutes, due to their rarity and value.

Post-war booms in travel and trade following on the economic strains of the recent war made fertile ground for new evolutions in styles of music that were once unique to specific cultures and places. During the war Jamaica was a shipping transit point, and as a hub of global shipping was shaped and coloured by the many fragments of other cultures that passed through and left their imprint. In the period directly following the war, the

sudden availability of cheaper radios and their capacity to tune to the more distant frequencies of Florida and Louisiana stations exposed Jamaicans to American rhythm and blues music, along with American jazz, gospel, and importantly the newer jump blues.

As radios became more available, American R&B artists like Amos Milburn, Fats Domino, Jelly Roll Morton, and others were a strong influence on local musical styles. Due to the expense of both records and their attendant players, a common business model of urban Jamaicans at the time was the truck-mounted sound system. Basically a record player, amplifier, and speakers on a pickup truck, it was used for street parties filled with dancing, food, and beer sales—in essence a kind of early iteration of the outdoor rave scene. Naturally, there was a great deal of competition between operators for territory and clientele, somewhat like the feuds between modern food trucks in urban city centres.

This business model was such a large contributor to the evolution of ska music that it would later be memorialized in songs such as (80s ska-punk band) Operation Ivy's 'Sound System.' But because these street-based outdoor dance parties were becoming so profitable for the organizers, they also generated a fierce competition over who could provide the newest and most in-demand records for audiences. This led to a growing local industry in record production, with local bands and producers battling to be the next new thing. Popular R&B styles were given a uniquely Jamaican flavour, and the quick, jumpy rhythms of the snappy guitars and piano stylings made for a music that was perfect for dancing.

Many early record producers started out running sound systems, like Arthur 'Duke' Reid, who was an important producer and studio owner. He ran one of the most popular sound systems of the 1950s, called Reid's Sound System, whilst Duke himself was known as The Trojan— possibly named after the British-made trucks used to transport the equipment. In the 1960s, Reid founded record label Treasure Isle (named after his liquor store) which produced ska, early rocksteady, and reggae music. Another important figure to emerge from the sound system business was Coxsone Dodd. Dodd used to play records to the customers in his parents' shop. During a spell working in the American south he became familiar

ROLL ON CHARLES STREET

20 Buster's Fabulous Ska

Rock A Shacka

PRINCE BUSTER

Prince Of Peace - Buster All Stars
Don't Throw Stones - Buster All Stars
Hey Train - Buster All Stars
Roll On Charles Street - Roland Alphonso
Vietnam - Don Drummond

RSPBLP-001

with the R&B music popular there at the time. In 1954, having returned to Jamaica, he set up the Downbeat Sound System, being the owner of a sound system and a collection of US records which he imported from New Orleans and Miami. With the success of his business, and in a competitive environment, Dodd would make regular trips through the US looking for new tunes to attract the Jamaican public. Dodd over time opened five different sound systems, each playing every night.

There is no one creator of the first wave of homegrown ska, but several musicians can certainly be said to have played key parts in its formation. Most agree for example that guitarist Ernie Ranglin invented the 'Ska Chop', and Cecil Bustamente Campbell, AKA Prince Buster, is often listed as the father of the Kingston ska scene. Even the word ska has complex origins that are widely debated. The full flowering of early ska would arrive in the early sixties with the 1963 formation of The Skatalites, whose members included Bob Marley and the notorious Don Drummond.

Early ska travelled rapidly to England with the post-war wave of immigration, where it was first known among the West Indian population as bluebeat. A critical figure in the early English scene was a white Jamaican, Chris Blackwell, who is often credited with much of ska's early British popularity. He started a record label and small-scale distribution network focusing on 'ethnic' music and, realizing how much appeal Jamaica's answer to the blues would have with the younger crowd, brought over to England the sounds of Bob Marley, The Skatalites, Jimmy Cliff, and Millie Small. Meanwhile back in Jamaica ska faded away, being replaced first by a style called rocksteady, and then by early reggae. But in the fertile ground of working-class England, ska found a new life and, taking influences from early punk rock, began to evolve further.

The ska style known as 2 Tone developed in the late 1970s and early 80s in England. Based in the working-class areas of Coventry, this second wave of ska produced some of the 2 Tone bands we still know and love today, like The Specials and The Beat. The British 2 Tone movement promoted racial unity at a time when immigration-driven racial tensions were unquestionably high. There were for example many Specials songs that dealt with the issues of racism, fighting, and friendship. Periodic riots in English cities were a common thing during the summer in which The Specials' song

'Ghost Town' was a hit.

Although bands like the The Specials, The Selector, The Belle Stars and The Beat were visibly interracial, the predominately white public image influenced American adoption of ska-punk. The strong political messaging of early ska-punk resonated with both American and English punks during their years living under the resurgent conservatism of Ronald Reagan and Margaret Thatcher, and many bands developed in resistance to this conservatism. One of the more influential early bands was the incredibly short-lived but iconic Operation Ivy, from America's west coast scene. Op Ivy's potent anti-racist message reflected much of the early American ska-punk attitude as well as the radical lens of their punk contemporaries. The ongoing east-west competition in the US stimulated changes in ska, along with the American exchanges of ideas with British punk, with groups like The Clash taking inspiration from ska and reggae sounds. In the United States, however, the political element of British ska became diluted by the more celebratory party tones of middle-class American bands.

Third wave ska sprang up in a wide variety of countries and was fuelled in part by the increase in global travel and communication. It was embraced by a new generation of immigrant children who grew up exposed to multiple cultures and had a knack for mixing influences. Although third-wave ska originated in the post-punk, industrial, and grunge scenes of the late 1980s, it became commercially successful in the 1990s. Some third-wave ska retains a traditional 1960s sound, though most is characterised by a blend of powerful guitar riffs and large brass sections, hearkening back to the big band era of the mid-twentieth century. By the mid-nineties ska had become an important player in the American rock scene, and on the west coast had absorbed some of the Latin American sound as well. At the same time, it lost much of the political intensity that drove earlier ska music and often became almost comedic in tone and content.

A standout example of the American taste for more light-hearted ska is found in the Aquabats, a ska-punk band from the west coast who dress as parodic superheroes onstage, have fights with villains as part of the performance, and even starred in a short-lived TV series on The Hub Network. Third wave ska is so diverse that the same band may be listed as 'ska' in one source and merely 'influenced by ska' in another (No Doubt are a well-known example of this trend). Another American oddity, Fishbone, perform an eclectic hybrid of styles, including ska, punk, funk, metal, reggae, and more.

Many important Ska musicians cover the full historical range of styles, such as Stranger Cole. Cole began his career in Jamaica, making his recording debut in 1962, finding instant success with singles such as 'Rough and Tough' and 'When You Call My Name,' and working as a songwriter and producer in the days of the sound systems. He moved to England in the early seventies to participate in the 2 Tone movement, and then moved on to Canada to start a small record company in Toronto serving third wave Canadian ska bands. He worked as a machinist in the Tonka toy factory in Toronto and later opened a record store—the first Caribbean shop in Toronto's Kensington Market area. His first album, *'Forward' in the Land of Sunshine*, was released in 1976, with a handful of further albums released over the next ten years, mostly on his own label. His sons also work in the ska business, Squiddly Cole working as a drummer for artists such as Ziggy Marley, and Marcus Cole (AKA KxritoXisen) producing music for his father.

Third wave ska is a truly global phenomenon, with ska bands in many countries all over the planet. The existence of a strong movement in Japan, calling itself J-ska, is illustrative of the wide appeal of ska in the modern age. The Tokyo Paradise Ska Orchestra is still putting out albums and doing soundtrack work for movies and television, such as 2020 the television show *Kamen Rider Sabre*. In the mid-nineties ska was for a while one of the most popular genres in American music, and a clear sign of this mainstream knowledge of ska is the parody song 'Your Horoscope for Today' on Weird Al Yankovic's 1999 album *Running with Scissors*.

Evidence of a slowly growing fourth wave can be seen as recently as the summer of 2019, when The Interrupters became the first American female-fronted ska band to have a radio hit since No Doubt. In Britain, the Ministry of Ska shows no sign of fading away, and over in Canada new ska groups are forming and putting out albums every year. Down in Australia the recently formed Melbourne Ska Orchestra is very active, with its most recent album coming out in 2020, and the Russian ska-punk band Distemper, founded in 1991 and with its roots in the third wave, released its most recent album in 2013. Looking at the many outlets of this longstanding genre, there seems every likelihood that modern ska will continue, evolve, and grow its audience in the years to come.

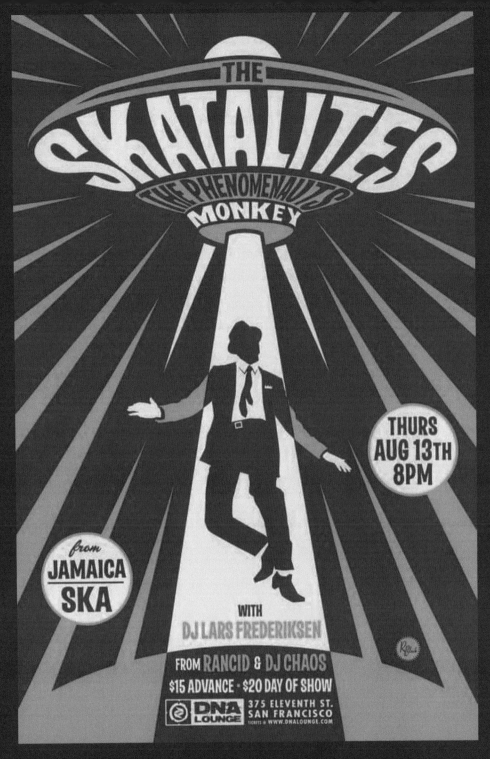

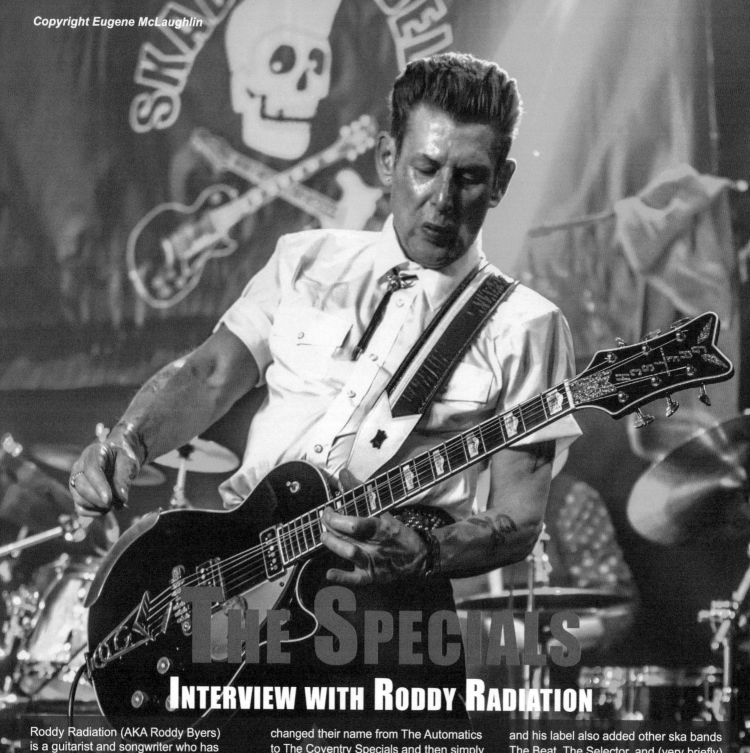

THE SPECIALS

INTERVIEW WITH RODDY RADIATION

Roddy Radiation (AKA Roddy Byers) is a guitarist and songwriter who has played with The Wild Boys, The Specials (and Special AKA), The Tearjerkers, The Bonediggers, and The Skabilly Rebels. He wrote several songs for The Specials including 'Concrete Jungle,' 'Rat Race,' and 'Hey Little Rich Girl' (later covered by Amy Winehouse).

Forming in 1977, they were arranged as a group by Jerry Dammers, who was the principal songwriter and keyboard player, The Automatics (not to be confused with an earlier band of the same name) were originally a punk band with reggae influences but soon switched to a more refined and upbeat ska sound. They

changed their name from The Automatics to The Coventry Specials and then simply The Specials. The band consisted of Lynval Golding, drummer Silverton Hutchinson, bassist Horace Panter, and vocalist Tim Strickland. At this time the band had a shifting lineup, with vocalist Tim being replaced by Terry Hall, drummer Hutchinson leaving and being replaced by John Bradbury, and Roddy latterly coming on board to add a more up-tempo guitar sound. Neville Staples was originally a roadie but his impromptu decision to join the band on stage and offer adlibbed vocals led to his inclusion in the group fulltime. Jerry Dammers set up 2 Tone Records to publish the band's music,

and his label also added other ska bands The Beat, The Selector, and (very briefly) Madness to the stable.

The Specials had much chart success, beginning with 'Gangsters'—a take on the Prince Buster single 'Al Capone'—peaking at 6 in the UK Singles Chart. This was followed by 'A Message to You, Rudy' (10), 'Too Much Too Young' (1), 'Rat Race' (5), 'Stereotype' (6), 'Do Nothing' (4), and 'Ghost Town' (1), after which Terry, Lynval, and Neville left to form Fun Boy Three. The band continued for a time under the moniker Special AKA, though their only big hit following the breakup was Top Ten single 'Free Nelson Mandela.'

Where did you grow up and what was your early life like?

Well, I grew up in a little coal mining village, called Keresley, just outside of Coventry. We lived in a Council owned property, and most of the other houses were 'pit' houses.

You were from a very musical family, weren't you?

Yes well, my father was a trumpet player. Originally in The Salvation Army, and later in pop bands, show bands, and soul bands, in the 60s. His father, my grandfather played the trombone in the Newcastle Orchestra, before he moved down to Coventry.

Were you encouraged to play?

My dad tried to get myself on trombone, and my brother Chris on trumpet when we were 11 and 10 respectively. But he wasn't very good at teaching. He was a bit rough. He would beat out the beats in the bar with a shoe on our heads. I think it's mostly due to that that I have such a good sense of timing!

Anyway, when I was 13 a couple of years later, I packed in the Trombone and took up the guitar. This is so that I could teach myself. I got hold of my first guitar from a school friend for £8. It was an acoustic guitar – a Spanish Selmer. My friend showed me a few chords, and I had a few lessons from someone else. But I was mostly self-taught.

What were your musical influences back then?

Well, it was late 60s. So, it was mostly chart music. Small Faces, The Who. I really liked The Monkees. Somehow, I went from The Monkees to Jimi Hendrix. Much rockier stuff.

Wasn't your first band The Wild Boys?

No, I had a Youth Club band before then. That was with the kid that sold me the guitar and a couple of other lads… We would transport our little amps and guitars over to the youth club in a wheel barrow. We were called 'The Undead' [laughs]. We played all the pop stuff and tried to play the blues as well. A friend of mine actually has a reel-to-reel tape of us playing. We were just 13-year-old kids trying to play the music that older black men were very good at. It was hilarious! I really need to get hold of a copy.

Well, when I was 17 a friend of mine got me an interview with a local cover band that played a lot of gigs in working men's clubs. And I sort of bluffed my way in playing lead guitar. The bass player in that band used to arrange sessions with me to go and jam together. And out of that came the new band The Wild Boys – must have been around the mid-1970s.

The Wild Boys were a mixture of rock and roll covers, Bowie and Lou Reed. Glam Rock I suppose? Then we got into Iggy Pop and The Stooges – 'I wanna be your dog' and all that sort of stuff, and 'No Fun' (which 'The Pistols' later covered). And when the 'punk' thing later came along, it wasn't a lot for us to change to that sort of sound.

What did your family think about you being in a punk band? As it had very negative connotations back then, didn't it?

Well, my dad was always out playing in different bands, so he didn't really take a lot of notice. But I don't think they thought much of it. It was a change from glam rock through to punk. I think that he was glad that I wasn't still a glam rocker though.

Is the name Roddy Radiation sort of a punk thing like Johnny Rotten?

Well, my brother Chris (as a joke when I was a big Ziggy Stardust fan) called me 'Roddy Radiation' as I would sometimes get a hot flush in the face when I drank a lot. When the Punk thing came along, I decided to use it as a stage name and I've been regretting it ever since!

How did you get involved with Jerry Dammers and the band that eventually became The Specials?

Wild Boys split up in 1977. And I was kind of at a loose end. And I'd just got married as well. Jerry was a keyboard player and I'd see him around the pubs and he liked a drink the same as I did. We were in a dodgy nightclub one night, and he asked me if I wanted to go to Soho in London the next day and record a demo? The singer of the band (the original singer before Terry Hall joined) was a good friend of mine. And I'd seen what was then called The Automatics playing around Coventry. They even supported The Wild Boys a couple of times. So, I was definitely interested.

Anyway, after the beers, I'd forgotten all about it, but the next morning, I woke up and there was a kicking and banging on my front door. So, I looked out of the window and saw Jerry Dammers and Pete Waterman (of all people), with a taxi waiting for me to get up and get my gear in the back to get to the train station. I had to explain to my wife within 5 minutes that I was off to London.

The rest of the band were already down there. Nothing really came of these demos. At the time we did take the tapes around all of the record companies – and no one was interested. But that's when I was apparently part of the band.

What was the band like in terms of a unit?

Well, it wasn't one really. Not to begin with anyway. I think Jerry had a vision and cherry-picked people from all of the local bands to create this new band. But that resulted in us just being this really mixed bunch. And we all thought were playing in a different type of band. I kind of thought I was in a band like The Clash. Horace [bass guitar] thought he was in a sort of funky disco band, Lynval Golding [vocals and guitar] thought he was in a reggae band, and Brad thought he was in a Motown band. Jerry himself was really into jazz, and had played a lot of jazz in other bands around Coventry. Terry Hall had by now joined on lead vocals too, and he thought he was in a punk band. He had that monotone voice thing that Johnny Rotten started off doing.

We were touring the pub and club circuit at the time after this – didn't make any money out of it. Couple of free beers if we were lucky. The cost of the van hire and the petrol ate up all of the cash that we did make.

How did the crowds in Coventry take to you initially?

We didn't get a lot of black fans initially. The older Rastafarians couldn't stand us. A lot of the black kids initially thought that our merging of punk and reggae was insulting the reggae roots. Neville [Staples] and Lynval [Golding], the two black guys in the band were getting a bit of stick from their black friends about it. Asked them why they were playing that horrible punk stuff with those white boys? But we started to get mixed white and black crowds later on.

Gangsters was your first hit – how did you manage to get that record recorded?

We'd borrowed some money from a local 'business man' to record 'Gangsters' – the original drummer had left by then and we had Jerry's flat mate join us on drums – a bloke called Brad [John Bradbury]. We couldn't afford the money to mix a second track for the B side. However, Brad had already recorded a record, along with his

The Specials - Roddy Radiation, Lynval Golding, Terry Hall,Horace Panter, Jerry Dammers, John Bradbury, and Neville Staple

cousin on trombone, and a friend called Neol Davies. That was given to us as the B side.

We put out a couple of thousand copies, and… John Peel started to play it on his late-night DJ show. We were suddenly a band that people wanted to listen to.

You wrote a few songs, such as 'Concrete Jungle' and 'Rat Race' for the band?

I had written songs for my previous band, The Wild Boys, and one of our songs 'Concrete Jungle' was one of the songs that Jerry wanted for his own band. I think he respected me as a songwriter. And that song was used in a slightly changed format from my original, on the first 'Specials' album with me as the singer (but uncredited for some reason), and I was writing more – Rat Race was one of them.

I tended (by pure accident) to use old song titles to name my own songs, and Jerry was very conscious of the fact that 'Concrete Jungle' was the title of a Bob Marley song, and asked me to change it if I could. He suggested 'Asphalt Jungle', but it just didn't work lyrically, so we ended up leaving it as it was.

With 'Rat Race', a few people in the band didn't want us to record that record. Coventry is taken up by the university in the centre of town, and they thought the lyrics were attacking students. But it wasn't. I used to regularly go and drink in the student bars (mostly cos the beer was cheaper). I used to overhear a handful of these posh students talking about which jobs their parents had lined up for them, and it annoyed me. These people didn't need to go to university – those places could have been taken by poorer people that did need qualifications. That's what the song is about.

The lyrics in 'Concrete Jungle' are quite bleak. Was Coventry quite a rough place?

Well, I lived in a rough area. I mean the mining village I grew up in was a pretty tough place. I grew up into rock and roll and had long hair. All of the guys that worked down the pits and their sons all seemed to be skin heads. I was regularly beaten up by skin heads because I looked different. Not that they needed an excuse. I was robbed three times – hit on the back of the head with a house brick. I've got numerous scars… Teeth knocked out. All

of this was strange a few years later when a lot of our audience *were* skinheads…

When do you think the band moved up a gear?

Jerry laid the law down and said we all had to 'go professional' now, and pack our part time jobs in. He'd managed to get us a supporting role on The Clash's new tour – he'd become friends with Bernie Rhodes, their manager.

I'd just got married too. And I'd just taken on a mortgage. wife wasn't too pleased about it. I could see her point, but it did work out eventually. Once Two Tone had signed a deal with Chrysalis, we were all put on £400 a month, which seemed like a fortune to us at the time.

Did you think that the band would identify as ska on your first album?

I wouldn't have said so, no. A lot of journalists tend to label things in certain ways and I don't think personally we were actually ska. They even labelled The Beat as a ska band, but to me they were a more a rock steady, new wave thing. In the early days we thought of ourselves as a punk band. Well, me and Terry Hall did.

I think what happened was that Elvis Costello produced our first album, and he'd seen us a few times live. He'd recently gotten into reggae and the early ska stuff. And he told us at the time that he didn't see how the early punk stuff was going to survive. And as a band, we weren't trying to revive that early 60s ska sound. We were using elements of it, with the new wave thing and punk influences.

What were The Clash like to tour with?

They were very very good to us. They were into a lot of reggae, and Paul [Simonon] the bass player was into ska. As was Joe [Strummer]. They were pretty friendly. The story goes that once the band found out how much money we were getting per show, they got their manager Bernie Rhodes to double it.

But we were sleeping in the van on a judo mat that we'd stolen at one of the gigs. Five of us and two roadies. Plus, the driver. If we were lucky someone at one of the gigs would let us sleep on their floor in a sleeping bag. But when you are 21 or whatever age we were, you can do those kind of things… It doesn't bother you… Going without food for a couple of days, you know?

Do you think the dynamic changed in the band when Neville joined after being a roadie?

Yes – Neville was pretty irrepressible. He still is. He's a very pushy character. He'd previously made his own sound systems, and he used to 'toast' over records. [Footnote – 'Toasting' was an early form of rapping – adding voice overs to songs to compliment them]. On one of the gigs, he'd found a microphone from somewhere, and he dashed onto the stage and started to add improvised Dub lyrics to different parts of our songs. Dub at the time was very fashionable, and we were all into it. I was the second singer in the band until then, so I decided to just play guitars from then on, and moved further back on the stage to give Neville more room, as he tended to throw himself around quite a bit!

I think what worked well was the contrast. Terry's performances were pretty static, and almost droll, in that punky way, and Neville's shouted words and energetic dancing.

How did the tour change the band?

Well Neville started to sing, obviously, and we *did* change our image. Or rather gained an image. And that was down to Bernie Rhodes who said 'The trouble with you guys is that you all look as though you're all in different bands. You need to adopt some sort of unifying look,' So, Jerry (our nominated leader) decided that we should all adopt that look that the mod revivalists were doing – those suits that The Jam were wearing at that time. There was also the SKA rude boy look coming in – which I wasn't very keen on… But we all adopted it and it clicked with the general public.

There's the famous story about the French Hotel…?

This was when The Clash's manager Bernie Rhodes was supposedly looking after us. We'd been sleeping rough at The Clash's rehearsal rooms. In chairs and on sofas. And I think he wanted to give us a treat, so he got us a couple of gigs in Paris.

Bernie was trying to persuade our driver to take us to Paris, and he'd pay him when he got back. But the driver wasn't having it, and demanded to be paid before he went. Nothing was sorted, so he left us and went back to Coventry.

Bernie asked Mickey Foote (who was the sound engineer for The Clash) to drive, and he drove us down to the ferry at Dover. Once we were there, they told us to put our gear on a trolley, wheel it onto the ferry, and another van would meet us in France at the ferry terminal.

Once we got to France, this tiny little van turned up. Barely enough room for the gear to go in. and perhaps a couple of people. But there was six of us. So, it was decided that the Neville and Lynval would go in the van, as the white guys would have better chance of success hitchhiking it.

Me, Jerry, Terry and Horace set off down the motor way, with our thumbs out. And the first lift we got was a Rolls Royce! It was a chauffeur on his way to pick his boss up, and he let us in and gave us cigarettes and drove us almost all the way there. After that we split into two groups and begged lorry drivers to take us the rest of the way. By the time we got to Paris it was morning and so we slept on park benches. We later found the club we were meant to be playing at later, and tried to get in, but the caretaker set his dog on us!

We finally found the hotel that Bernie Rhodes had set up for us and given us the money for, which was a relief, and we checked in – our guitars and stuff were already there. We'd been there about 15 minutes when the French woman who ran the hotel started to demand that we paid our bill. Which we'd just paid. We said 'we've just paid it?' and she said 'no – that paid for the band that stayed here before. Now you must pay your own bill.' Apparently The Damned had been there the week before us, and smashed the place up! And now she wanted us to pay for the damage. And so they confiscated our guitars.

So… We went back to the club. Told the manager of the club, who told *his* bosses, and a couple of Italian looking gentlemen in sharp suits and camel hair coats turned up and went back to the hotel with us. One of these gentlemen offered me and Terry a mint, and as he opened his jacket, we could see a gun in a shoulder holster. So, they went in and threatened the manager, and so we got the guitars back.

How did the gig go after that?

It went Ok – Ian Dury's band came to see us. So, we hung out with them. But we needed to get home after a couple of days, and we managed to bum enough money for a train. Horace managed to persuade a friend of his to pick us up at Dover.

The band had a lot of sudden success, and you were on Top of the Pops a few times, weren't you? What was that like?

Yes, and I was kind of disappointed really. After seeing it all those years on TV as a kid, you have this impression of it being this massive studio, and loads and loads of kids there. But it was quite a small affair. There were these plywood stages. And about 40 kids that were sort of herded from one stage to another to give the impression of it being a much bigger crowd.

They made you do several run throughs. We had tried to break the stage when we performed 'Gangsters', by stomping, but couldn't. By the time of the final dress rehearsal, the BBC bar had opened. I got thrown out when I complained when one of the big BBC bosses pushed in front of me. He got one of the doormen to escort me out.

Going on the show was a bit like being back at school, but it pushed a lot of records. At that time everyone watched the show and it reached millions of people. All your friends and family would see you.

You never cracked the States as a band – why do you think that was?

No, well we did go over there a couple of times. But Jerry Dammers, our 'leader' hated America. He had very strong political views and was very anti-capitalist. When we played LA, The LA Times interviewed Jerry, and he told them he'd 'had more fun on a school trip to Russia…' Which didn't go down very well obviously. Then when our American record company, Chrysalis, came to see us when we were doing two shows a night at the Whisky-Go Go club, they came into the dressing room, cigars in mouth, and told us to put our stage outfits (our suits) back on, so they could take some photographs of us. Jerry told them to 'fuck off'. And so, we all joined in. [laughs]. And after that incident they stopped pushing our records over in the states.

But I think we influenced some of the bands that were coming through at the time. Rancid and No Doubt had seen us live, and they developed their own ska scene over there. Rancid claimed that I invented 'ska punk' but I think that's stretching it a bit. I just played as I knew how to play. Lynval our guitarist did the reggae stuff and I added the Chuck Berry and Johnny Thunders rock and roll licks over it.

Did any major labels try to sign The Specials?

Mick Jagger turned up at one of the gigs, and offered to sign us to Rolling Stones Records. Which Jerry turned down. He wanted to have his own label on the back of a major. And to be fair he did actually achieve that in the end with the Two Tone label.

It was just after this release that the band came to a halt – Terry, Neville and Lynval left to form Fun Boy Three – was that a surprise?

No not really. It had gotten to the stage where we didn't really speak to each other. I mean as I said before, we were such different people that we never really hung out together anyway you know? Apart from when we had to…

By this time, we'd started work on the third album, and Jerry wanted that to have a few more jazz influences. He wanted to get away from the ska and rock and roll style, which I wasn't very happy about. The first album he was a lot more open to our input, but with the second album I think he had a much clearer idea of what he wanted to do. By the third album Jerry just wanted us to do what he said, basically.

Terry, Neville and Lynval had sort of been working as a unit within the band, and coming up with ideas, which were getting knocked back. So, they just left to do their own thing.

I'd formed my own band by then, though I was still playing with The Specials in the studio, so I didn't care.

It was around this time when the royalty cheques started to roll in, and it was the first time that we were starting to see real money. So It was a shame.

When the band eventually did split up, I was on the dole five years later. My neighbour at the time said 'You must be a millionaire Roddy!' and I said 'If I was why would I be living next door to you?' [Laughs].

Years later, you joined up with members of the band to reunite for a few tours?

Yeah well, what happened was that someone was trying to get a few of The Specials together to be a backing group for Desmond Dekker. And we had fun doing that. Then apparently this big ska thing was taking off in the USA, so we toured over there without Jerry or Terry. We did talk to Jerry about another reunion in later years but he wanted to be the one in charge again, so that just didn't happen.

What are you up to these days?

I have a band over in California, and I'm over there next week to do some touring. It's called Roddy Radiation and the Skabilly Rebels.

Daniel 'Woody' Woodgate is the drummer of Madness and also added percussion for Voice of the Beehive during the former's hiatus.

Madness formed in London in 1976, drawing on earlier Jamaican artists such as Prince Buster and Desmond Decker and became prominent in the early 80s ska revival. They first gained a dedicated local following as regular players at the Dublin Castle pub in Camden Town. They had a surprise hit with their first single (and tribute to Prince Buster) 'Prince' reaching 16 in the UK charts in 1979, though this was the only of their singles published by 2 Tone Records. This led to an approach from Stiff Records.

They toured with other 2 Tone and ska revival bands The Specials and The Selector before releasing their debut album *One Step Beyond*, which containing future singles 'One Step Beyond' (7) and 'My Girl' (3) which moved in a slightly more pop-oriented direction though maintaining the ska sound. Next album *Absolutely* reached number 2 in the UK Albums Chart and spawned the hits 'Baggy Trousers' (3), 'Embarrassment' (4), and 'The Return of the Los Palmas 7' (number 7). Their third album 7 reached number 5 in the charts in 1981 and again spawned three new hit singles 'Grey Day' (4), 'Shut Up' (7), and 'Cardiac Arrest' (14) and had an emphasis on social commentary, retreating from the more dance-oriented sound of previous work. This was perhaps their peak year as they concluded it with 'It Must Be Love' (4) and 'House of Fun' (their only number 1 single) along with compilation singles album *Complete Madness* which also reached number 1.

1983 saw 'Our House' released, and whilst only rising to 5 in the UK charts it hit number 7 in the USA and was their highest-ranking international hit. Following from this were the singles 'Wings of a Dove' (2) and 'the Sun and the Rain' (5). But Mike Barson announced that he would fulfil all band commitments including the next two singles 'Michael Caine' and 'One Better Day' before leaving in 1984. From here the band slowly descended the charts with the single 'Yesterday's Men' being particularly prophetic. The band officially split after the era's final single '(Waiting For) The Ghost Train.'

1992 saw the re-release of 'It Must Be Love,' which reached number 6 in the UK and led to several open-air gigs. These so called Madstock events still pull in massive crowds, rude boys and girls attracted to the fun and frolicsome antics of the Nutty Boys as they grace the stages once again.

MADNESS
INTERVIEW WITH WOODY WOODGATE

COMPLETE MADNESS

Complete Madness - Licensed courtesy of BMG Rights Management (UK) Ltd

So how did music start to manifest itself in your life?

Well, I grew up in West London with my brother Nick. He's fifteen months younger than me. It was a good upbringing really, but my Mum and Dad had their issues, and it was a bit confusing for both of us. I remember that they were arguing a lot and we didn't really know what was happening at the time, then my mum left and we were suddenly living with my dad. My mum became a mum that we saw only on weekends. It was a bit confusing for us as we were just little kids really. It was great though in a few ways, because my brother and I lived a quite bohemian lifestyle. My dad was working a lot and often had to spend nights away—he was a professional photographer. We were mainly brought up by nannies and au pair girls. We were quite free spirits; we did whatever we wanted. It was pretty good even though we missed our mum being around.

Living in Camden was great. We used to play with all the kids on the estate across the road off Agar Grove. I think music was a way to keep us amused. When Nick started to play the guitar I picked up the one thing which I was good at, which is drumming, then we formed pretend bands

of sorts. Then when we got old enough we formed an actual band.

Can you remember your first gig?

Yes! After a couple of gigs in schools we formed a little band called Steel Erection and played our first gig at a pub in Chalk Farm in London. When we went over to visit mum near Baker Street the first part of the Westway was built around the Baker Street area, and there was a load of this scaffolding stuff. They had hundreds of signs that said BEWARE STEEL ERECTION. I just thought it sounded hysterical. The actual gig wasn't very good, but it was a useful experience.

I was a huge Madness fan when I was growing up and I suppose that I imagined certain character traits for everyone. I had you pegged as the sensible one, perhaps a bit less crazy than the others in the band—do you think that's accurate?

[Laughs] That's something I hear quite a lot actually. The other members in the band weren't particularly crazy though; all of the Nutty Boys stuff was just a bit of a laugh really, and we were all quite serious about making music. As a kid I suppose I was intelligent enough and

eloquent enough to talk my way out of bad situations if things got violent—I was never really big or tough for sure. But I was sort of a bad kid in many ways, didn't go to many of my lessons at school. I don't know if that's being good or bad. I'm certainly not violent and I've never stolen anything. I was lucky enough to not be in want for anything in the sense that my dad was well-paid and we lived in a nice house in Camden. It rubs against me a little bit when Madness is regarded as all coming from a working-class background. The truth of it is that *most* of the band came from parents who worked in decent jobs and were quite well educated, artistic, and went to nice schools.

How did you join Madness?

I met Bedders [Mark Bedford] years before; he turned up at my mates' houses with me and Nick and he was beginning to learn to play the bass guitar at the time. Garry Dovey was also a good mate of mine; he was a drummer. And they were the two founder members of what later became Madness, along with Mike Barson, Chris Foreman, and Lee Thompson. I saw them play a gig at Willy Nilly's under the name The Invaders. My brother was in another band by then and they were playing at the same venue. There were two things that struck me; first was that they were bloody awful. But I really liked them, I really did, they had something about them that was just so different. It wasn't just the fact that they weren't polished musicians like everyone else, they just had something special. The other thing that really struck me is how frustrated I was with Garry Dovey, the drummer. I was thinking 'I'm better than him! I could do that.'

Soon after that I heard that Garry had left the band. I rang Bedders and I said 'Any chance of me getting in?' He said 'Yes, come on down,' so I went down to the rehearsal room and then I met these kind of threatening, unfriendly people—Mike Barson was very brisk in particular. I'd heard about this singer called Suggs that they had. I'd heard that he'd been sacked because he wanted to watch football instead of going to practice with the band, but he was now back in the band again. He was a Chelsea fan which was good because so am I, so I felt I had at least two people there that would be on my side—that was a positive point there. But Suggs walked in flanked by two rather large skinheads. They looked awfully aggressive. I kind of wondered what the hell have I gotten myself into, but actually they were a really nice bunch once the atmosphere thawed out.

They gave me a test: they played a few of the songs that I'd witnessed at the gig and asked me to play as I would normally. They had the songs on cassette and the sound quality was not that great. The people at the front of the stage on the recording were drowning out what the drummer was doing, and I had a hard time picking out what the hell to do. It was doubly awkward because I'd never really listened to reggae or bluebeat or ska much, and so getting the beat right was hard. I think Mark [Bedford] was the most demanding. I suppose it was also easier for him to talk to me as we already knew each other, if you see what I mean; he was a lot more comfortable with giving me suggestions. I think out of the other band members he had a better grasp of what they needed musically, too. I was a bit of a flare drummer and tried to show off a bit, as you would in that sort of situation, but Mark wanted it simple. He had to kick me off the stool a few times to demonstrate what was needed, and the mantra was 'keep it simple,' and he was correct—I had to rein myself in. They seemed satisfied at the time and accepted me into the band, but I did have an overwhelming sense of being strictly on probation!

We did a series of gigs in London following this, and we began to get a following in one of the smaller venues in London at the time, a place called the Dublin Castle in Camden. It had a little stage; it was absolutely tiny. It had a few beer crates stacked together with a board over the top in a corner of a room in the back. It was a very folky, crafty venue for individuals playing with acoustic guitars, but by word of mouth we got very popular, and we eventually had queues around the block. That got us noticed locally in London.

We then did a gig opening for The Specials—who were a massive band at the time—and another ska band. Things seemed to be taking off, but we needed an actual record, a single, and we somehow got the money together to make 'The Prince.' That was put out by Two Tone Records, which had been formed previously by Jerry Dammers of The Specials.

Dave Robinson, who was the head of Stiff Records, also saw us live and was impressed enough to invite us to play at his wedding. He seemed very—what's the phrase—'particularly in touch and in tune with us', and offered us a recording contract the same day. So the other singles and albums were published through his company. Soon afterwards we recorded 'Madness' and 'My Girl.' We recorded those at Pathway, which is where Elvis Costello did his first album, a tiny eight-track studio in North London.

Why do you think ska music became so popular at this time?

It was quite fast paced and fun. There was us, The Specials, The Selector, Bad Manners, The Beat. Out of all of them at the time I think I liked The Beat the most, but over time that switched to The Specials.

I think that punk created a bit of seriousness to music in the late 1970s and early 1980s. Do you think people craved a bit of fun after that?

We all knew where the punk ethos came from; that feeling of isolation from society in a certain set of disaffected youths. I never became a punk myself—it was interesting though and I liked a lot of the music. But at the same time, by the early to mid 1980s we just needed to be cheered up. It was hard times and the punk thing opened up other attitudes. It also opened up music to smaller bands. The DIY punk ethos opened up a lot more venues too; before that you couldn't get gigs for a lot of money unless you had an agent. How in the world could you get an agent unless you'd done some gigs? Record companies were signing dinosaurs and all the big rock bands were really getting self-indulgent. Punk kind of swept that away.

I suppose like everything we go through a lot of cycles, and whilst we appreciated the ideas and seriousness of punk we also needed to just relax again, we wanted to laugh again as a music listening community, and the music scene found a special zone for us and didn't really analyze us too much (initially at least); I think they assumed we were a bit of a novelty band. But we weren't.

How did the songwriting work in Madness—did you all have input?

Everyone used to come in with snippets of songs or whole songs, or Chris would whistle a tune. We were just quite lucky to be in a band full of writers, I suppose. Suggs liked to write the lyrics but we all liked to chip in with ideas.

You became very successful as a band very quickly—how did you cope with that?

It was great. We had so many hits and were on *Top of the Pops* and on other shows too. It was a little bit surreal to see yourself on something you had watched as a kid for years. And yes, the studio is a lot smaller than you think it is. You couldn't play live on the show even if you wanted to as there was no space to put amps and speakers.

Alamy Photo Library

Leaning on a Lamp Post - Madness in 2020 - © Grace FairChild

One thing that I used to love were the pop videos, because they looked so much fun to make. They were obviously quite low budget for the time but great to watch. How did you come up with the ideas?

Although we had numerous hits we never seemed to have money to spend on glorious videos. It did strike me as unusual that other bands were on yachts in Rio doing videos and we were asked to get ideas for places locally or somewhere on the cheap! The 'Baggy Trousers' video was fun, that was brilliant. Lee Thompson [the saxophonist] said 'I want to fly,' but the poor sod had no idea what we had in store for him!

We talked to Kathy Wise, a professional stunt performer from the theatre. We discovered that it costs a fortune to make someone look like they were flying in a safety suit using wires, but I think someone in the band knew how to hire a crane cheaply. We put a coat hanger in the back of his suit or something and dangled him from some old shipping wire. I don't think he suggested anything else after that. It actually looked great in the end; the lighting bleached out the wire so you couldn't see it. But to be honest we didn't care if it was visible—it would have been funnier if it had been. We filmed that at a local school. We shot other videos at theme parks and so on too, or just in the street.

The style of Madness changed from the early days to the latter days and **became a bit more reflective and less fast paced. Do you think the band began to get a bit jaded? and do you think that this led to the eventual breakup?**

I think when you're on the road all year round you lose touch with reality a bit; your only interaction with life is what you see on the news and what's around in the media at the time. We began to reflect on the world around us as opposed to our experiences in day-to-day life because our experiences in day-to-day life, unfortunately, narrowed down to getting on a tour bus, going up a motorway, doing a gig, and then staying in a hotel. Then the next thing you're stuck in a studio writing new songs and performing them live and the cycle goes round. It's difficult to connect to the real world again when you don't really experience it. This prompted Mike to leave the band in 1984. He couldn't do it anymore. I can look back at that time and think 'You know what? He was right.' All we needed was a break. We needed a break and to go and live in the normal world for a while so we could start writing about our experiences with people and life again.

The music industry has changed a lot hasn't it since those days. Do you think music is a bit too formulaic now?

That is the way it's gone with chart music. It's like anything; you fine tune things as you go along. Similar to car manufacturing they've sorted everything out from the windscreen wipers right down to the aerodynamic shape of the car. They're refining it to such a point that every single car looks the same. It's the same with the music industry. Great music is still out there, but finding it is the problem. Punk came along in the late 1970s to shake everything up, and I think in the music industry there will always be more people who will come along and shake everything up again (I'm an eternal optimist really), but I hope it happens again.

Music in the 1960s, 1970s, and even up to the 1990s was quite diverse. On *Top of The Pops* every week there was always a large range of music. It was a family program. You could have a punk band, heavy metal, reggae, pop, all in the same Top 20 charts and in the same TV show. But now the charts seem to be purely R&B.

What do you think of Madness and your legacy with them?

Well, obviously we reformed and still make albums. We do a lot of Madstock festivals, which are very popular. I think we have entertained a lot of people and I just hope that people got us as a band. That we make a lot of people happy; that's all that matters in the end.

Photo by Jo Brent

BELLE STARS

INTERVIEW WITH JENNIE MATTHIAS

Jennie Matthias was the lead singer of The Belle Stars and has worked on several other projects—including forming The Dance Brigade with Madness saxophonist Lee Thompson and Keith Finch — and currently fronts Bad Barbee along with Elizabeth Westwood. She also volunteers with several charities, has written a self-help book, and is a noted poet.

The Belle Stars arose from the remnants of The Bodysnatchers, who disbanded after insuperable internal conflicts. Jennie was recruited as their new lead vocalist, with Lesley Shone as the new bass player, joining remaining members Stella Barker,

Sarah-Jane Owen, Miranda Joyce, Penny Layton and Judy Parsons. The new line-up's first gig came at the end of 1980.

Having gained a following around London, they were featured on the cover of *Sounds* and soon signed to Stiff Records where they supported several other ska bands including Madness and The Beat. The first few singles didn't garner much attention but this changed in 1982 with a cover version of 'Iko Iko' that peaked at 35 in the UK charts, not helped by a rival version of the song released by Natasha England at the same time. The Belle Stars followed up with 'The Clapping Song,' which was their

first Top 20 success, and 'Mockingbird'. In 1983 they released what was to be their signature song 'Sign of the Times,' which rose to number 3 in the charts with the album of the same name reaching 15 in the Albums Chart.

Lesser success followed with 'Sweet Memory' (22) and 'Indian Summer' (52), with their only other minor hit being '80s Romance' in 1984, which reached number 71. In 1989, 'Iko Iko' was used in the soundtrack of *Rain Man,* enjoying a renaissance and reaching 14 in the US Billboard chart.

What was your early home life like?

Harrowing to say the least. My mother was quite violent and most of my early days were miserable because of it, but when away from home and spending time in children's homes I was able to have some respite from all that. I simply loved music back in the 1970s onwards, which helped me to get through it.

What sort of music were you listening to?

Anything and everything. As a person born in the 50s, I would listen to some of my family's faves from that era, but as a young child in the 60s mod music was popular and my first ever record was by a band called The Move: 'Fire Brigade'. I progressed from there and got into early Motown, ska, glam rock, Roxy Music, Bowie, Suzi Quatro, Slade etc. Later on I got into Jimmy Hendrix, Black Sabbath, Pink Floyd and then American bands like Cheap Trick. Moving on from there I got into punk, new wave, which led me into the 1980s, which was the new resurgence of ska, pop, new romantics—bands such as Visage etc. I have an eclectic taste and the genres are a mix of many cultures. I am also a great fan of doowop, reggae, jazz and Latin . . .

When did you know you wanted to be a performer?

I didn't, it fell into my lap by accident. The story goes like this: I was hanging with a new friend I had met in a bar, and she mentioned that she was going to a studio to do some vocals, and she asked me if I would come with her to give her some moral support. I was pretty reluctant about going because I had a sore throat and didn't feel up to it, but she was persistent so I caved in and off we went to this studio in Waterloo where we met up with this really nice chap called Ian. Anyway, when it became my friend's turn Ian asked me if I could sing, and I told him 'No,' because I was not a singer. He said that I had a great speaking voice and asked me to give it a try. He then passed me the lyric sheet, and I went in to do some backing vocals. Once that was done, he then asked me to sing the main vocal. This was my first ever experience of being in a studio and all the while I was reluctant to do it.

When I had finished, Ian put the whole recording onto a cassette and said 'You're actually a good singer—would you like to learn this track properly?' with a view to coming back into the studio again. I went home, and my boyfriend at that time said 'What have you been up to?' I passed him the cassette and he played it. He said 'I never knew you could sing,'

to which I replied 'Nor did I!' The following morning his ex-girlfriend called him up and mentioned that she was looking for a new lead singer because the last one had just left the band. She said the band would prefer to have someone of a darker skin, and he said 'I have the perfect person; my new girlfriend has a great voice,' and the rest is history. His ex was the lead guitarist of The Body Snatchers, and the track I sang in the studio was 'Iko.' This is a true story.

How did your family react?

Pretty shocked, but by then I wasn't living with them, and I was just doing my own thing. Yes, my dad was very supportive, but my mother wasn't as much.

They had changed their name by now from The Bodysnatchers to The Belle Stars. What were your first impressions of the band?

It was all new to me and I just went with the flow; I was totally naïve to it all. They had done it all before, but I soon got the hang of it, and they liked me as the front person. I was petrified at first of playing live but I guess I just grew into it as time went by. I integrated very quickly. We were getting a lot of bookings because we were an all-girl band, and there were not many of those out there at the time. We had no time to even think about it.

How did songwriting work—did you have a natural leader or did you all assume roles?

It was quite democratic; we all chipped in to make the sound that we had. Yes, at times one person may have written lyrics, but everyone chipped in with their own styles and creativity.

Do you think all-female bands had a harder job succeeding in music in the 1980s? If so, why? Do you think that's better now in any way?

Yes I do, as many males did not take us seriously as players. I think it has always been that way. But now we see males and females together in bands, and I like that.

How do you compare writing songs to the ska beat compared to other types of music? Is it easier or more difficult?

It is easier to write ska because the beat allows you to come up with various melodies. Having said that, I have since written songs with many other artists in all sorts of styles: not only ska, but also reggae, blues, rockabilly, ballads . . . and as a prolific writer I find it easy to come up with melodies and lyrics for all styles, but

ska and reggae are by far the easiest.

Ska music was amazingly popular. Do you think that people needed to have fun again after the seriousness of punk?

Yes. A world without music is dead; ska is great uplifting music, and every age gets up to the beat that you get with that type of music.

What is your favorite memory of this period?

I would say the style and the way of life. We were young and full of energy. Ska was our favoured music in the early years—when the schools had their monthly dances on this is what would be blaring out of the sound system. I remember the smell of brut cologne lingering throughout the dance floors, Brutus and Ben Sherman shirts, pristine along with the 16- or was it 32-hole high-leg bovver boots that went with the bleached, turned-up Levi's held up by braces, a number one haircut for the lads and the girls with a number one and a shaggy front. Priceless days they were!

You had some amazing exposure early on, touring with The Clash, The Police, Madness, The Beat, and others. What was touring like? Did you have comfortable accommodation and travel?

The time spent with all those bands was indeed an experience I shall never forget—and all positives. The lads treated us all very well, and I ended up having a very long relationship with Chrissy Boy from Madness, who is still my dearest friend today. There are so many fabulous stories about our time with The Clash that it would take far too long to write. We were invited by them to do a mini European tour, and since it was my first time abroad it was one of the most exciting times of my life. We traveled with them everywhere on their coach, and all of us got on really well. That was an experience I shall never forget.

How did you get on with the other bands, especially Madness—were they really 'nutty boys?'

The Body Snatchers had done gigs with them before, and the sax player Miranda went out with the bass player of Madness. The rhythm guitarist went out with Neville [Staple] from The Specials, and I ended up going out with Chrissy Boy as I mentioned. We were all mates and so the answer to that is we all got on really well. And yes, the Madness Boys were really nutty, especially Chris and Lee, who eventually

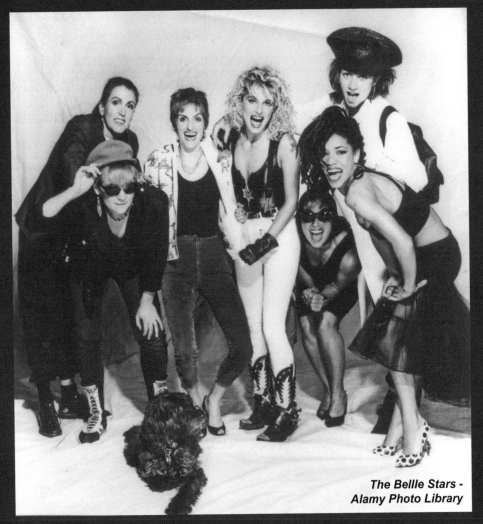

*The Bellle Stars -
Alamy Photo Library*

it was a fresh idea and different from what was then the norm. It also had its own creative style, and their audiences were totally different to anything that went on before. It's natural for people to try new things. Steve Strange [lead singer of Visage] was my best friend in those days.

There seemed to be a slow disintegration of the band. Why did you eventually leave The Belle Stars?

Our tastes changed musically, and we began drifting apart. And on a personal level I had become a pain in the arse for the band due to my drug taking (which thankfully I no longer do).

You're still making great music. You were recently number 1 in the Legacy charts for a number of weeks with your single 'Don't Watch TV.' What were your influences when you wrote that song?

Having been in the business for over forty years I have picked up many influences, and those have shaped me musically then as now, so I guess the answer to that question would be that it depends on what music I am given. If it's a reggae track like 'Don't Watch TV,' then I will of course add the knowledge I have picked up over the years within that genre of music. I was also a commercial pop artist and so I add that to the frame—then coupled with my own style and original lyrics I create tracks in this way.

What advice would you give to singers or bands starting out now in the industry?

Avoid taking drugs, be original in all that you do, rest your vocals, pace yourself on tour, always be on time in the studio, and when you get in there know the track better than the people that gave you the music to sing over it. You will never be without work if you follow that lead.

You've worked on a lot of charity work—how did you get into that? It must be very rewarding.

I am still doing that today. In 1999 I became a Community Champion for creating a drug awareness program for school children. I created interactive and informative projects relating to drug prevention, using art as a tool to educate the masses. It's my way of giving back to the community.

Do you think you'll ever retire?

Only when I am dead!

went on to create a spinoff project called The Nutty Boys.

You had quite a few record companies chasing The Belle Stars. Why did you decide to sign with Stiff Records?

Because they were by far the coolest company of that time. To be on Stiff Records was an honour, and we were in great company with the likes of Madness, Elvis Costello, Ian Drury and the Blockheads, Kirsty MacColl, Tenpole Tudor, Desmond Dekker, and endless others. Also, they were amazing when it came to marketing.

How did 'Sign of The Times' become a song: where did it originate and how did it evolve?

The lyrics were written by Stella, and it was the story of her then relationship with Neville Staple of The Specials. They had a very long relationship and are still good friends today. Stella brought this to the band and then the band added their input.

Were you surprised at how successful it was?

Yes, we were pleasantly surprised. What

followed on from that was a lot more work and recognition due to our many times on *Top of the Pops*.

When your follow-up single 'Iko Iko' originally was released, there was direct competition from a rival version by Natasha England. Was this quite annoying at the time? Did you think your version was superior?

Natasha knew we were putting it out as a single, and while we were in Spain she got her boyfriend to help her to record it, and so her version came out first, and her's did do a little bit better in the charts at the time. But years down the line our song was chosen for all the adverts and was used on the soundtrack to the film *Rainman*, so we ended up having the biggest success with it overall. Everyone plays our version and not many people know her version. I was happy for us all and the fact that a track that I had brought into the band by accident became our biggest hit of all.

Why do you think New Romantic music eventually began to take over the charts?

Because it was great music—and because

101

New Romantics

The so-called New Romantic movement was more of a fashion than a style of music. Originating in London in the late 1970s, first at Billy's nightclub and then Blitz, the 'scene' started when Steve Strange and Rusty Egan began hosting nights with a strict dress code. This code, which fashion students at the two local art schools would live or die by, was often satisfied by foppish clothing and extravagant makeup. Heavily inspired by the glam rockers of the early 70s and such stars as David Bowie, Marc Bolan, and Wizzard's Roy Wood, New Romanticism was a reaction to the austere anti-fashion of punk. Frilly shirts, Regency- or pirate-influenced costumes (mimicking Vivienne

Westwood's *Pirate* collection), and a generally androgynous look were de rigueur. Bandanas, kilts, and trilby hats were also much in display. Over time these outlandish costumes would be replaced by cool designer suits.

As far as the music went, the instrumentation of New Romantic bands was also somewhat reminiscent of glam rock, with sharp, bright guitars, melodic synths, and sometimes booming drums. Glam was a common soundtrack to nights at the Blitz, where future members of Spandau Ballet and Ultravox were regular attendees. The club's hosts, Strange and Egan, would later with Midge Ure

form Visage, a band which very smoothly melded synthpop music with New Romantic dress. Many New Romantics were keen to shun this moniker, seen somewhat pretentious even by the standards of the 80s, while patrons of the Blitz may have been happier to be known simply as 'Blitz Kids'. 'Gender benders' Boy George and Marilyn worked the cloakroom at the Blitz for a time, handling the sartorial extravagances of those bright young things. The guest list on any given night may have read: Visage, Adam and the Ants, Spandau Ballet (house band), Ultravox, Japan, Culture Club, Simple Minds, A Flock of Seagulls, ABC, and Duran Duran.

Spandau Ballet - Alamy Photo Library

VISAGE

INTERVIEW WITH DAVE FORMULA

Dave Formula is a keyboard player probably best known for his work with post-punk band Magazine and New Romantic electronica group Visage, though he embraced early chart success with his first band St Louis Union. Dave continues to produce music both as a sound engineer and musician.

Visage began in 1978 as a collaboration between Midge Ure (then fronting Ultravox) and ex-Rich Kids drummer Rusty Egan, who was now DJ at influential London nightclub Billy's (in Soho, then Covent Garden). They enlisted the aid of Ultravox keyboardist Billy Currie and three members of Magazine: Dave Formula also on keyboards, guitarist John McGeoch, and bass player Barry Adamson. Steve Strange became their vocalist.

Record producer Martin Rushent was a regular at Blitz and upon hearing this music was keen to sign the band to his nascent label Genetic Records, even financing more songs which were recorded at his home studio for the album *Visage*. However, the label collapsed before it could properly take off, and the album was instead taken up by Radar Records. It sat unpublished until 1980 when its release coincided with the band's new single 'Fade to Grey,' released on yet another new label: Polydor. Success was almost immediate, however.

Helped by exposure gained by the flamboyant Steve Strange—who once arrived by camel at a Visage party in New York City—and some stunning (for the era) special effects-laden pop videos,

they became one of the most identifiable bands in Europe. *Visage* reached 13 in the UK Albums Chart, number 1 in Germany, and graced the Top 20 across most of Europe. 'Fade to Grey' reached 8 in the UK and was Top 10 across most of Europe (1 again in Germany). 'Mind of a Toy' (13), 'Visage' (21), 'The Damned Don't Cry' (11), and 'Night Train' (12) were all successful in the UK during '81 and '82, after which a gradual decline began with 1984's 'Pleasure Boys' only reaching number 44. Later singles sank lower following a change in musical direction and the departure of some key members. Under the leadership of Rusty Egan and with a shifting roster of temporary youths, however, Visage continues to tour.

What was your upbringing like?

Manchester was quite bleak back in the 50s, like many other cities. I grew up in Whalley Range (on the outskirts) but I went to local schools, and I was an only child. At times I felt quite isolated. My refuge was the family next door, an Irish Catholic family with four very attractive daughters and a son who remains a very good friend of mine. There was nothing wrong with my own family, but this family always seemed to be full of laughter—everything seemed so free and easy. They were my second family in a way.

I had a very musical family background. My dad was a very good piano player, semi-pro. All his brothers also played piano. He used to play in dance bands. My mother was a great singer. My grandmother was in concert parties. Because of this background it was sort of inevitable that I'd be lumbered with piano lessons. I quite enjoyed them to be honest, though I didn't practice very much, a quick hour just before I went for the lesson usually. The woman that taught me was quite interesting though, as she was mostly an accordion player. When I would be playing her this week's lesson she could write out next weeks lesson for me on musical notation paper by hand. She was also quite progressive in that if a student wasn't really picking up on the theory, she would quietly drop it. And if you weren't doing well with the standard children's songs or neoclassical pieces, she would switch to pop songs instead, which was great because I could impress my friends at school.

I kept this up till I was fourteen, but before then, when I was eleven, I went to a secondary school and the literature teacher was the director of a youth theatre in Manchester. He was always looking for children that might be interested in joining. So I joined that, started my theatre life at the bottom as an eleven-year-old spear carrier in Hamlet or something like that and really got the bug for it. That was a real freedom thing as I was going out two or three times a week to rehearse and then we had a week of shows. I gained some independence through that, and it was great for confidence.

I was still involved with the music side of things too as the theatre had its own band, and I was the second piano player. It was there that I met Tony Cassidy, who would become the singer in my first band, St. Louis Union. We became friends and we would go into Manchester to the Left Wing Coffee Bar when we were sixteen. We met the guitar player and bass player just going home on the all-night bus. That was the beginning of me being in proper bands.

You had a lot of success with the St. Louis Union?

Yes, we did well locally and we were persuaded to enter a national *Melody Maker* competition. We beat an early version of the band Pink Floyd on the way to winning it. They were called The Pink Floyd then I think. Which just goes to show (for them at least): you win some, you lose some.

Good things came out of that, including getting a recording contract. Our manager signed us up to what was called The Kennedy Street Artists - A big agency in Manchester. And they persuaded us to record 'Girl,' which is a Beatles song from *Rubber Soul,* which was a hit record for us reaching number 11 in the UK Singles charts, but it forever tainted us as being seen as a ballad pop band. But it was so out of character—we were more of a bluesy soul band. It did open a few doors for us though. We were doing a lot of touring and appearances on TV, including *Top of the Pops,* and our fees went up, but everyone wanted us to play the Beatles cover. But there you go—an early taste of stardom!

St. Louis Union came to an end, and I was doing anything to keep myself in the world of music—cabaret gigs… Awful stuff! One of the better ones was getting to play with legendary blind jazz saxophonist [Rahsaan] Roland Kirk in a gig in Liverpool. He'd been playing another gig at the local university and had decided to come along to the cabaret club where we were playing for a drink afterwards. Suddenly four or five guys came in, in full African robes. We were like *What the…?* It was an amazing sight. And then one of his entourage came over to the side of the stage and told us that Roland would like to come on stage and play a few songs with us. 'Wow—get him up!' So, we played a couple of blues and a couple of soul standards with him. I was about twenty-one or twenty-two and suddenly I'm sharing a stage with a jazz legend.

Punk was happening around this time—what was your reaction to it?

I was too old for the punk thing. I thought it was, musically, very limiting. I was interested in the excitement it was causing though, and I've always been interested in photography. I'd often visit clubs simply to take photos of punks—more so the crowds than the actual bands.

How did joining the band Magazine come about?

That was through my friend Martin Hannett, the record producer [now famous for working with Factory Records, Joy Division, and Happy Mondays] whom I'd met around 1974, probably in the pub or something. Martin was also a bass player

and was trying to help me develop as a musician. One night he called me and told me to watch a band on a local Manchester music programme on Granada Television presented by Tony Wilson, *So It Goes.* He told me that I might find them interesting and that they were looking for a keyboard player.

So, I tuned in at half past ten and it was Magazine. It was very different to the entire punk thing that I'd been seeing in Manchester up till then; it was a revelation. It was a nice change to see something different from the two- or three-cord wonders that I was used to seeing. The band were very theatrical, which obviously appealed to me due to my previous theatre experience. So, the next day I called Martin back and told him I loved it, and he arranged a meet up between myself and Howard [Devoto], which was a three-hour chat about the music that I enjoyed, and to check if I was an idiot or not I guess. Then I had a playing audition. I guess I passed this first stage, as it led to a week of rehearsals with them, and the I 'got the gig' as they say.

How did the songwriting work in Magazine?

Well, when I joined a lot of the songs had already been written; I was replacing another keyboard player [Bob Dickinson] who had left the band. Their first single ('Shot by Both Sides') had already been released and had really taken off during this time, reaching number 41 in the UK charts, but we had just started working on the first album, *Real Life*. I was contributing a lot to the songs and arrangements that we already had—I decided that I really wanted one of my own songs on there too, and I wrote 'Parade.' By this time I was sharing a flat with my girlfriend over in Didsbury, Manchester, with Martin Hannett (who owned it). I had my synth over there and I came up with the chords, showed the song to the band later on, and it was used. And because I was now a permanent member of the band and had contributed my own song, it made it easier to get more ideas into the other songs.

Howard told us all from the beginning though that he was the one that wrote the lyrics and that he wasn't interested in anyone else writing them. But to be fair he was the lead singer and he was very good at writing lyrics. But he always emphasised that the music side of it was open, and it was very democratic in that respect.

What was your keyboard set up at the time?

Hammond organ, a Fender Rhodes [electric piano], and the Korg ARP Odyssey. Although I've always been a Hammond fan, that and the Rhodes were sort of hangovers from a slightly older era, and I thought that the sound didn't quite fit with the music that we were now producing. So after the first handful of gigs I got rid of that and the Fender and got a Yamaha organ on a chrome stand. We did a deal with Yamaha to get a Yamaha Electric Grand, as a lot of the songs demanded an acoustic piano. I got a Yamaha String Machine as well.

How did you all get to gigs? Was it the classic clapped-out minivan experience?

Ah, no; our original manager, a guy called Andrew Graham-Stewart, had been recommended to Howard by Virgin, and he would drive us around in his Range Rover. When that manager didn't work out we always managed to get to gigs in relative comfort, even if it meant travelling in separately.

How did your participation with Visage come to be? Was it a side project from Magazine initially?

Well, we met Rusty Egan in the now infamous Blitz Club. He told us he was a huge Magazine fan, and then John [McGeoch, guitarist in Magazine] started to join us when we went to the club. Rusty told us that he had a music project just starting and that he'd love us all to be involved with it. Was it a side project? Yes, for sure. We were just about to do our first US tour with Magazine at the time and we were constantly either making albums or on the road, so from a purely physical perspective it was definitely a side project, as Magazine was taking up so much of our time. We certainly began working on the first Visage single, 'Tar,' before recording the Magazine album *Secondhand Daylight*, and we recorded the Visage self-titled album once that Magazine album was completed and we were back in the UK. It was a side project for most of us, as Midge Ure and Billy Currie were still with Ultravox. Rusty was a drummer, so he took that role, and Steve Strange came in to do the vocals.

What did you think of all of the bizarre fashions you saw in Blitz? Did you participate?

Innovative - some of them. A lot reminded me of the sort of outfits the drag queens in Manchester wore and that was just the blokes. A blue leather coat was as close as I got to a new romantic outfit.

How did you get on with Steve Strange, and what was he like to work with? Were you there in NY when he rode the camel?

Steve, although a brilliant fashion leader, and not without a healthy ego, a very nice fella. No, I missed the camel ride.

How was working with Midge Ure? Did he have any idiosyncrasies?

Midge was always very businesslike and efficient in the studio. Not a great surreal sense of humour though.

How did it work putting the records together for Visage? Because you were a floating pool of musicians on the Magazine side of things, did it cause problems?

Well, 'Fade to Grey' had already been written by the time we got involved, but the B-side hadn't. We basically all got together in a rehearsal room and wrote the songs in a couple of weeks for the first album. The second album worked in the same way—we'd find a gap in the Magazine and Ultravox schedules, and then we'd all meet up. A lot of the development of the songs happened later in the recording studio. New parts came up and were added, as they do. As the band had two keyboard players both me and Billy Currie would spend a lot of time in the studio adding new things with Midge who would produce them and try out new ideas.

And what was your keyboard set up like at this point?

Pretty much the same as I was using for Magazine. The Fairlight [an early synth/sequencer that enabled sampling and had a library of voices] had arrived on the scene by now, which was a revelation. Also, various big Moogs and Polymoogs had been developed. Billy Currie, who by now had had a lot of success with Ultravox, had managed to get a super-duper deal with Yamaha to get some top-end keyboards—CS80s and so on—so we had access to these from time to time.

Did you ever get to play around on a Fairlight?

I did! Rusty knew Richard Burgess [of synth band Landscape], and Richard was also the UK representative for Fairlight. So, after the first Visage album I went over to his place one day and just recorded lots of weird stuff. The Fairlight stuff I recorded was used as a link between the tracks on the first Visage album. I was very keen to get one for Magazine because I could see the potential. I went to see Simon Draper, our A&R guy at Virgin, told him how much (£26,000), and he said 'No.' [laughs] It was along the same lines as when we wanted to get John Barry [composer of famous film scores, including the original James

Bond theme] in to produce our second album, and Virgin weren't completely against the idea. But John was a tax exile who was based in California, and it would mean us going out there to record it—and they didn't want to pay for that either.

Visage dominated the charts for a few years as the New Romantic movement took off—was it a surprise to you?

The album recording just sat on the shelf for months. Then later I was walking through Soho, and someone shouted at me—it was one of Ultravox's managers (who had also taken on Visage). They asked if I knew that we had a number one album and single in Germany, and I said 'No, I didn't,' and that's when it became a bit more serious for everyone. Germany at the time was the third biggest marketplace in the world. I suddenly realised that there was money being made here. And then it took off in lots of other places: Australia, UK . . . I thought 'Wow, how strange!' [laughs] There's still a lot of royalties floating around in the ionosphere that I'll probably never see. It would be lovely if they would appear in my bank account but they probably never will now.

Are there any tracks that you would have done differently now?

No, I don't think so. I've not really thought about it. It was what it was and it captured the moment I think. We get a lot of requests to remix a lot of Magazine singles, but again I can't see the point. People liked it then, and both bands haven't dated—they sound from today.

You left Visage during the early recordings of the third album Beat Boy due to musical differences with Rusty—was that right?

Well, it wasn't just Rusty and I, although that was part of it. By this time it wasn't Visage anymore; John McGeoch had already left, Midge had gone, Barry had left after the first album (though he added some session work later). I probably should have moved on before I did but it was no real effort to contribute, so it was the path of least resistance really until it became no fun anymore. So that was the end of it really. We've been on speaking terms for quite a few years now.

A lot of good came out of it. I'm proud of the songs of course, but it also allowed myself and Richard Boote to go into partnership and build a studio together. It was something I always wanted to do, and even now though it's a different studio I spend my time recording either my own music or for other people and helping with production.

Do you think there's an overreliance in modern music on the use of pre-sets and libraries?

I think it can bland things out—I have to be careful myself of becoming too lazy—but if you use the libraries and pre-sets correctly you can make some amazing stuff. I've recently tried to make music that sounds like a large ensemble using jazz voicings, strings, and electronics all together. It's difficult to get something that sounds right and not just a mishmash of things, and I'm not saying I've achieved that yet, but I'm pleased with the way it's going.

I think that the technology we have now compared to what we had back in the Fairlight days is lightyears ahead; it's almost unfeasible. When I first saw a Fairlight I came away thinking 'Everything has changed now,' but it was pretty crude compared to what we have these days.

Do you think that, very generally speaking, popular music just now is very generic sounding?

I think things such as Spotify and so on are pretty bad. I think that it's one of the reasons, going back to your earlier point, that things sound very formulaic these days. There was a program on the BBC the other day that was looking at the way modern music had changed, and one of the things that they were examining was how the intros to songs had shrunk and there are very little in the way of solos on records now. One of the reasons for this apparently is that if a track is played on Spotify, the musician won't get paid unless the song gets past the 30 second mark, so the songs have to grab you during that time.

One other drum I keep banging is the lack of musical movements these days. Everything sounds the same and all the musicians (particularly female ones) tend to look almost identical. Back in my era, during the 60s, 70s and 80s, the charts had a lot of variety. You would have punk, heavy metal, reggae, a novelty act, and even choirs and opera, all in the Top 40 at the same time. You don't get that now—it's just R&B with the odd Ed Sheeran song thrown in.

Yes, I experienced a similar thing in the 1960s; the charts were full of that diversity of music. You'd still get the Ken Dodds and other terrible music but you are right, there was that variety. And it all sat side by side, and families would watch shows together. All of that has gone now.

I think it's that mixture of the ability to now make music when you have no talent to do so, due to the technology we have, as well as the streaming and so on. It's a bad load of chemistry, and in a lot of ways the record companies can only blame themselves, can't they? I mean the fact that there's only really three record companies left. It's very, very sad. And you know, it's easy to be a Cassandra and moan about it, but the fact is that's how bad it is, isn't it? I have a drummer friend that moved over to Louth where I now live and where my studio is, and he was shocked at how few bands there were around now. Usually even in small towns you'd have a handful of local bands, but that's all gone as well now.

I think half the problem is the talent shows such as X Factor, where you get people from boy bands and girl bands, who made a career singing cover versions, teaching new generations to be as bland and unmusical as they were—that good singing means trying to fit as many notes into a song as possible.

Yes, we're in complete agreement here. It's self-propagating, isn't it? And as you said, that's teaching them how to sing badly. It's unlistenable. Compare that to Aretha Franklin and people like her and it's completely different. It's the vocal equivalent of sampling, isn't it? . . . Oh I dunno, we're just a bunch of moaning old gits, aren't we? [laughs] The sad thing is that hidden away in all of this there *is* still great stuff out there, if you look for it, it's just that it doesn't get exposed. There are some decent music shows still out there though. Once in a while Jools Holland will have a band on that you've never heard of. We're lucky in that we have a decent record store in Louth and he gets in stuff that's quite obscure, which is great to see happening.

If you wanted to give the best advice you can for any aspiring musicians, what would it be?

Keep at it. You need talent and so on but by far the best quality is determination. You see so many people that give up at the first hurdle.

Visage - Midge Ure, Rusty Egan, Steve Strange, Dave Formula, Billy Curry - Alamy Photo Library

LIVE AID

No book about the history of music would be complete without a passage on the Band Aid single and the Live Aid concert.

In 1984 Bob Geldof, lead singer of Irish band The Boomtown Rats, had seen yet another news report on an ongoing famine in Ethiopia and decided that enough was enough. He cajoled, bullied, or sometimes simply asked popular bands from the UK (mostly) to join him in a charity single under the banner of Band Aid. Among them were members of Duran Duran, Simple Minds, Heaven 17, Big Country, Culture Club, Spandau Ballet, U2, Wham, Status Quo, The Police, Bananarama, The Style Council, Kool and the Gang, Paul Young, Phil Collins, Midge Ure, and Marilyn. Together they performed the single 'Do They Know it's Christmas?' which was penned and produced by Midge Ure and Bob Geldof. 'Do They Know it's Christmas' was a huge hit, though disappointingly it did not generate enough cash to bring and end to the famine that Geldof and co. had hoped for. Nowhere near enough.

To complicate matters, there were concerns following the release of the single about how the money was being used and if the aid was getting through to those who really needed it. Evidence arose of government officials in Ethiopia syphoning cash off to their personal accounts.

It was decided by Bob, that what was needed was an organization based in Ethiopia with its own distribution network, its own planes carrying shipments, and its own trucks delivering this aid to those most in need. And so, in 1985 Geldof set about organizing what would become the largest music event ever—Live Aid.

Simultaneously broadcast from Wembley Stadium in the UK and the John F. Kennedy Stadium in Philadelphia, USA, Band Aid featured UK artists Status Quo, The Style Council, The Boomtown Rats, Adam Ant, Ultravox, Spandau Ballet, Elvis Costello, Nik Kershaw, Sade, Sting, Phil Collins, Howard Jones, Brian Ferry, Paul Young, U2, Dire Straits, Queen,

Davie Bowie, The Who, Elton John, and other members of Band Aid for the finale. The US broadcast featured Billy Ocean, Black Sabbath, The Hooters, Joan Baez, Bernard Watson, The Four Tops, Crosby Stills and Nash, REO Speedwagon, Run D.M.C., Rick Springfield, Judas Priest, Bryan Adams, The Beach Boys, Eric Clapton, Simple Minds, Santana, Madonna, The Pretenders, Tom Petty and the Heartbreakers, The Cars, Neil Young, Thompson Twins, Led Zeppelin, Phil Collins, Duran Duran, Hall and Oates, Mick Jagger, Bob Dylan, and Patti LeBelle. There were also performances from other countries: Australia, Germany, the Soviet Union, Holland, Austria, Japan, and Yugoslavia.

The concert raised $127 million for the famine relief, and further funds were made from sales of the video. Live Aid showed the world that, when enough people care and make enough noise about it, large scale events can be organized for the good.

Electronic Body Music

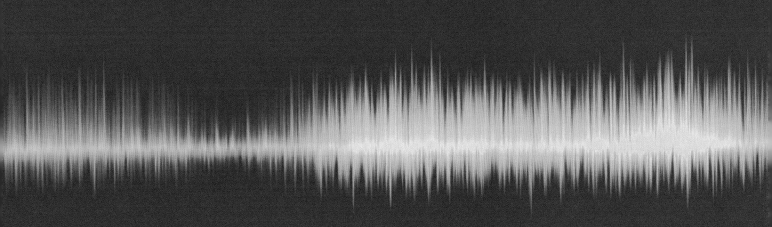

Electronic Body Music (or EBM) is where industrial music meets dance and synth pop. Taking some cues from industrial groups like Cabaret Voltaire and Throbbing Gristle but generally having a more defined structure, it uses drum machines, danceable rhythms, and repetitive sequencer lines with lyrics that are often shouted or aggressively asserted.

The term EBM was first used by German band Kraftwerk (though really an electronica group) when describing their album *The Man-Machine*. It was later adopted by bands such as Front 242 in Belgium and England's Nitzer Ebb, as well as DAF and Die Krupps. EBM is a predominantly European phenomenon and is a mutation of krautrock in many

respects. It could be argued, however, that many US industrial rock bands went through an EBM phase. The Nine Inch Nails album *Pretty Hate Machine* as well as Ministry's early synthpop arguably have roots in the earlier music of Front 242, and the latter made the shift to industrial rock only after touring with Front 242.

FRONT 242

INTERVIEW WITH PATRICK CODENYS

Patrick Codenys is a founder member and keyboard player of Front 242, a band that grew from the early 80s delivering a high-powered dance beat over stark atmospherics. They referred to their particular subgenre of electronic music as 'Electronic Body Music.'

Their visual aesthetic depended on the concept of anonymity, incorporating sunglasses and sometimes even military uniforms in their stage and video presence. This intriguing presentation caught the public imagination, and the band's first self-published album *Geography* was released in 1982.

They began to accrue international recognition when they signed to record label Wax Trax! in 1984 and were asked to support Ministry's tour in the same year at the behest of Al Jourgensen, the band's legendary lead singer. As the popularity

of industrial rock grew, they were asked to support Depeche Mode's Music for the Masses tour in 1987. Depeche Mode were slowly moving away from the synthpop they had broken through with and were developing a darker sound. 1988 saw the release of what is probably Front 242's most well-known single 'Headhunter,' the video for which received heavy airplay on MTV.

In 1991 the album *Tyranny (For You)* became the band's highest charting release to date, and they signed to Sony/Epic, who bought their back catalogue, re-releasing the albums with new covers and extra tracks taken from unused material or EPs. As the 90s progressed the band was influenced by techno (especially The Prodigy) and concentrated more and more on esoteric multimedia art projects. Their energies remain largely devoted to the latter, though Front 242 continue to gig.

What attracted you to electronic music and a career in music?

I was interested in creating a mixture of various media types into one experience. I was a Graphic Designer and saw possibilities with mixing strong artwork and branding with music and film. The problem was that I couldn't play an instrument. I didn't really want to learn to play the guitar because by now guitar music was getting very boring and predictable. The entire idea of the usual way of making music, with guitars as well as a drummer and a singer, didn't interest me. But my timing was fortunate. The synthesiser, an instrument that became available at an affordable price in the 1980s, allowed us to discover totally new sounds, a new universe.

It wasn't just synthesisers but also sequencers and the ability to twin this to early computer systems to help to compose. It was an open field. We were forced to create a new aesthetic and something far away from traditional musical genres. We were more inspired by architecture and cinema than any music of the time. To me, cinema has much more cultural importance than jazz or blues music.

Another thing that attracted me was the fact that it was an opportunity to explore my own roots. As Belgians, and as Europeans, we had enjoyed English bands (and still do), but again, they were known primarily for creating rock and roll music. But we are not Anglo-Saxons. Electronic music is international, and we could make our own mark. In the early 80s the UK-US record companies didn't know how to handle this new genre growing throughout Europe and left us alone. So, it became a chance for us to emerge.

What was the live music scene like in your area at the time?

Totally chaotic. There was no music scene as such. We did have a few live venues, but Belgium was a little bit odd, and people didn't really socialise in the same way that perhaps the English or Americans do. There were bands but they were experimenting at home, isolated without contact with other bands. The easiest way to do this was to do things electronically.

You and Jean-Luc De Meyer originally formed a band called UnderViewer. How did you guys meet?

I was at school with Jean-Luc's brother, and he introduced me to him. We decided to join creative forces and instruments to have more possibilities – technology could be a reason to associate yourself with somebody before you really knew what musical direction to follow. At the time in Brussels, there wasn't a facility to find local musicians. In the UK or the States, you could put an advert in Melody Maker or something like that and get a few people applying to be in your band. It wasn't like that in Belgium, finding other musicians was nearly always word-of-mouth. Therefore, a lot of people oriented their choices to machines. A rhythm box to replace a drummer, a synth for bass lines, etc. So, I was working with small synths—MS 20, MS 50 and SQ 10—and Jean-Luc had just bought a rhythm box with a bass guitar and distortion for some post-punk experimentation.

What sort of groups influenced your very early music?

Initially krautrock bands like Kraftwerk, Can, Neu. Later, Throbbing Gristle, Cabaret Voltaire, Joy Division, Einsturzende Neubauten, and many others. We liked anyone that sounded different. And that usually either meant experimental, electronic, or someone that had a darker sound. But we liked bands that had structure to their music.

How did you meet the other member of Front 242 and why did you join forces?

A small label liked some of UnderViewer's tracks and wanted to release a single. But back then Jean-Luc and myself had no idea how to do the mastering of tracks. The label suggested we contact Daniel Bressanutti, who was in a band called Front 242 and had already released the first Front 242 single and knew how to handle this side of production. Daniel was also working in the music shop where I bought my first synths. When we first met Daniel, we realised we had matching tastes in terms of music and incorporating music into something resembling a cinematic experience, what would now be called 'multi-media'. Also, he was looking for a partner and a singer.

We started to work together and released the UnderViewer single 'Nobody but You' – that single was a real alternative hit in Belgium. But we dropped the idea to release more UnderViewer music to begin work on a Front 242 album, and we became part of the band.

Were there any conflicts within the band when you and Jean Luc first joined?

Daniel basically did the first Front 242 single alone and was truly looking for new people to help. Jean-Luc and I were a complementary match; it was never a

conflict at the time. In fact, hopefully it was quite the opposite.

How did you share the song writing in the band?

Jean Luc would be the one to do the singing. He had a lot more confidence in the role and I think that helped. Jean Luc also seemed to write most of the lyrics. But the lyrics weren't particularly deep, and we made a conscious decision to steer away from that sort of thing. Lyrics and words became their own instrument.

We were each working on a specific field; each of us was concentrating on our individual strengths. We never needed to place our ego in another band member's task, but we had moments where we were all in the studio deciding about the concept, the construction, and possible direction of a track. Musically and in general, we all had our own musical set up in our own homes. But Daniel seemed to have the best one, so we used to work in his home for the most part.

I think in many ways it was a blank canvas for us. We didn't have a musical heritage as such to copy from or fall back on when true electronic music became possible. In the older days, electric guitars were just more powerful versions of acoustic and bass guitars, electronic keyboards were obviously just pianos that had a lot of different sounds that you could generate, but pure electronic music—taking samples and manipulating them—this was new, there were no formulas to be influenced by.

At the time there were no pre-sets to fall back on. You had to create through your modulator. Our first experiments were just abstracts. Interesting in their own way, but we realised that other people were not wanting to listen to them, so we had to introduce rhythm to them. We didn't really aim for a dance music sound, but sometimes one evolved out of the chaos.

You were previously a Graphic Designer. Do you think that this helped when you began to decide on the look of the band?

We were lucky in that all members in the band came from a strong visual background, be it graphic design, art, or craft. We wanted to have a strong visual presence because at the time we didn't think our music was strong enough. And we were also very much part of the punk 'do-it-yourself' ethos. We thought it was vital to develop such things as a logo. We needed a 'brand' if you like, a certain look and way of doing things. We needed a strong image. We didn't have a lot of money, but we did have a lot of ideas, for sure.

We wanted to have an air of mystery, which is partly why we all dressed alike and wore sunglasses. We chose to wear military clothing simply because we wanted to be stripped of personality, which is partly what they do to you in the military by giving everyone the same clothes and haircuts. We also thought it would be easier for any potential fans to look like us quite cheaply if they wanted to.

What did you think of the concerns people were having that you were a 'fascist' band?

If you didn't know anything about the band, you would perhaps make a few erroneous conclusions. The 'Front' part of our name was to show that it wasn't us; it was a front. It was something we hid behind as part of the mystique. We didn't associate it with political groups such as The National Front and other fascist organisations. And the '242' part was just a nice-looking number from a graphic design point of view. None of the 242 lyrics have any racist, xenophobic or hatred connotation.

How did the band evolve after the first steps?

Well, the band never really stops evolving; each album uses different technology. But the first steps were making music that was interesting, and although we were using electronics to make music, the process remained analogue for at least the first two albums. 4-track recorders were used on the first album and 8 track on the second. As new technology became available though, we utilised it where and when we could or felt like it was necessary. Our first album, *Geography*, was quite popular, but it was just a starting point for us. Our sound was beginning to develop, we were gaining in confidence. We also began to use samples of guitars around 1983-84, which gave us a rockier sound, though obviously a million miles from the way a traditional rock band would sound.

After a point we decided to move to live performances, but it took us a while to gain the courage. We were not identifying as musicians still, and to bring music to the stage took us a while. Which is why I think adding visual elements helped. We had a movie reel of little clips of news reels and war films and so on, which helped the audience to be distracted from us as actual people on stage. Later, Richard [Jonckheere], who later used the stage name of Richard23, joined us and brought a powerful live dimension to the band. He was on drums and backing vocals and it was clear that he revelled in the limelight, which was a relief to everyone else in the band. He had previously experimented with noise collages and would add a lot

of atmospheres to our recordings. Poor Daniel hated performing live and often hid completely behind equipment.

The band began to get very popular, but were you surprised when you were asked to tour the USA in 1984 with Ministry?

Well, we had completed our second album, *No Comment*, and had just finished a European tour, and we were gaining popularity, so yes and no. Remember, we were signed by Wax Trax! – a record company that had also released music by Ministry. The real surprise came through the excitement of touring in the US, a new territory with another culture. We would have to confront a very different type of crowd and convince them that we would entertain them!

The tour was difficult as no venue was equipped for electronic music concerts. The staff could not believe we had no drums and no guitars; we were not considered as a real band by them. It was sort of funny but perplexing for us.

As for Al Jourgensen, Ministry was kind of new wave, perhaps even a pop band at the time. And Al was watching Front 242's performance every night. We could feel he wanted to go that direction, our direction, more tough, and loud, and physical. I think we really affected how he saw music, which you can definitely see in how Ministry changed almost over night into a more industrial, thrash metal band.

The tour led to the formation of the on/off band The Revolting Cocks with Al and Richard from Front 242. Were you asked to take part?

The Revolting Cocks were initially just Richard23 and Luc Van Acker (Big Sexy Land). They had an idea to try something new. Al Jourgensen of Ministry was the producer. I joined them in Chicago for a

brief moment in the studio to work with them and was credited on the record, but my contribution was not substantial. We all had a lot of fun with it, and it was good to work with new people.

Front 242 have been identified as an industrial rock band. Would you go along with the description?

There seemed to be a fight between the US and European definition of 'industrial music'. In Europe, industrial does not include having guitars other than sampled ones. And if you go back to the original definition, no real instruments at all if you pare it back to basics. In the US though, industrial rock bands are synthesiser-led heavy metal music.

I would say we are an electronic industrial band although we created a specific genre to name what we do: electronic body music (EBM).

The Single 'Headhunter' in 1988 was the big breakthrough hit that made you international stars. How did it feel to be such big stars?

I think if you ask the man in the street, he or she would immediately associate us with 'Headhunter'. That had extensive airplay on MTV and is the record we are most heavily identified with.

We felt flattered when the success elevated us, but never went crazy about it. I believe this is the reason why Front 242 still remains successful with the same 4 people since 1981, [laughs]. We keep on doing what we believe in and [are] not heavily influenced by the sales, media, music industry, etc.

The bold use of graphic design set the tone for other bands who saw how powerful branding could be, and the look and image of your band were successful in making you stand out.

Do you see yourself in any band that followed, either musically or visually?

Not really, Front 242 is unique and specific at what we do. From the start we presented a strong concept [and] logo, with particular graphics and live attitude. I am still shaped by my first love. Other bands came before us when it came to elements such as these and others followed, from a visual sense. I don't think other bands really tied in the visual and musical elements to the same degree that we did, but that is just my opinion.

Your style gradually drifted into an almost techno sound. What inspired you to follow this path?

The 80s were a period of experimentation for electronic music, with negative and positive outcomes. The major labels (UK-US) did not really know how to handle those more extreme bands. In the 90s, with bands like Underworld, The Prodigy, The Chemical Brothers, etc., a way to exploit electronic music was found. Furthermore, in a parallel way, the techno music appeared also as a good money maker.

We were lost in the nineties, and the live tours had more of a techno sound. But today, Front 242 live is vintage/analogue and back to our origins, with a touch of modernity.

Do you think that the download culture is good or bad for music in general?

No, because it does not pay the artist for their work. Yes, because of the facility to access new music and the discovery of new talents.

Will you ever stop working do you think, or is there simply too much fun to be made experimenting with new formats?

I love my life; I will never stop.

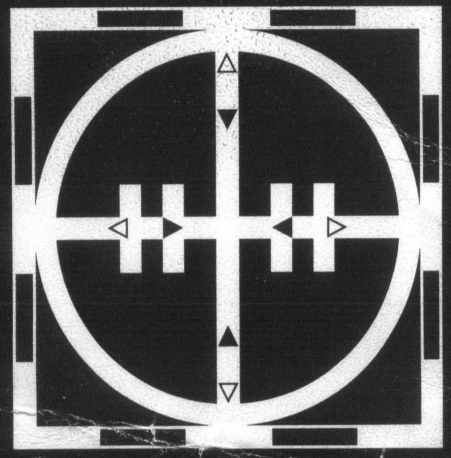

FRONT 242

TYRANNY ▶ **FOR YOU** ◀

Mittwoch, 20.3.91, Einlaß: 20.00 Uhr, Beginn: 21.00 Uhr

HAMBURG-DOCKS

VVK: 26,– DM, zzgl. VVK-Gebühr, incl. 7% MwSt.
ABK: 30,– DM, incl. 7% MwSt.
Örtlicher Veranstalter: Scorpio

Allg. Geschäftsbedingungen des Veranstalters
siehe Rückseite.

MCT

1 № 0483

NEW WAVE

Post-punk refined the political messaging of punk and developed musically in many different directions. It was still often politically charged and very cynical in outlook. Ska music brought some relief from this and an upturn in happier-sounding music, but when they were not singing many ska bands were fighting a war against racism. The mercurial attitude of the general public was becoming tired with 'causes.'

'New wave' was a catch-all description applied to many bands appearing after in this period—bands offering a sound that was more lighthearted and less political. Many very different acts were categorised as new wave, but what connected them was quirkiness and a sense of humour. Often, they very well dressed and had a touch of glamour about them also. Emigrants from punk and post-punk—such as XTC, Talking Heads, and Blondie—

were being rechristened as new wave bands along with other undefinables like The B-52s, Devo, Elvis Costello, Squeeze, and the Vapors. Even The Pretenders, Madness, The Police, U2, and a medley of synth bands would eventually be herded under this banner, as well as the entirety of the surviving New Romantics. 'New wave' was, for all intents and purposes, another name for pop.

THE HOOTERS

INTERVIEW WITH ERIC BAZILIAN

Eric Bazilian is a multi-instrumentalist and founder member of The Hooters, a new wave rock group who emerged in Philadelphia in the early 1980s. Rob Hyman formed the band with Eric, and they were joined by David Uosikkinen, John Lulleym, and occasionally Fran Smith Jr. Their sound is notable for its ska and folk influences.

After earning popularity in their home city, The Hooters soon rose to prominence in the US with the high-charting single

'All You Zombies', also making waves in Europe with 'Satellite' and 'Karla with a K.' Albums *Nervous Night* and *One Way Home* followed in 1985 and 1987 respectively, and both were certified platinum. They played in the USA segment of Live Aid in 1985 despite objections from organiser Bob Geldof, who famously asked 'Who the fuck are the Hooters?', unaware of *Rolling Stone's* nomination of them as 'Best New Band' of that year. In 1990 they also played at The Wall concert

in Berlin along with Roger Waters of Pink Floyd, Cyndi Lauper, The Scorpions, and numerous notable solo musicians.

Eric is now better known as the Grammy-nominated singer-songwriter and producer behind Joan Osborne's debut album *Relish,* and specifically the single 'One of Us' which he wrote. He has collaborated with many others including Cyndi Lauper, Robbie Williams, The Scorpions, and Billie Myers.

HOOTERS
ONE WAY HOME

How did you become a musician?

I had a typically atypical upbringing. My mother was a concert pianist, and my father was a psychiatrist, so I grew up surrounded by music and deep thought. My parents had a lot of odd friends, and I was surrounded by very interesting, unusual people, who I think opened my mind for the future, because I still like to be surrounded by unusual and interesting people. I grew up with my mother's piano. I was drawn to that, drawn by her passion for it.

I started taking piano lessons at six and found that I didn't have the discipline nor the desire, really, to play classical music. I gave that up at seven or eight years of age. At nine years old though, my uncle taught me some guitar cords. He was a folk musician. Aged nine, I performed on TV for the first time. I did a Joan Baez song on local TV.

Then, February 1964, aged ten, I was one of the millions of young boys who saw the Beatles on *The Ed Sullivan Show,* and my life was changed forever. I looked at those guys and I said, 'That's what I want!' I remember, first I looked at Paul and I said 'I want to be like him,' because he was charismatic and having a good time. Then I looked at John and I thought 'No, I

want to be him,' because he was deep and sarcastic. Then I looked at George and I thought 'No, I want to be him,' because he was just nerding out on the guitar. Then I looked at Ringo and I said 'No, actually, I want to be him because nobody is having more fun than he is.' I realized I wanted to be all four Beatles! That really set the trajectory.

Since I already had some facility in playing the guitar, I was able to start picking up The Beatles' songs very quickly. I started my first band the next day with my friend Bernie, who, since he didn't play an instrument, was going to 'play' the drums. It was called the Limestones. I thought of that name because it was like The Beatles' first band name, The Quarrymen. The band didn't get so far. We did the best we could, considering we were just ten and eleven years old at the time.

I spent years looking for the right combination of people to add to my band. The hardest thing was to find somebody who could really sing. Then, when I was fifteen years old, we found a young man who could not only play really good rhythm guitar, but he could also sing amazingly, and he wrote songs. We formed a band called Evil Seed. That was the first real band I had where we had real songs and

real arrangements. At that point, we'd do a lot of covers of Cream, Hendrix, Jeff Beck, and all the British blues rock that followed in the wake of The Beatles. That band took me through high school.

I went off to university at eighteen because that's what you did. I tried studying music but wasn't particularly inspired by what they had to offer, so I ended up getting a degree in physics, because I'd had this whole parallel life as a science geek. I was a HAM radio operator from the time I was nine years old. I always built my own equipment. I always had a scientific bent – before The Beatles, I was going to be the first pre-pubescent in outer space! Anyway, it was in my first week at university that I met Rob Hyman. I recognized him; as he was in a band called Wax that was already getting some notoriety around Philadelphia, which I joined until the Rob graduated and the band split.

After that Rob continued writing songs with David Kagan, the singer in Wax. Rick Chertoff, the drummer in the band, decided that he wanted to be a producer and got a job working for Clive Davis' new label, Arista. Fast forward to 1975, when I was just about to graduate, and Rick had signed Rob and David as Baby Grand. They brought me aboard as guitarist, third voice, and general agent of chaos.

We recorded two albums. We were either ahead of our time or behind our time, but it wasn't the right time for those records. They didn't make much of an impact and sounded a bit like Steely Dan on steroids. In 1979, we were trying to write a third album and realized that this just wasn't the vehicle for us. The singer in the band decided that he wasn't born to rock, which was true. Brilliant, brilliant writer, he had a very distinctive voice but was never comfortable being the front man in a rock band. Rob and I looked at each other and said 'Can you sing?' 'I don't know, can you?' 'I don't know. Let's try it.' Try it we did, and both of us could sing, so we shared the role. But something else was missing, and we felt that the band didn't have an identity. This was right around the time that the second British Invasion was happening. We thought 'You know what? Let's do what the Brits are doing. The world doesn't have to know that we are virtuoso instrumentalists. Let's dumb it down in a smart way and write some really cool ska and reggae songs,' which we did. That takes us to 1980.

So why did you call the band The Hooters?

We were looking for a plural noun that was not a household object, so that everyone

The Hooters - Alamy Photo Library

in the band could say 'I am a' – not a shoe or a chair, but like a Beatle or a Rolling Stone or a Wailer. With this thought in the back of our minds, we went in to do our first demo recordings as a new look band. We had borrowed a melodica. At the same time, we borrowed a mandolin to see how that would work, because Rob was always curious about the mandolin. Ironically, I ended up playing the mandolin and he ended up playing the melodica. We were getting set up and the engineer spoke to us through the talk-back, he said 'Let me get a level on that hooter.' So, the melodica became the hooter, and it didn't take more than a couple of days for us to realize, 'Hey, there's our plural noun that's not a household object.' It was a great idea! Had the restaurant of the same name not come along later, it would have remained a good idea.

You got quite popular very quickly in Philadelphia.

We did. We had added a couple of people to the band and done some demo recordings. One of them was a ska instrumental by Don Drummond called 'Man in the Street'. Through happenstance, we ended up getting that recording played on a local radio station, WMMR, which supported local musicians back then. A disc jockey named Michael Pierson played it once, and as they said back then, the phones went crazy. The song went into regular rotation. All of a sudden, we went from playing five nights a week at biker bars in the suburbs to playing clubs in the city. Then, we did a residency every Monday night at this one club called Grendel's Lair. It was sort of like The Beatles at the Cavern Club. The first time we played we had fifty people in the audience, then we had seventy, and within a couple of months, the line was literally around the block.

How did the song-writing work in the band? Did you have certain roles or was it more democratic?

It was absolutely not a democracy; it was a benevolent oligarchy. It was Rob and I that were in charge. That was the idea from the beginning, that we were the writers and leaders of the band, the directors. We were open to suggestions from the other members—if somebody came in with a great idea, we were certainly all ears—but I think we had to identify early on who was in charge.

What was the music scene like in Philadelphia at the time? Was your music different to the mainstream groups around in that area?

There were a lot of bands, a mixture of either that classic 80s big shoulder pads yuppy pop thing that was in vogue back then, or wannabe punk and pop punk bands. We were the only ones really doing ska and reggae. That set us apart from the pack. And I think, mostly, we wrote better songs.

There were clubs everywhere. We would play four or five nights a week at different clubs and people would come. It was a golden age for live music in Philadelphia.

What was your 'break out' moment?

The first song that we wrote, 'All You Zombies', which is probably the song that we're most universally known for, but one that we didn't think much of ourselves. When we played live, we would start our first set with that to get it out of the way because it never occurred to us that anyone would actually like it. It was a weird song, a weird Bible story with a reggae beat.

We played a live session for the local radio station. We were opening for the English band The Beat, which was very exciting for us because I think of all the two-tone ska bands, they were our favourite, just because of the way they incorporated rock elements – and musically they were really interesting. We again opened with 'All You Zombies', and all of a sudden, the same radio stations started playing the live recording of it, and it just had a life of its own. So, we actually released that as a single, and it really took off. Not so much in the USA where it would only get to 58 in the charts, but it was Number 1 in Australia. We also had minor hits with 'Man in the Street', 'Fightin' on the Same Side', and 'Rescue Me'.

You opened for The Who, on the Farewell Tour in 1982? That must have been amazing?

It was The Who, The Clash, Santana, and The Hooters. To me, it felt as though we were opening for Santana and The Clash were opening for the Who.

If a big band was touring the States, it would be city-to-city. So probably to save money, a local popular band would be added to the set, and we got chosen for the Philadelphia gig. I could barely believe it. As mentioned, I was heavily into the British music scene, and to be on the same stage as The Who and The Clash as well as the legend that is Santana, well, I talk about The Beatles as being the reason I play music, but it was actually The Who album *Tommy* that really entranced me in my teen years. And seeing The Who live onstage was a moment as strong as seeing The Beatles for the first time.

I have many photographs from that 1969 show. I was riveted watching The Who from my seat three feet from the stage. I had never seen anything that loud, that powerful, that much visual information on stage at the same time. I felt myself looking at John Entwistle a lot because I got physically tired of watching Pete and Keith and Roger... How did they had that much energy? It was amazing... Back stage at the show we did with them at JFK Stadium I never dared talk to any of them. I couldn't get the courage to walk up to Pete, who was sitting quite close by. He did not give off a vibe of 'Hey, come to talk to me.' But not in a rude way; he just seemed completely focused on the performance they were about to do... They all did.

Since then, due to the power of the internet, we have had a few email communications, which came about in a roundabout way. He's very, very nice on

email. He always answers them and has complimentary things to say. I don't think that he really wants to hear me fanboy out on him though so much, so I try to keep that to a minimum.

Soon after this you got to work with Cyndi Lauper? How did this come about?

We were contacted by Rick Chertoff, who is a music producer and friend of ours. This was 1983. Cyndi was not well known at that time, and it was felt that she needed input from other song writers – to bounce ideas off. It was for her first album, *She's So Unusual*. Both myself and Rob Hyman co-wrote 'Time after Time' and 'Girls Just Want to Have Fun' with her.

How did you find working with Cyndi?

It's like any kind of a relationship, you have your times when it's a love-fest, and then suddenly the boxing gloves are on. Cyndi's a very dynamic person. You really didn't know what you were going to get from one minute to the next. When we resonated, it was amazing. Then she'd sometimes come back and say 'No, I hate it. It's all wrong. It's stupid, I hate it,' and you are back to square one...

There was a lot of back and forth on that album, but great art can come from that. I think we made a record that was certainly ground-breaking. It wasn't a record that I would have made on my own. My instincts musically are much rockier; I like dirtier guitars. She didn't want to make a rock record, she wanted to make a dance record. I think what we made was something that totally defies categorization.

Interestingly, for 'Girls Just Want to Have Fun', she originally swore she would never sing that song. She thought it was demeaning to women. Rick Chertoff has a great instinct for A&R though; and could match a voice and a song. He knew that her voice singing that song was a hit, but it was turning the music into something that would work with the voice and lyrics. That's what Rob and I were there for.

We tried everything to get it to sound right: we tried doing it as a rock song, we tried doing it like Cat Stevens, we even tried doing it as a reggae song... We came in one day and we were talking about 'Come on Eileen', the song by Dexy's Midnight Runners, which was ubiquitous at that point. It's just one of the most, if not *the* most likeable record ever. Cyndi said 'Well, can we make it like 'Come on Eileen?' and I said 'Okay. Let's try it!' I remember I had an 808 drum machine

at the time, and I programmed in the kick drum from the song, that *boom bah-dah, boom bah-dah*. Then I picked up my guitar, and we were off and running. A little four-track demo was made, and after that we knew it was a hit. And suddenly Cyndi was saying 'I always wanted to sing that song.'

The album title *She's So Unusual* is pretty appropriate; Cyndi *is* unusual. She's brilliantly talented, not always the easiest to work with, but usually worth it.

You played Live Aid in 1985 too – that must have been amazing!

Well, yes! That was a last-minute coup on the part of our management and the local promoter in Philadelphia, Larry Magid, who just thought that we deserved to be on that show. Sir Bob Geldoff, who had obviously instigated the entire Live Aid event, wasn't so happy with that, apparently. In fact, he left us off the official DVD. I think he just didn't feel that we had earned a right to be on the show at that point in our careers. The quote from him was 'Who the fuck are the Hooters?' But you know what, it was his right. It was his baby; if he didn't want us on the DVD later, then fair enough.

It was a crazy day. I barely remember it; we were on and off stage. We were on for literally ten minutes, but apparently a billion people saw us all over the world that day. They can never take that away from us! I have a big picture of it in my studio.

Ironically, a week after the Live Aid DVD came out, Bob Geldoff opened a show for us in Germany with his band The Boomtown Rats. He was a bit sheepish that night...

I think I first became aware of The Hooters when I heard your One Way Home album, with your hit single Satellite.

I remain fascinated with how people became aware of us. People in the UK tend to have discovered us much like yourself – we were on the *Top of the Pops* and *Friday Night Live* TV shows. We were also getting a lot of video time on MTV back when it was a music channel. 'Karla with a K' was also a big hit for us in Europe.

What was it like working with Robbie Williams?

He was great. This was the very beginning of his solo career; he had just left Take That and his record label had sent him to the producer Desmond Child to help kick off his 'new phase'. I don't think they really believed in him at that point. I remember Desmond talking about a 'boy band refugee' having 'a short shelf-life,' and the record company just wanted to get something out in a hurry before the public forgot who he was.

Desmond and I had a small catalogue of songs, and we thought we'd run it by Robbie and see what would fit. But Robbie wanted to write his own songs, which really impressed me.

'Old Before I Die' actually started when Robbie and I were sitting in a room with a guitar. I had just gotten a new little effects box that could make a guitar sound like anything. It had all these pre-sets, and I was scrolling through them, and there was one called *Start Me Up*, and I played *Start Me Up*. Then there was one called *Day Tripper*, and I played *Day Tripper*. Then there was one called *Generation* – this inspired me to start playing 'My Generation' by The Who, and Robbie and I both started singing it, verse and chorus. At the end of that, Robbie looked at me and said 'Wouldn't it be great to write a song that says 'I hope I get old before I die?'' and I sang 'I hope I'm old before I die.' We wrote that chorus in minutes and then Desmond came in and said 'That's gold, right there!' We wrote the verses together and put the song together. We actually did a full production.

Robbie was great, he was delightful. He actually rang me later to work some more, but for whatever reasons, it never happened again. I have great memories of working with him, and I'm very proud of the artist he became. I think he really rose above and beyond.

Of all of the songs that you've written, including for other artists, which one is your favourite?

Of the ones that people know, I hate to be obvious here, but I would have to say 'One of Us', written in 1995. It seemed to come out of nowhere; I literally just sang it. I created a musical track because my then girlfriend (now wife) asked me to show her how my four-track porta studio worked. I'd been playing that guitar riff all day, so I built a little arrangement, a little track around it. Then she said 'Sing it,' and I sang 'What if God was one of us? Just a slob like one of us?' That's literally what came out. I listened back and thought 'Wow'. The entire thing took about four minutes.

It was just happenstance that I was working with Joan Osbourne, and again Rick Chertoff, on Joan's new album *Relish,* because the next day I played the demo for Joan and Rick Chertoff. I was pretty excited about it. Rick looked up and

he said 'Joan, you think you could sing that?' It was the last thing I would have imagined, but she said 'Yes, I can sing the phone book if I put my mind to it. Write out the lyrics.' I played the music and Joan sang the song. The song had found its voice and the voice had found its song. We were going to be hearing that for a very long time. It was a huge hit and was nominated for a Grammy.

How are The Hooters doing these days?

The Hooters still tour. Germany's the gift that keeps on giving. We tour at least a month there every summer. The US tour is mostly Philadelphia now, as local boys done good. We've entered into a new phase now where we are rediscovering our Ska and Reggae roots. Expect something exciting in the near future.

If you could give some honest advice to up-and-coming musicians now – what would it be?

Expect nothing. If you have any other option, take it. If not, give it everything and maybe something good will come.

Live on stage - Alamy Photo Library

BIG COUNTRY
INTERVIEW WITH TONY BUTLER

Tony Butler was the bassist of Big Country, having played also for On the Air, Rhythm for Hire, and as a session musician for many others including The Pretenders, to whom he declined full-time membership before joining Big Country. He has taught music courses at Petroc College in Devon and now records as a solo artist.

Big Country was founded in 1981 by vocalist and lead guitarist Stuart Adamson (who had already tasted success with The Skids) and Bruce Watson on guitar and backing vocals. They were joined by Tony on bass and Mark Brzezicki on drums, both of whom were brought in to help on initial single 'Harvest Home' in 1982 but offered full-time membership soon afterwards.

The band enjoyed considerable commercial success almost immediately. 'Harvest Home' (91) did moderately in the charts, but it was the single 'Fields of Fire (400 Miles)' which broke the Top 10. Debut album *The Crossing* was a big hit too, selling over a million copies in the UK alone. 'In a Big Country' (17 in the UK) followed, which was their only Top 20 US single (19). Their second album *Steeltown* reached number 1 in the UK Albums Chart and spawned three hit singles: 'East of Eden' (17), 'Where the Rose is Sown' (29), and 'Just a Shadow' (26). 1986 album *The Seer* reached number 2 in the charts, with single 'Look Away' peaking at number 7. The band were failing to break through in the USA despite a final attempt with a new musical direction on *Peace in Our Time* in 1988. Dwindling sales followed in the USA, though the album did reach 9 in the UK charts. *The Buffalo Skinners* would reach 25.

Final studio album *Driving to Damascus* fared badly in 1999, spurring a fit of deep depression in Stuart Adamson, exacerbated by severe alcoholism which caused him to disappear without notice for days at a time. In 2000 the band played a final concert in Kuala Lumpur despite Stuart arriving late (and 'under the influence'). Some months afterwards he disappeared again; an appeal went out to fans to alert the band if they saw him or were harbouring him. He was found dead in a hotel room in Honolulu, Hawaii in December 2001. The band continued with Tony taking lead vocals for a time and Mike Peters of The Alarm joining briefly. Big Country now tour with an altered line-up that includes Bruce's son Jamie Watson.

What led to you wanting to be a musician, Tony?

My father was a musician. He was originally a trumpet player on the island of Dominica where my family originated. He was regarded as the pop star on the island and my mum was a follower of his music and they ended up marrying! They came over to England with my mum pregnant with me at the time. I grew up in a little West London town called Shepherd's Bush, and it was a typical multi-racial area back in those days.

I started dabbling with musical instruments from the age of about—I should say, five, six, around the time when my father died. My dad bought me a piano and I plonked on that for about ten minutes and decided I didn't like it. I didn't really look at any other sort of instrument until I was about ten. That corresponded with discovering rock music. Black kids back in those days were supposed to like reggae and such like but I started listening to Jimmy Hendrix when I was young. I would pore over album sleeves and just dream that I would be in a band with him.

When I was in secondary school I started learning how to play bass because of my music teacher, a guy called Ken Williams, who is a fantastic man (and a Welshman) who asked us, if we *were* to play a musical instrument what would we like to play? It just so happened the previous night I was watching *Top of the Pops* and there was Norman Greenbaum playing 'Spirit in the Sky.' The camera did a close-up on a Fender Jazz Bass and I looked at it in wonderment and amazement and I said 'I want one of those. I want to play one of those.' When my teacher asked me 'What instrument would you like to play?' I immediately said 'I would like to try the bass.' He got hold of a bass guitar and I was able to learn and practice from that point onwards and got pretty good.

When I was around twenty-two years old one of my school friends said that he had a friend who was looking to put a band together. I was asked to go to a house in Ealing Common, West London, to see if they would accept me. So off I went. I knocked on the door of a house and this old, dishevelled lady answered the door, accused me of being a drug dealer and told me to 'fuck off!' I said 'No, I'm here to audition!' then she apologised and she let me in. The lady that had opened the door was Betty Townshend, Pete Townshend's [of The Who fame] mum. Simon Townshend, Pete's younger brother, was the one that wanted to start this new band.

We had a chat and he seemed to like me. I joined and we eventually became a five-piece with three more guys. We now had a band which we called Clear Blue Sky. The flavour of the day was bands like Genesis. We wanted to be like them because we wanted to play 'intelligent' music. We weren't into the three-minute ditties that were part of the music scene at the time, particularly the popular mainstream types of music. We tried to pass ourselves off as 'proper musicians' playing 'proper music.' After about two years we became a three piece and that is when we changed the name of the band to On the Air.

The band then went on to become a sort of Simon Townshend vehicle. Simon Townshend himself started getting some interest from record companies and we went from being an autonomous group to becoming Simon's backing band, which we didn't like very much because we didn't like the idea of trading on the name Townshend. Simon himself didn't really want to do it but he had no option because that's the way that his family had promoted him, and his brother Pete was quite a large part of that influence. But Pete, to be fair, really did have our best interests at heart. He saw us as a new band struggling along and he gave us opportunities to develop.

On one occasion Pete invited us to his studio in Goring-on-Thames where he had just installed a quadraphonic system and we were one of the first bands to record music using these new recording methods. That was a nice experience and it made us feel special. He even let us hang around at his house. It was a shrine to Pete's musical career; gold and platinum discs all over the walls. It was all very integral to my idea that music was something that I very much wanted to be involved with.

We went from On the Air to The Simon Townsend Band, but then we went back to being called On the Air again and we finally got our own record deal with WA Records. We recorded a couple of singles with a producer called John Burns who was, at one time, the Genesis producer. The records didn't sell very well. All good experience though.

We started to look at our own band in a different light, style wise. So rather than being a Genesis-influenced band we slowly turned into a three-piece with a more aggressive rock-pop attitude, and we decided we needed a decent drummer. And this is where Mark Brzezicki came into the picture. We had put an advert in

Big Country, 1984 - Left to Right - Tony Butler, Bruce Watson, Stuart Adamson, and Mark Brzezicki - Alamy Photo Library

Melody Maker—we were asking for a 'Phil Collins, Bill Bruford-type of drummer.' We held the auditions at Shepperton Studios and we had about ten turn up. Mark had wangled himself to be the last one to be auditioned. He was earwigging to what the others were doing and listening to our songs. By the time he came in to play he was shit-hot and seemed to know our songs off by heart. Mark joined and was playing on our first single, 'Ready for Action' on WA Records, which was released not long afterwards in 1980.

We had a manager now who was just sort of a friend of ours really, but he managed to get us signed up for a tour with a band called The Skids, which I hadn't really known much about previously. They were a Scottish punk band but they had been moderately successful and we saw it as useful experience.

What were your first impressions of Stuart Adamson and The Skids?

I remember the first night of the tour because it was just so awesome, for a few different reasons. We turned up at the gig—it was in a Leicester Polytechnic building called the De Montfort Hall—I walked in with our band and we were all excited. There was a guy fiddling with bass guitars on the stage and I went up to him and said 'Hey, we're the support act. Where are we supposed to be?' This rather angry Scottish bloke turned round and said 'Get out of my fucking way.' That person I found out subsequently was Russell Webb, The Skids' bass player at the time. We eventually managed to introduce ourselves to the rest of the band, they let us have a sound check, which was nice of them, and we did our own first gig very nervously.

It was watching The Skids after our show that I really noticed Stuart, who was their lead guitarist. I thought he was awesome. I thought he was incredibly unique in his guitar playing technique. I loved the songs that I was hearing from his band. I didn't particularly like the vocalist [Richard Jobson] though because I couldn't understand a word he was singing!

As the tour went on I made sure I got to know Stuart. He was a very quiet chap who, I learned, was very much into practical jokes! We got on well throughout the tour. He seemed to be the contemplative one whereas the others were a bit more vocal and had a bit of attitude. Russell Webb I got to know well because he was their bass player and I was our bass player. We spent about two or three weeks touring around Britain and it was a great experience.

When the tour finished, I remember talking to Stuart and saying 'Look, if you ever need a rhythm section, myself and Mark would be available.' We had slowly realised that Simon was being set up *again* to be a solo artist. His family, I presume, had gotten him a deal with Warner Brothers. I thought 'The band's going to come to an end. I might as well start punting for something else.'

And this led to you eventually joining Big Country?

Yes. Stuart duly left The Skids a few months later to form his own band, Big Country. Although they were under the radar at this point, himself and Bruce Watson were working on some songs together. And by this time myself and Mark were working as session musicians, often together, as On the Air had now parted ways with each other.

Lo and behold, 18 months later I got a call from Ian Grant [Big Country's manager]; 'We'd like you and Mark to come down to Phonogram's studios and do some stuff.' I cheekily said 'Yes, how much are we getting paid? He told me to 'fuck off!'

Mark and I duly turned up at the studios in London and it was just awesome. We got to hear the songs that we were going to be playing on a tape deck and it was very different to what The Skids had been performing; melodic, closer to rock and away from the punkier sound of the previous band. Big focus on the guitars. And then we were in the studio, and though it took us a few goes as we hadn't played together before, we finished the demo. I was trembling. Everything sounded so great—we'd played a song called 'Heartless Soul' and my bass line was absolutely fantastic.

Ian (the manager) was hanging about whilst we were recording and then this guy from the record company had a listen. He was just sitting there and he had a huge smile on his face. I asked Stuart who he was and he said 'His name's Chris Briggs and he's the A&R man for Phonogram.' By the end of the session Big Country had a record deal—brilliant! Me and Mark still didn't get paid, by the way, but we *were* asked to join the band and I said yes immediately.

Driving home from the session I said to Mark 'I think we're onto something here! but Mark was very apprehensive. Mark was married to his drums; drums meant everything to him. He loves playing with whoever wants him to play. I think he didn't want to be tied down to just one band. I had to coerce him over the following

period to get him to agree to sign the record contract. And that was it, we were on our way as Big Country.

How did this work out with your session work? Did you have anything booked?

Just before we got together to start rehearsing with Stuart and the others I had to go and do a session that was previously booked with The Pretenders. We recorded 'Back on the Chain Gang.' Afterwards I was asked if I wanted to join The Pretenders there and then, but I said to Chrissie, 'I'm just about to start with this new band and I'm really into it. I'd love to be your bass player but I've committed to these other guys.'

Big Country seemed to come out of nowhere. It was instant success; one minute I'd never heard of the band and the next minute you were everywhere. Was it really like that though?

It was just a matter of months. Stuart and Bruce came down from Scotland and lived at my house in West Ealing. Mark was already in London. Soon we were playing gigs and before we knew it we were on tour, releasing records, and then we were on bloody *Top of the Pops*. It was all within about ten months. It was extraordinary, it just took off and we were all quite bewildered. Stuart had been here before of course with The Skids, so he was a bit more used to it.

What was the music writing like inside the band? Did you all have input?

To start off with, no not really. Mark and I were just catching up and working on rehearsing for the tour that Stuart and Bruce Watson, the other guitarist, had put together. We were learning the existing songs. I think the first song that we started looking at as a unit was the track 'The Crossing' from the album of the same name. Because of Mark and my self's joint background, it was the nearest thing to what we had known previously as musicians. The song has different parts with different rhythms (it's polyrhythmic) and they're quite extended rhythms. That's where Mark and I had come from in terms of music and because we were the rhythm section, Stuart and Bruce listened to us. That was when we started to think that we could have a lot more input, song writing-wise. Stuart and Bruce were still the focus of the writing at that time. As the rest of *The Crossing* album shows, it was very much Stuart and Bruce who were the driving force then.

There was a media thing where they

BIG COUNTRY

THE CROSSING
40TH ANNIVERSARY TOUR 1983-2023

PLUS VERY SPECIAL GUESTS

SPEAR OF DESTINY

Stuart Adamson - Alamy Photo Library

kept going on about the Big Country records all sounding the same. Did that become annoying?

Yes, and it was complete rubbish. I think Mark was on record saying that you can't really win because if you try something different then you get criticised for not sounding like Big Country and if you don't then it 'sounds exactly the same as the other records.' You *do* strive to be creative; you strive to move yourself forward as an individual and as a writer, in life and in general, and you try to do what you do best. I think that we sometimes fell into the trap of having such a defined sound and sticking roughly to it. That was a struggle but at the end of the day we were happier trying to be creative.

The 1984 album Steeltown had a much different atmosphere to previous albums. Were you trying to get away from the rockier sound of before?

I think it was the atmosphere and the temperature politically then. Everything was quite glum, everything was down, dowdy, grey, it was weird. Also, after two years of touring around the world basically, we were all fucked—completely fucked. We were tired and *then* we had to go and

start working on the new album. That was a real chore. Stuart was just wasted; he was empty I think is the word. Going back into the studio to start writing and rehearsing new stuff I think was a bit too soon for us. We just needed a rest really.

We went to Stockholm to record it at Polar Studios, which belonged to Björn and Benny from ABBA. It was a very strange place for us to be recording but it gave myself and Mark an opportunity to really expand in terms of what we played in arrangements and stuff like that. I think there was a real knitting together of what was going to be the Big Country sound post-*The Crossing*. That was the band growing.

Chris Thomas, who was the original producer on it, really didn't identify with the Scots in the band at all, and it was a very Scottish sounding album. We weren't gelling with him. Chris Briggs from Phonogram was magnanimous enough to say 'Let's scrap that, we'll start again.' That's when we got a hold of Steve Lillywhite, who has produced so many fantastic bands such as U2, Simple Minds, Peter Gabriel, Talking Heads and many, many others. That's how our relationship started with Steve, and he was perfect for

that album, absolutely perfect.

Why do you think Big Country never really took off in the States?

We knew that we had an opportunity to go and break America. Obviously, U2 did their live *Red Rocks* televised show in 1983, which was very successful and opened the door for them to get noticed in the States, and it really opened the door for other bands to attempt the same thing. And we had a not-dissimilar style to that incarnation of U2; we were quite rock orientated and we thought we could match what U2 had done.

It didn't take off purely and simply because Stuart was very difficult to deal with at that time. I think that Stuart's problems were really starting to manifest themselves around then. Anything that the management were trying to organise ended up being thwarted. I just think, after *Steeltown*, Stuart's problems were becoming exacerbated. He would go missing and could not be contacted. He hid his alcoholism well and so it was confusing.

What do you think contributed to Stuart's problems? Was it just the pressure, do you think?

Yes, the pressure—and alcohol was a release from it. Although he was the lead singer in the front line, he didn't enjoy it and he didn't relish being in that position. He just wanted to be a writer and play his guitar.

When do you think that the band began to deteriorate?

I think it was just before we started recording *The Seer* in 1986, as both Stuart and Bruce declared that they were alcoholics and they were attending AA meetings. We wanted to support them as much as we could—we need to support people—and things began to improve. We were happier as a band after they told us about their problems and we were glad that they were trying to get help. But then a few things happened which began to put pressure on everyone. We started having record company problems once we'd finished the [Seer] album—an aggravating issue for everyone. That's when Stuart really started to feel the pressure, and that usually led to another secret drinking session, and things were slowly coming to a head.

What happened with the record company? What was causing the problems there?

Chris Briggs, who was the original A&R,

was very supportive, but he subsequently left. He was replaced by someone new and certain decisions were being made after we had recorded *The Seer* regarding the mixing of the album that were worrying. The record company had drafted in some guy that we didn't know to mix the album. We started hearing all these horror stories, that he was replacing our guitars and getting other people to do guitar overdubs and stuff like that. But because we were on the road and couldn't step in to fix the situation, relations were strained. It was just horrible, no one wanted to be in that sort of position. We were excluded from the final polish. I am still proud of that album though, despite these experiences, and it was great to have Kate Bush singing on one of the tracks.

You carried on as a band for quite a few years?

We continued onwards and made a few more good albums but I think Stuart's heart wasn't really in it towards the end. I think he'd always wanted to be a country musician and had even moved to Nashville. He was struggling with things.

A couple of years later, when we were recording *Driving to Damascus* in 1999 in Wales—we didn't know at the time obviously but it was to be our last album—Stuart seemed to be in good form and good shape. We were all into each other's songs that we'd put together for that album and we were all enjoying recording. Stuart was supposedly dry at this point. But we were informed by one of the studio cleaners that Stuart's room was 'a shrine to alcohol.' We did not think he was drinking yet the room was full of bottles, beer cans, all sorts of things. We realised, yes, he was in bad shape.

Sometime later, after he'd gone missing again, we were contacted by somebody from the public who'd seen Stuart in a bar passed out on a table covered in empty bottles. When the album was completed Stuart went home. He was no longer interested in mixing records. He'd relocated to Nashville as I said previously. So he went back there once the studio sessions were completed and we carried on mixing without him.

But the final crack for Stuart, I think, was when we released the lead single from *Driving to Damascus*, 'Fragile Thing.' We all got really excited. We had Eddi Reader do some female vocals on it. It was great radio fodder. We needed that exposure to climb back to where we were and reclaim all the ground we'd lost over the intervening years. The BBC had added it to the playlist and the sales were

initially fantastic. We didn't know the exact chart position but we were told we were definitely in the Top 40 again. We looked like we were back on track and Stuart was really happy.

Then we had a catastrophe. We were all touring to promote the record and Stuart flew back in to join us. We were doing a record signing in Glasgow, at Tower Records, and we were told that the organisation [CIS] who put charts together had banned one of the formats of the CDs the single was published under, so any sales of that format would not be counted towards chart numbers. The upshot was that the sales of the special edition CD were struck from the chart total—it had one too many gatefolds or something like that. And worse, some big retailers such as HMV completely misunderstood and thought that the album in any CD format had to be removed from sale. It was devasting. It went from being a Top 40 record to barely reaching number 70. It had a really bad effect on everybody, particularly Stuart, probably more than us, and the end was on the cards. I could tell he was at breaking point. I think he wanted to end the band but didn't want to be the one to do it, and it was breaking him apart.

I had a bit of a summit meeting with Stuart. We were in Germany at the time, at the end of the tour. I went to his room in the hotel and had a heart-to-heart with him. I said 'Look, I'm not into doing this anymore. You're obviously in a complete and utter mess, you need to go and get yourself sorted out. Even if it means *me* leaving the band so you have the excuse to stop, that's what I'm willing to do because this is not good, you're not in a good place.' He didn't reply and I left the room.

Basically, after that tour, for all intents and purposes I'd left the band. It wasn't something that I was going to publicize or make an announcement about but the band as a unit had come to a halt. We were all doing our separate projects and I didn't see Stuart again for ages, until we were invited to play at a concert in Malaysia which corresponded with the Grand Prix out there at the time. I was persuaded to come back to do a final gig. It was quite a good money-maker and we were all getting a bit skint. We thought 'It's a money gig, let's do this and then see where we go with the band.'

When we all arrived in Kuala Lumpur, we were hanging around waiting for Stuart for hours in the airport. Basically, he'd somehow gotten himself lost because he was drunk and ended up in Japan. By the time we met up with him he'd obviously been drinking heavily and he was in a

mess. The subsequent gig, for me, was a complete and utter embarrassment. He didn't know where he was, he didn't know what he was doing. He was completely screwed.

When we left Malaysia after the gig I didn't see him again. And then the news broke about Stuart's passing a while later and it was still a huge shock, even though we knew he had his share of problems.

Big Country continued onwards though?

It did but a number of factors made me decide to leave the band, a major one being some health issues that I had to contend with. They are still active and touring and I wish them the best.

After you left the band, you moved into teaching?

I needed to think about my future. I really enjoyed what I did throughout my career but I didn't fancy continuing. I didn't want to be part of any supergroup, I didn't want to be touring, I didn't want to do anything like that because my time doing that was with Big Country.

In 2002 I completed a degree and ended up teaching in a college in Barnstaple. To me that was the best place for me to spend my time and experience, and I loved it. I really got off on being able to show people the way to do things because I'd done it myself. I thought it was a very unselfish gesture as well as a job. I like working in a studio with the younger people coming through and it was a very satisfying part of my life that I really enjoyed.

Since Big Country have you worked on solo albums?

I didn't want to hang the guitar up just yet and I wanted to mix teaching with writing and playing on solo work. It was my time to write something like this, it was my time to show the world what I could do. This is my time, in terms of where I am in my own life. I've written a bunch of good songs and I really like doing that! Guess what the album is called? *My Time*.

[Tony has also released a book about his experiences, called *Then Came the Great Divide*, available from all good stockists. I've read it—it's excellent].

125

THE STORY CONTINUES IN...

VOX·ROX 2

A BRIEF HISTORY OF THE EVOLUTION OF MUSIC
IN THE LATE 20TH CENTURY

SHAUN MCCLURE   LAURIAT LANE III

Printed in Great Britain
by Amazon

23791494R00075